easy to make
Complete
Cookbook

Delicious everyday recipes for all occasions

Good Housekeeping

easy to make
Complete
Cookbook

Delicious everyday recipes for all occasions

COLLINS & BROWN

This edition published in Great Britain in 2011
by Collins & Brown
10 Southcombe Street
London W14 0RA

An imprint of Anova Books Company Ltd

The Good Housekeeping website is
www.allaboutyou.com/goodhousekeeping

10 9 8 7 6 5 4 3 2 1

ISBN 978-1-84340-667-9

A catalogue record for this book is available from the British Library.

Reproduction by Dot Gradations Ltd, UK
Printed and bound by Everbest Printing Co Ltd, China

This book can be ordered direct from the publisher at
www.anovabooks.com

NOTES

- Both metric and imperial measures are given for the recipes. Follow
  either set of measures, not a mixture of both, as they are not
  interchangeable.
- All spoon measures are level.
  1 tsp = 5ml spoon; 1 tbsp = 15ml spoon.
- Ovens and grills must be preheated to the specified temperature.
- Use sea salt and freshly ground black pepper unless otherwise
  suggested.
- Fresh herbs should be used unless dried herbs are specified in a recipe.
- Medium eggs should be used except where otherwise specified. Free-
  range eggs are recommended.
- Note that certain recipes contain raw or lightly cooked eggs. The
  young, elderly, pregnant women and anyone with an immune-
  deficiency disease should avoid these, because of the slight risk of
  salmonella.
- Calorie, fat and carbohydrate counts per serving are provided for the
  recipes.
- If you are following a gluten- or dairy-free diet, check the labels on all
  pre-packaged food goods.
- Recipe serving suggestions do not take gluten- or dairy-free diets into
  account.

Contents

Foreword

Cooking, for me, is one of life's great pleasures. Not only is it necessary to fuel your body, but it also exercises creativity, skill, social bonding and patience. The science behind the cooking also fascinates me, learning to understand how yeast works, or to grasp why certain flavours marry quite so well (in my mind) is to become a good cook.

I've often encountered people who claim not to be able to cook – they're just not interested or say they simply don't have time. My sister won't mind me saying that she was one of those who sat firmly in the camp of disinterested domestic goddess. But things change, she realised that my mother (an excellent cook) can't always be on hand to prepare steaming home-cooked meals and that she actually wanted to become a mother one day who was able to whip up good food for her own family. All it took was some good cook books (naturally, Good Housekeeping was present and accounted for) and some enthusiasm and, sure enough, she is now a kitchen wizard, creating such confections that even baffle me.

I've been lucky enough to have had a love for all things culinary since as long as I can remember. Baking rock-like chocolate cakes and misshapen biscuits was a rite of passage that I protectively guard. I made my mistakes young, so have lost the fear of cookery mishaps. I think it's these mishaps that scare people, but when you realise that a mistake made once will seldom be repeated, then kitchen domination can start.

This Good Housekeeping *Easy to Make! Complete Cookbook* is filled with hundreds of tantalising recipes that have been triple tested (at least!) in our dedicated test kitchens. They have been developed to be easily achievable, delicious and guaranteed to work – taking the chance out of cooking.

I hope you enjoy this collection and that it inspires you to get cooking.

Meike.

Meike Beck
Cookery Editor
Good Housekeeping

starters, canapés and nibbles

Cook's Tips

'Peppadew' is the brand name of preserved sweet and spicy red peppers from South Africa; they are available as mild or hot, and are sold in jars.

Chillies vary enormously in strength, from quite mild to blisteringly hot, depending on the type of chilli and its ripeness. Taste a small piece first to check it's not too hot for you.

Jalapeño chillies are from Mexico; they range from hot to fiery hot and when ripe they can be dark green or red; they are usually sold in jars.

Be extremely careful when handling chillies not to touch or rub your eyes with your fingers, as they will sting. Wash knives immediately after handling chillies for the same reason. As a precaution, use rubber gloves when preparing them if you like.

Tahini is a paste made from finely ground sesame seeds. It is sold in jars.

Hummus with Rocket and Mint

3 tbsp sherry vinegar

75ml (2½ fl oz) extra virgin olive oil

150g (5oz) wild rocket

12 small fresh mint leaves

12 Peppadew peppers (mild) (see Cook's Tips)

6 tbsp sliced jalapeño chillies (see Cook's Tips)

sesame seed flatbreads and lemon wedges to serve

For the hummus

400g can chickpeas, drained and rinsed

juice of 1 lemon

4 tbsp tahini (see Cook's Tips)

1 garlic clove, crushed

75ml (2½ fl oz) extra virgin olive oil

salt and ground black pepper

1 To make the hummus, put the chickpeas, lemon juice, tahini, garlic and oil into a food processor. Season well with salt and pepper, then whiz to a paste. Spoon the hummus into a non-metallic bowl, then cover and chill overnight.

2 To make the salad dressing, mix the vinegar with a pinch of salt in a small bowl, then add the oil and whisk to combine. Chill overnight.

3 To serve, divide the hummus among six 150ml (¼ pint) pots. Put on to six plates. Put the rocket and mint leaves into a bowl, then drizzle the dressing over them. Divide the salad, peppers, jalapeño chillies and flatbreads among the six plates. Serve with lemon wedges.

30 Minute Recipe

Serves	EASY		NUTRITIONAL INFORMATION	
6	**Preparation Time** 15 minutes, plus chilling		**Per Serving** 399 calories, 30g fat (of which 5g saturates), 25g carbohydrate, 0.6g salt	Vegetarian Dairy free

Cook's Tip

Prosciutto is Italian dry-cured ham. It is available from Italian delis and most supermarkets. Parma ham is a type of prosciutto, but other types are less expensive.

200g (7oz) smoked salmon slices

100g (3½ oz) cream cheese or goat's cheese

1 tbsp dill-flavoured mustard or creamed horseradish

1 large courgette

about 2 tbsp hummus

200g (7oz) prosciutto (see Cook's Tip)

about 2 tbsp fruity chutney, such as mango

1 small bunch of chives, finely chopped

1 roasted red pepper, finely chopped

ground black pepper

30 Minute Recipe

Cocktail Rolls

1 Lay the smoked salmon on a sheet of greaseproof paper. Spread with a thin layer of cheese, then a layer of mustard or horseradish, and roll up.

2 Using a vegetable peeler, pare the courgette into long, wafer-thin strips. Lay the strips on a board, spread with cheese, then hummus, and roll up.

3 Lay the prosciutto on a board. Spread thinly with cheese, then with the chutney, and roll up.

4 Stand the rolls on a greaseproof paper-lined baking sheet (trimming the bases if necessary), cover with clingfilm and chill for up to 8 hours.

5 About 2 minutes before serving, top each roll with a little cheese. Dip the salmon rolls into the chopped chives, the prosciutto rolls into the red pepper and the courgette rolls into coarsely ground black pepper.

EASY	NUTRITIONAL INFORMATION		Serves
Preparation Time 20 minutes	**Per Serving** 117 calories, 7g fat (of which 3g saturates), 4g carbohydrate, 1.7g salt	Gluten free	**10**

Chicken and Salsa Verde Crostini

50g (2oz) walnuts
1 loaf walnut bread, cut into 15 × 1cm (1/2 in) slices
2 tbsp olive oil
1 tbsp sea salt flakes
175g (6oz) cooked chicken breast, thinly sliced
125g (4oz) sun-dried tomatoes in oil, drained and thinly sliced
fresh flat-leafed parsley leaves to garnish

For the salsa verde

3 tbsp each freshly chopped coriander, mint and basil
1 garlic clove, roughly chopped
2 tbsp Dijon mustard
3 anchovy fillets
1 tbsp capers
50ml (2fl oz) olive oil
juice of 1/2 lemon

1 Put the walnuts into a dry pan and toast over a medium-high heat, tossing regularly, for 2–3 minutes until golden brown. Chop finely and put to one side.

2 Put all the salsa verde ingredients into a food processor or blender and whiz until smooth. (Alternatively, use a pestle and mortar.) Cover and chill.

3 Preheat the grill to high. Put the bread on a baking sheet, brush with the oil and sprinkle with sea salt flakes. Grill for 1 minute on each side or until lightly toasted.

4 To serve, put two or three chicken slices on each crostini base, top with a spoonful of salsa verde and slices of sun-dried tomato, then garnish with a sprinkling of walnuts and flat-leafed parsley.

Makes 15	EASY		NUTRITIONAL INFORMATION	
	Preparation Time 20 minutes, plus chilling	**Cooking Time** 2 minutes	**Per Serving** 208 calories, 9g fat (of which 1g saturates), 24g carbohydrate, 1.7g salt	Dairy free

Try Something Different

Use mini poppadoms instead of croustades.
Replace the chutney with cranberry sauce.
Instead of roast chicken, use turkey.

30
Minute
Recipe

Tangy Chicken Bites

2 × 50g packs mini croustades

about 275g (10oz) fruity chutney, such as mango

2 roast chicken breasts, skinned, torn into small pieces

250g carton crème fraîche

a few fresh thyme sprigs

1 Put the croustades on a board. Spoon about ½ tsp chutney into each one. Top with a few shreds of chicken, a small dollop of crème fraîche and a few thyme leaves. Transfer the croustades to a large serving plate and serve immediately.

Makes 48	EASY	NUTRITIONAL INFORMATION
	Preparation Time 10 minutes	**Per Serving** 43 calories, 2g fat (of which 1g saturates), 4g carbohydrates, 0.1g salt

Cook's Tip

Tahini is a thick, creamy paste that is made from ground sesame seeds. You can buy it in supermarkets and health food shops.

Mini Poppadoms with Aubergine Purée

2 large aubergines

1–2 garlic cloves, crushed

1 tbsp tahini (see Cook's Tip)

juice of ½ lemon

3 tbsp freshly chopped coriander, plus extra sprigs to garnish

1 pack mini poppadoms (40 in pack)

salt and ground black pepper

paprika to garnish

1 Preheat the oven to 200°C (180°C fan oven) mark 6. Pierce the aubergines several times with a sharp knife, put on a baking sheet and cook in the oven for about 1 hour or until very soft. Leave to cool.

2 Peel the aubergines. Wrap the flesh in a clean cloth and squeeze to remove any excess juice. Add the garlic, tahini and lemon juice and mash well with a fork or blend in a food processor. Stir in the chopped coriander and enough water to give a dipping consistency. Season with salt and pepper.

3 Put a little purée on each of the poppadoms and garnish with paprika and coriander sprigs.

EASY		NUTRITIONAL INFORMATION		Serves
Preparation Time 5 minutes, plus cooling	**Cooking Time** about 1 hour	**Per Serving** 128 calories, 6g fat (of which 1g saturates), 16g carbohydrate, 0.4g salt	Gluten free Dairy free	**8**

30 Minute Recipe

Chicken Caesar Salad

2 tbsp olive oil

1 garlic clove, crushed

2 thick slices country-style bread, cubed

6 tbsp freshly grated Parmesan

1 cos lettuce, washed, chilled and cut into bite-size pieces

700g (1½lb) cooked chicken breast, sliced

For the dressing

4 tbsp mayonnaise

2 tbsp lemon juice

1 tsp Dijon mustard

2 anchovy fillets, very finely chopped

salt and ground black pepper

1 Preheat the oven to 180°C (160°C fan oven) mark 4. Put the olive oil, garlic and bread cubes into a bowl and toss well. Tip on to a baking sheet and bake in the oven for 10 minutes, turning halfway through.

2 Sprinkle the Parmesan over the croutons and bake for 2 minutes or until the cheese has melted and the bread is golden.

3 Put all the ingredients for the dressing into a bowl, season with salt and pepper and mix.

4 Put the lettuce and sliced chicken in a bowl, pour the dressing over and toss. Top with the cheese croutons.

Serves 4	EASY		NUTRITIONAL INFORMATION
	Preparation Time 15–20 minutes	**Cooking Time** 12 minutes	**Per Serving** 482 calories, 27g fat (of which 8g saturates), 8g carbohydrate, 1.4g salt

Cook's Tip

Caesar Dressing: Put 1 egg, 1 garlic clove, juice of ½ lemon, 2 tsp Dijon mustard and 1 tsp balsamic vinegar into a food processor and whiz until smooth, then, with the motor running, gradually add 150ml (¼ pint) sunflower oil and whiz until smooth. Season with salt and pepper, cover and chill. It will keep for up to three days.

30 Minute Recipe

Warm Spiced Salmon Niçoise

350g (12oz) new potatoes, thickly sliced

175g (6oz) fine green beans, halved

175g (6oz) cherry tomatoes, halved

1 small red onion, cut into thin wedges

4 × 150–175g (5–6oz) salmon fillets, skinned

15g (½ oz) butter, melted

1 tbsp coriander seeds, crushed

½ tsp dried crushed chillies

4 tbsp Caesar Dressing (see Cook's Tip)

flaked sea salt and ground black pepper

fresh chives to garnish

1 Cook the potatoes in lightly salted boiling water for 8–10 minutes until just tender, adding the beans for the last 2 minutes. Drain well, then transfer to a bowl with the tomatoes and onion wedges. Meanwhile, preheat the grill.

2 Cut each salmon fillet into three strips. Place the strips in four piles on a baking sheet and brush each pile with the melted butter. Mix the crushed coriander seeds with the chillies and a little sea salt and sprinkle evenly over the salmon. Place under the hot grill for 4–5 minutes until just cooked through.

3 Add 1 tbsp water to the dressing to thin it slightly (it should be the consistency of single cream). Spoon three-quarters of the dressing over the vegetables and toss to coat. Season well.

4 Divide the vegetables among four plates, top with the salmon and drizzle the remaining dressing around the edge of the salad. Garnish with chives and serve.

EASY		NUTRITIONAL INFORMATION		Serves
Preparation Time 15 minutes	**Cooking Time** 15 minutes	**Per Serving** 480 calories, 28g fat (of which 6g saturates), 18g carbohydrate, 0.6g salt	Gluten free	**4**

Healthy Tip

Tofu is rich in high-quality protein. It is also a good source of calcium, B vitamins and iron. Tofu is also very low in fat and sodium, making it a perfect food for people on sodium-restricted diets.
Fennel is a good digestive aid, helping reduce gas and bloating.
Butter beans provide good amounts of protein and iron as well as fibre.

30
Minute
Recipe

Warm Tofu, Fennel and Bean Salad

1 tbsp olive oil, plus 1 tsp

1 red onion, finely sliced

1 fennel bulb, finely sliced

1 tbsp cider vinegar

400g can butter beans, drained and rinsed

2 tbsp freshly chopped flat-leafed parsley

200g (7oz) smoked tofu

salt and ground black pepper

1 Heat 1 tbsp oil in a large frying pan. Add the onion and fennel and cook over a medium heat for about 5–10 minutes until soft.

2 Add the cider vinegar and heat through for 2 minutes. Stir in the butter beans and parsley, season to taste with salt and pepper, then tip into a bowl.

3 Slice the smoked tofu horizontally into four and then into eight triangles. Add to the pan with the remaining 1 tsp oil. Cook for 2 minutes on each side or until golden brown.

4 Divide the bean mixture among four plates, then add two slices of tofu to each plate.

Serves 4	EASY		NUTRITIONAL INFORMATION	
	Preparation Time 10 minutes	**Cooking Time** 15 minutes	**Per Serving** 150 calories, 6g fat (of which 1g saturates) 15g carbohydrate, 0.8g salt	Vegetarian • Gluten free Dairy free

Healthy Tip

Cannellini beans are a good source of iron needed to prevent anaemia; folate and magnesium needed for energy and cardiovascular health. They also contain fibre, which is needed to regulate bowel function. Their combination of fibre, carbohydrates and protein makes these beans good for prolonged energy and stable blood sugar levels.

Cannellini Bean and Sunblush Tomato Salad

½ red onion, very finely sliced

2 tbsp red wine vinegar

a small handful each of freshly chopped mint and flat-leafed parsley

2 × 400g cans cannellini beans, drained and rinsed

4 tbsp extra virgin olive oil

4 celery sticks, sliced

75g (3oz) sunblush tomatoes, snipped in half

salt and ground black pepper

1 Put the onion into a small bowl, add the vinegar and toss. Leave to marinate for 30 minutes – this stage is important as it takes the astringency out of the onion.

2 Tip the onion and vinegar into a large serving bowl, add the remaining ingredients, season to taste with salt and pepper and toss everything together.

EASY	NUTRITIONAL INFORMATION		Serves
Preparation Time	**Per Serving**	Vegetarian	**6**
5 minutes, plus marinating	163 calories, 8g fat (of which 1g saturates), 17g carbohydrate, 1.3g salt	Gluten free • Dairy free	

Get Ahead

To prepare ahead Complete the recipe to the end of step 2 and store in an airtight container in the fridge for up to two days.
To use Complete the recipe.

30 Minute Recipe

Vietnamese Rice Salad

225g (8oz) mixed basmati and wild rice
1 large carrot, coarsely grated
1 large courgette, coarsely grated
1 red onion, finely sliced
4 tbsp roasted salted peanuts, lightly chopped
20g ($^3/_4$ oz) each fresh coriander, mint and basil, roughly chopped
100g ($3^1/_2$ oz) wild rocket

For the Vietnamese dressing
2 tbsp light muscovado sugar
juice of 2 limes
4 tbsp fish sauce
6 tbsp rice wine vinegar or white wine vinegar
2 tbsp sunflower oil

1 Put the rice into a pan with 500ml (18fl oz) water. Cover and bring to the boil, then reduce the heat and cook for 20 minutes until the rice is just cooked. Tip on to a plastic tray, spread out and leave to cool.

2 Meanwhile, make the dressing. Put the sugar into a small pan and heat gently until it just begins to dissolve. Add the lime juice, fish sauce and vinegar. Stir over a low heat to dissolve the sugar. Take off the heat and add the oil. Stir into the rice with the grated carrot, courgette and sliced onion.

3 Spoon the salad into a large bowl and top with peanuts, herbs and rocket. Cover and keep chilled until ready to serve.

Serves 6	EASY		NUTRITIONAL INFORMATION	
	Preparation Time 10 minutes	**Cooking Time** 20 minutes	**Per Serving** 294 calories, 14g fat (of which 2g saturates) 38g carbohydrate, 0.6g salt	Gluten free Dairy free

Cook's Tip

Leftover mackerel fillets can be turned into a quick pâté. Whiz in a food processor with the zest of a lemon and enough crème fraîche to make a spreadable consistency.

30 Minute Recipe

Smoked Mackerel Citrus Salad

200g (7oz) green beans

200g (7oz) smoked mackerel fillets

125g (4oz) mixed watercress, spinach and rocket

4 spring onions, sliced

1 avocado, halved, stoned, peeled and sliced

For the dressing

1 tbsp olive oil

1 tbsp freshly chopped coriander

grated zest and juice of 1 orange

1. Preheat the grill. Blanch the green beans in boiling water for 3 minutes until they are just tender. Drain, rinse under cold running water, drain well, then tip into a bowl.

2. Cook the mackerel under the hot grill for 2 minutes until warmed through. Flake into bite-size pieces, discard the skin and add the fish to the bowl with the salad leaves, spring onions and avocado.

3. Whisk all the dressing ingredients together in a small bowl. Pour over the salad, toss well and serve immediately.

EASY		NUTRITIONAL INFORMATION	Serves
Preparation Time 10 minutes	**Cooking Time** 5 minutes	**Per Serving** 299 calories, 26g fat (of which 5g saturates) 4g carbohydrate, 1g salt	Gluten free Dairy free	**6**

Crispy Duck Salad

6 duck legs, about 200g (7oz) each

1 tsp black peppercorns

2 fresh thyme sprigs and 2 bay leaves

125g (4oz) pecan nuts

finely grated zest and juice of 2 oranges

225g (8oz) cranberries

125g (4oz) caster sugar

4 tbsp white wine vinegar

9 tbsp sunflower oil

3 tbsp walnut oil

125g (4oz) kumquats

salt and ground black pepper

salad leaves, such as frisée, to serve

1 Preheat the oven to 180°C (160°C fan oven) mark 4. Put the duck legs into a large flameproof casserole, cover with cold water and bring to the boil. Reduce the heat and simmer for 10 minutes, then skim the surface of the liquid and add the peppercorns, thyme, bay leaves and 2 tsp salt. Transfer to the oven and cook for 45 minutes–1 hour until tender. Cool quickly in the liquid and chill overnight.

2 Preheat the grill. Put the pecan nuts on a baking sheet and toast lightly under the grill.

3 Put the orange zest into a frying pan with 200ml (7fl oz) orange juice, together with the cranberries and sugar. Bring to the boil, then reduce the heat and simmer gently for 5 minutes or until the cranberries are tender. Drain the cranberries, reserving the juice, and put to one side. Bring the juice to the boil and bubble until syrupy, then add the cranberries. Put to one side.

4 Put a good pinch of salt and pepper into a small bowl, then whisk in the vinegar, followed by the oils. Cut the kumquats into quarters, then add to the cranberry mixture with the dressing and pecans. Put to one side.

5 Skim the fat from the surface of the jellied duck liquid and put to one side. Cut the duck into thick shreds, leaving the skin on.

6 Just before serving, heat 1 tbsp reserved duck fat in a large non-stick frying pan and fry half the duck for about 5 minutes or until very crisp and brown; set aside in a warm place. Repeat with the remaining duck. To serve, carefully toss the duck with the cranberry mixture and serve with salad leaves.

Serves 8	A LITTLE EFFORT		NUTRITIONAL INFORMATION	
	Preparation Time 30 minutes, plus chilling	**Cooking Time** 1½ hours, plus cooling	**Per Serving** 655 calories, 65g fat (of which 11g saturates), 22g carbohydrate, 0.2g salt	Gluten free Dairy free

30 Minute Recipe

Warm Bacon Salad

4 handfuls of soft salad leaves
1 small red onion, thinly sliced
75g (3oz) cubed pancetta
1 thick slice white bread, diced
2 medium eggs
25g (1oz) Parmesan shavings
salt and ground black pepper
fresh flat-leafed parsley sprigs to garnish

For the dressing
1 tbsp Dijon mustard
2 tbsp red wine vinegar
2 tbsp fruity olive oil

1 Put the salad leaves and onion into a large bowl. Fry the pancetta in a non-stick frying pan until it begins to release some fat. Add the diced bread and continue to fry until the pancetta is golden and crisp.

2 Put all the dressing ingredients into a small bowl, season with salt and pepper and whisk together.

3 Half-fill a small pan with cold water and bring to the boil. Turn the heat right down – there should be just a few bubbles on the base of the pan. Break the eggs into a cup, then tip them gently into the pan and cook for 3–4 minutes, using a metal spoon to baste the tops with a little of the hot water. Lift the eggs out of the water with a slotted spoon and drain on kitchen paper.

4 Tip the pancetta, bread and any pan juices over the salad leaves. Add the Parmesan, then pour the dressing over the salad. Toss well, then divide between two plates. Top each with an egg, season to taste, then garnish with flat-leafed parsley sprigs and serve.

EASY		NUTRITIONAL INFORMATION	Serves
Preparation Time 10 minutes	**Cooking Time** 10–15 minutes	**Per Serving** 375 calories, 29g fat (of which 9g saturates) 11g carbohydrate, 1.7g salt	**2**

Pear, Grape and Parmesan Salad

125g (4oz) white seedless grapes, halved

2 large ripe pears, peeled, cored and thickly sliced

150g (5oz) rocket

175g (6oz) Parmesan, pared into shavings with a vegetable peeler (see Cook's Tip)

50g (2oz) walnut pieces

For the dressing

1 tbsp white wine vinegar

½ tsp Dijon mustard

3 tbsp walnut oil

1 tbsp sunflower oil

salt and ground black pepper

1 Whisk all the dressing ingredients together in a small bowl and season with salt and pepper.

2 Put the grapes and pears into a bowl, pour the dressing over and toss together. Leave to marinate for 15 minutes.

3 Just before serving, tear the rocket into smallish pieces, put in a large bowl, add the grape and pear mixture and toss together. Divide the salad among four serving plates and serve topped with the Parmesan shavings and the walnut pieces.

Try Something Different

Apple, Celery and Hazelnut Salad: Replace the walnut oil with hazelnut oil, the grapes with 2 sliced celery sticks, the pears with apples and the walnuts with toasted, roughly chopped hazelnuts.

Cook's Tip

Vegetarian cheeses: Some vegetarians prefer to avoid cheeses that have been produced by the traditional method, because this uses animal-derived rennet. Most supermarkets and cheese shops now stock an excellent range of vegetarian cheeses, produced using vegetarian rennet, which comes from plants, such as thistle and mallow, that contain enzymes capable of curdling milk.

Serves 4	EASY		NUTRITIONAL INFORMATION	
	Preparation Time 20 minutes, plus marinating		**Per Serving** 440 calories, 34g fat (of which 11g saturates), 13g carbohydrate, 1.3g salt	Vegetarian Gluten free

**30
Minute
Recipe**

Tomato, Rocket and Parmesan Salad

150g (5oz) mixed salad leaves

50g (2oz) rocket leaves

250g (9oz) baby plum tomatoes, cut in half lengthways

50g (2oz) pinenuts, toasted

3 tbsp extra virgin olive oil

1 tbsp balsamic vinegar

75g (3oz) Parmesan, pared into shavings
with a vegetable peeler (see Cook's Tip, page 26)

salt and ground black pepper

1 Put the salad and rocket leaves into a bowl of ice-cold water. Leave for a few minutes to crisp up, then drain through a colander and shake to remove excess water. Put into a serving bowl, add the tomatoes and pinenuts and toss well.

2 Mix together the olive oil and vinegar in a small bowl and season with salt and pepper. Pour over the salad, toss well, then scatter the Parmesan on top to serve.

Serves	EASY	NUTRITIONAL INFORMATION	
6	**Preparation Time** 10–15 minutes	**Per Serving** 176 calories, 16g fat (of which 4g saturates), 2g carbohydrate, 0.4g salt	Vegetarian Gluten free

Chicory, Fennel and Orange Salad

1 small fennel bulb, with fronds

2 chicory heads or ½ head Chinese leaf, shredded

2 oranges, peeled and cut into rounds, plus juice of ½ orange

25g (1oz) hazelnuts, chopped and toasted

2 tbsp hazelnut or walnut oil

salt and ground black pepper

1 Trim the fronds from the fennel, roughly chop them and put to one side. Finely slice the fennel bulb lengthways and put into a bowl with the chicory or Chinese leaves, the orange slices and toasted hazelnuts.

2 Put the orange juice, hazelnut or walnut oil and the reserved fennel fronds into a small bowl, season well with salt and pepper and mix thoroughly. Pour over the salad and toss everything together.

EASY		NUTRITIONAL INFORMATION		Serves
Preparation Time 15 minutes	**Cooking Time** 2–3 minutes	**Per Serving** 127 calories, 10g fat (of which 1g saturates), 9g carbohydrate, trace salt	Vegetarian Gluten free • Dairy free	**4**

soups

Carrot and Coriander Soup

40g (1½ oz) butter
175g (6oz) leeks, trimmed and sliced
450g (1lb) carrots, sliced
2 tsp ground coriander
1 tsp plain flour
1.1 litres (2 pints) vegetable stock
150ml (¼ pint) single cream
salt and ground black pepper
coriander leaves, roughly torn, to serve

1. Melt the butter in a large pan. Add the leeks and carrots, stir, then cover the pan and cook gently for 7–10 minutes until the vegetables begin to soften but not colour.

2. Stir in the ground coriander and flour and cook, stirring, for 1 minute.

3. Add the stock and bring to the boil, stirring. Season with salt and pepper, then reduce the heat, cover the pan and simmer for about 20 minutes, until the vegetables are tender.

4. Leave the soup to cool a little, then whiz in batches in a blender or food processor until quite smooth. Return to the pan and stir in the cream. Adjust the seasoning and reheat gently; do not boil.

5. Ladle into warmed bowls, scatter with torn coriander leaves and serve.

Serves 6	EASY		NUTRITIONAL INFORMATION	
	Preparation Time 15 minutes	**Cooking Time** about 30 minutes	**Per Serving** 140 calories, 11g fat (of which 7g saturates), 10g carbohydrate, 0.2g salt	Vegetarian Gluten free

Leek and Potato Soup

25g (1oz) butter

1 onion, finely chopped

1 garlic clove, crushed

550g (1¼lb) trimmed leeks, chopped

200g (7oz) floury potatoes, sliced

1.3 litres (2¼ pints) hot vegetable stock

crème fraîche and chopped chives to garnish

1 Melt the butter in a pan over a gentle heat, then cook the onion for 10–15 minutes until soft. Add the garlic and cook for a further 1 minute. Add the leeks and cook for 5–10 minutes until softened. Add the potatoes and toss together with the leeks.

2 Pour in the hot stock and bring to the boil, then reduce the heat and simmer the soup for 20 minutes or until the potatoes are tender.

3 Leave the soup to cool a little, then whiz in batches in a blender or food processor until smooth.

4 To serve, reheat the soup gently. Ladle into warmed bowls and garnish with crème fraîche and chives.

Serves 4	EASY		NUTRITIONAL INFORMATION	
	Preparation Time 10 minutes	Cooking Time 45 minutes	Per Serving 117 calories, 6g fat (of which 4g saturates), 13g carbohydrate, 0.1g salt	Vegetarian Gluten free

Cook's Tip

Parmesan Crisps: Preheat the oven to 200°C (180°C fan oven) mark 6 and line two baking sheets with baking parchment. Put heaped tablespoonfuls of freshly grated Parmesan on the sheets, spacing them well apart, and spread each one out. Sprinkle with poppy seeds and bake for 5–10 minutes until lacy and golden. Leave on the baking sheet for 2–3 minutes to firm up slightly, then transfer to a wire rack to cool.

Cream of Watercress Soup

250g (9oz) watercress

50g (2oz) butter

1 onion, finely chopped

700g (1½lb) potatoes, cut into small pieces

900ml (1½ pints) milk

900ml (1½ pints) vegetable stock

6 tbsp single cream

salt and ground black pepper

Parmesan Crisps (see Cook's Tip and on page 26) to serve (optional)

1 Trim the watercress and discard the coarse stalks. Reserve a few sprigs to garnish, then roughly chop the rest.

2 Melt the butter in a large pan, add the onion and cook gently for 8–10 minutes until soft. Add the potatoes and cook for 1 minute, then pour in the milk and stock and bring to the boil. Reduce the heat and simmer for 15–20 minutes until tender.

3 Take the pan off the heat. Stir in the chopped watercress, then transfer to a blender and blend, in batches, until smooth. Pour the soup into a clean pan, then add the cream and season with salt and pepper. Heat through, then serve garnished with the reserved watercress sprigs and the Parmesan crisps.

EASY		NUTRITIONAL INFORMATION		Serves
Preparation Time 15 minutes	**Cooking Time** 30 minutes	**Per Serving** 251 calories, 13g fat (of which 8g saturates), 26g carbohydrate, 0.4g salt	Vegetarian Gluten free	**6**

75g (3oz) butter

700g (1½lb) small onions, finely chopped

3 garlic cloves, crushed

1 tbsp plain flour

200ml (7fl oz) dry white wine (optional)

1.4 litres (2½ pints) vegetable stock

bouquet garni (1 bay leaf, a few fresh parsley and thyme sprigs)

salt and ground black pepper

French Onion Soup

To serve

1 small baguette, cut into slices 1cm (½in) thick

50g (2oz) Gruyère or Cheddar cheese, grated

1 Melt the butter in a large heavy-based pan. Add the onions and cook slowly over a very low heat, stirring frequently, until very soft and golden brown; this should take at least 30 minutes. Add the garlic and flour and cook, stirring, for 1 minute.

2 Pour in the wine, if using, and let it bubble until reduced by half. Add the stock, bouquet garni and seasoning. Bring to the boil, then reduce the heat and simmer gently, uncovered, for 20–30 minutes.

3 Discard the bouquet garni and let the soup cool a little. Whiz one-third in a food processor or blender until smooth, then stir this back into the soup in the pan.

4 Preheat the grill. Lightly toast the baguette slices on both sides. Reheat the soup and adjust the seasoning.

5 Divide the soup among four ovenproof soup bowls. Float two or three slices of toast on each portion and sprinkle thickly with the grated cheese. Stand the bowls under the hot grill until the cheese has melted and turned golden brown. Serve at once.

Serves 4	EASY		NUTRITIONAL INFORMATION	
	Preparation Time 30 minutes	**Cooking Time** about 1 hour	**Per Serving** 438 calories, 21g fat (of which 13g saturates), 45g carbohydrate, 1.3g salt	Vegetarian

Cook's Tip

Make the stock a day ahead, if possible, then cool overnight. The following day, remove any fat from the surface.

Cock-a-Leekie Soup

1.4kg (3lb) oven-ready chicken, including giblets if available

2 onions, roughly chopped

2 carrots, roughly chopped

2 celery sticks, roughly chopped

1 bay leaf

25g (1oz) butter

900g (2lb) leeks, trimmed and sliced

125g (4oz) ready-to-eat dried prunes, sliced

salt and ground black pepper

freshly chopped parsley to serve

For the dumplings

125g (4oz) self-raising flour

a pinch of salt

50g (2oz) shredded suet

2 tbsp freshly chopped parsley

2 tbsp freshly chopped thyme

1 Put the chicken into a pan in which it fits quite snugly, then add the chopped vegetables, bay leaf and chicken giblets. Pour in 1.7 litres (3 pints) water and bring to the boil, then reduce the heat, cover and simmer gently for 1 hour.

2 Meanwhile, melt the butter in a large pan. Add the leeks and fry gently for 10 minutes or until softened.

3 Remove the chicken from the pan and leave until cool enough to handle. Strain the stock and put to one side. Strip the chicken from the bones and shred roughly. Add to the stock with the prunes and softened leeks.

4 To make the dumplings, sift the flour and salt into a bowl. Stir in the suet, herbs and about 5 tbsp water to make a fairly firm dough. Lightly shape the dough into 2.5cm (1in) balls. Bring the soup just to the boil and season well. Reduce the heat, add the dumplings and cover the pan with a lid. Simmer for 15–20 minutes until the dumplings are light and fluffy. Serve the soup scattered with chopped parsley.

EASY		NUTRITIONAL INFORMATION	Serves
Preparation Time 30–40 minutes	**Cooking Time** 1 hour 20 minutes	**Per Serving** 280 calories, 4g fat (of which 1g saturates), 40g carbohydrate, 0.2g salt	**8**

30 Minute Recipe

Fast Fish Soup

1 leek, trimmed and finely sliced

4 fat garlic cloves, crushed

3 celery sticks, finely sliced

1 small fennel bulb, finely sliced

1 red chilli, seeded and finely chopped (see Cook's Tips, page 10)

3 tbsp olive oil

50ml (2fl oz) dry white wine

about 750g (1lb 10oz) mixed fish and shellfish, such as haddock, monkfish and salmon, raw shelled prawns, and mussels, scrubbed, rinsed and beards removed (see Cook's Tips)

4 medium tomatoes, chopped

1½ tbsp freshly chopped thyme

salt and ground black pepper

1 Put the leek into a large pan and add the garlic, celery, fennel, chilli and oil. Cook over a medium heat for 5 minutes or until the vegetables are soft and beginning to colour.

2 Stir in 1.1 litres (2 pints) boiling water and the wine. Bring to the boil, then reduce the heat, cover and simmer for 5 minutes.

3 Meanwhile, cut the white fish into large chunks. Add to the soup with the tomatoes and thyme. Continue to simmer gently until the fish has just turned opaque. Add the prawns and simmer for 1 minute, then add the mussels. As soon as all the mussels have opened, season the soup and ladle into warmed bowls. Discard any mussels that remain closed, then serve immediately.

Cook's Tips

Frozen seafood mix is a useful standby. Use it instead of the fish and shellfish in this recipe but take care not to overcook or it will become tough.

Mussels are sold either by weight or volume:
1.1 litres (2 pints) of mussels is roughly equivalent to 900g (2lb).
Do not buy mussels with cracked or open shells.
To prepare fresh mussels, rinse them under cold running water to help rid them of any grit and sand. Scrub the mussel shells thoroughly, using a small stiff brush to remove any grit and barnacles. Pull away the hairy 'beard', which protrudes from one side of the shell. Tap any open mussels sharply with the back of the knife or on the surface. If they refuse to close, throw them away. Rinse the mussels again under cold running water before cooking.

Try Something Different

To give the soup more of a kick, stir in 2 tbsp Pernod instead of the wine.
Garlic croûtes are traditionally served with fish soup; they can be made while the soup is simmering. Toast small slices of baguette, spread with garlic mayonnaise and sprinkle with grated cheese. Float in the hot soup just before serving.

EASY		NUTRITIONAL INFORMATION		Serves
Preparation Time 10 minutes	**Cooking Time** 15 minutes	**Per Serving** 269 calories, 10g fat (of which 2g saturates), 6g carbohydrate, 0.6g salt	Gluten free Dairy free	**4**

30
Minute
Recipe

Smoked Cod and Sweetcorn Chowder

130g pack cubed pancetta

50g (2oz) butter

3 leeks, about 450g (1lb), trimmed and thinly sliced

25g (1oz) plain flour

600ml (1 pint) semi-skimmed or full-fat milk

700g (1½ lb) undyed smoked cod loin or haddock, skinned and cut into 2cm (¾ in) cubes

326g can sweetcorn in water, drained

450g (1lb) small new potatoes, sliced

150ml (¼ pint) double cream

½ tsp paprika

salt and ground black pepper

2 tbsp freshly chopped flat-leafed parsley to garnish

1 Fry the pancetta in a large pan over a gentle heat until the fat runs out. Add the butter to the pan to melt, then add the leeks and cook until softened.

2 Stir in the flour and cook for a few seconds, then pour in the milk and 300ml (½ pint) cold water. Add the fish to the pan with the sweetcorn and potatoes. Bring to the boil, then reduce the heat and simmer for 10–15 minutes until the potatoes are cooked.

3 Stir in the cream, season with salt and pepper and the paprika and cook for 2–3 minutes to warm through. Ladle into warmed shallow bowls and sprinkle each one with a little chopped parsley. Serve immediately.

Serves	EASY		NUTRITIONAL INFORMATION
6	**Preparation Time** 5 minutes	**Cooking Time** 20 minutes	**Per Serving** 517 calories, 28g fat (of which 15g saturates), 35g carbohydrate, 4.7g salt

Cook's Tip

Fresh Pesto: Put a 20g pack of roughly chopped basil into a food processor. Add 25g (1oz) finely grated Parmesan, 50g (2oz) pinenuts and 4 tbsp extra virgin olive oil and whiz to a rough paste. Alternatively, grind in a pestle and mortar. Season with salt and plenty of ground black pepper.

2 tbsp olive oil

1 small onion, finely chopped

1 carrot, chopped

1 celery stick, chopped

1 garlic clove, crushed

2 tbsp freshly chopped thyme

1 litre (1³/₄ pints) hot vegetable stock

400g can chopped tomatoes

400g can borlotti beans, drained and rinsed

125g (4oz) minestrone pasta

175g (6oz) Savoy cabbage, shredded

salt and ground black pepper

Fresh Pesto (see Cook's Tip), toasted ciabatta and extra virgin olive oil to serve

Minestrone with Pesto

1 Heat the oil in a large pan and add the onion, carrot and celery. Cook for 8–10 minutes until softened, then add the garlic and thyme and fry for another 2–3 minutes.

2 Add the hot stock, tomatoes and half the borlotti beans to the pan and bring to the boil. Mash the remaining beans and stir into the soup, then reduce the heat and simmer for 30 minutes, adding the minestrone pasta and cabbage for the last 10 minutes of cooking time.

3 Check the seasoning, then ladle the soup into four warmed bowls and serve with a dollop of fresh pesto on top and with slices of toasted ciabatta drizzled with extra virgin olive oil on the side.

EASY		NUTRITIONAL INFORMATION		Serves
Preparation Time 10 minutes	**Cooking Time** 45 minutes	**Per Serving** 34 calories, 11g fat (of which 3g saturates), 47g carbohydrate, 1.5g salt	Vegetarian Dairy free	**4**

Cook's Tip

Dried peas form the base of this comforting soup. First, you need to soak them overnight in about 1 litre (1¾ pints) cold water. If you forget, put them straight into a pan with the water, bring to the boil and cook for 1–2 minutes, then leave to stand for 2 hours before using.

Split Pea and Ham Soup

500g pack dried yellow split peas, soaked overnight (see Cook's Tip)

25g (1oz) butter

1 large onion, finely chopped

125g (4oz) rindless smoked streaky bacon rashers, roughly chopped

1 garlic clove, crushed

1.7 litres (3 pints) well-flavoured ham or vegetable stock

1 bouquet garni (see page 36)

1 tsp dried oregano

125g (4oz) cooked ham, chopped

salt and ground black pepper

cracked black pepper to serve

1 Drain the soaked split peas. Melt the butter in a large pan, add the onion, bacon and garlic and cook over a low heat for about 10 minutes until the onion is soft.

2 Add the drained split peas to the pan with the stock. Bring to the boil and skim the surface. Add the bouquet garni and oregano, then season with salt and pepper. Reduce the heat, cover the pan and simmer for 45 minutes–1 hour or until the peas are very soft.

3 Cool a little, then whiz half the soup in a blender or food processor until smooth. Return to the pan and reheat, then add the ham and check the seasoning. Ladle into warmed bowls and sprinkle with cracked black pepper to serve.

Serves 6	A LITTLE EFFORT		NUTRITIONAL INFORMATION	
	Preparation Time 15 minutes, plus soaking	**Cooking Time** 1 hour 5 minutes	**Per Serving** 400 calories, 10g fat (of which 5g saturates), 55g carbohydrate, 1.5g salt	Gluten free

Healthy Tip

This highly nutritious soup provides an excellent balance of protein (from the chicken), carbohydrate (from the pasta) and healthy unsaturated fats (from the olive oil). The vegetables add valuable amounts of fibre, B vitamins, folate and iron, while the garlic provides numerous health benefits including protection against heart disease.

Chicken Broth

1 tbsp olive oil

about 300g (11oz) boneless, skinless chicken thighs, cubed

3 garlic cloves, crushed

2 medium red chillies, seeded and finely diced (see Cook's Tips, page 10)

1 litre (1³/₄ pints) chicken stock

250g (9oz) each green beans, broccoli, sugarsnap peas and courgettes, chopped

50g (2oz) pasta shapes or spaghetti, broken into short lengths

1 Heat the oil in a large pan. Add the chicken, garlic and chillies and cook for 5–10 minutes until the chicken is opaque all over.

2 Add the stock and bring to the boil. Add the vegetables, reduce the heat and simmer for 5 minutes or until the chicken is cooked through.

3 Meanwhile, cook the pasta in a separate pan of lightly salted boiling water for about 5–10 minutes, depending on the type of pasta or until just cooked.

4 Drain the pasta and add to the broth. Ladle into warmed bowls and serve immediately.

EASY		NUTRITIONAL INFORMATION		Serves
Preparation Time 30 minutes	**Cooking Time** 15 minutes	**Per Serving** 229 calories, 7g fat (of which 1g saturates) 16g carbohydrate, 1.2g salt	Dairy free	**4**

Chilled Vegetable Soup with Olive and Basil Cream

1.4kg (3lb) ripe tomatoes, halved
350g (12oz) shallots or onions, halved
275g (10oz) celery, chopped
4 small garlic cloves
275g (10oz) carrots, sliced
4 red peppers, seeded and chopped
4 tbsp olive oil
2 red chillies (see Cook's Tips, page 10)
750ml (1¼ pints) passata (see Cook's Tips)
1½ tsp sugar
grated zest and juice of 1 lime
salt and ground black pepper
crushed ice and Olive and Basil Cream (see Cook's Tips)
to serve

1 Preheat the oven to 200°C (180°C fan oven) mark 6. Divide all the vegetables between two roasting tins. Add the oil and chillies, then stir well. Roast for 1–1½ hours until the skins are charred, turning halfway through the cooking time.

2 Discard the chillies. Whiz the vegetables with the passata in a blender or food processor until smooth, then push the purée through a sieve.

3 Add the sugar, lime zest and 2 tbsp juice and plenty of seasoning. Cover and chill.

4 Ladle the soup into chilled bowls, sprinkle with crushed ice and top with Olive and Basil Cream.

Cook's Tips

Passata, a mixture of sieved tomatoes rather like tomato paste, is sold in cartons and bottles. Look out for it in supermarkets.
Olive and Basil Cream: Roughly chop 50g (2oz) pitted black olives. Stir into 150ml (¼ pint) crème fraîche with 2 tbsp freshly chopped basil and the grated zest and juice of 1 lemon. Season well with salt and ground black pepper. Cover and chill the cream until ready to serve, then spoon on to the soup.

Serves	EASY		NUTRITIONAL INFORMATION	
8	**Preparation Time** 15 minutes, plus chilling	**Cooking Time** 1–1½ hours, plus chilling	**Per Serving** 153 calories, 7g fat (of which 1g saturates), 21g carbohydrate, 0.2g salt	Vegetarian Gluten free

eggs and cheese

Eggs Benedict

4 slices bread

4 medium eggs

150ml (¼ pint) Hollandaise Sauce (see Cook's Tip)

4 thin slices lean ham

parsley sprigs to garnish

1 Toast the bread on both sides. Poach the eggs. Gently warm the Hollandaise Sauce.

2 Top each slice of toast with a folded slice of ham, then with a poached egg. Finally, coat with Hollandaise sauce.

3 Garnish each with a sprig of parsley and serve.

Cook's Tip

Hollandaise Sauce: Put 4 tbsp white wine vinegar, a blade of mace, 1 slice of onion, 1 bay leaf and 6 black peppercorns into a pan. Bring to the boil and reduce to 1 tbsp liquid. Cut 150g (5oz) unsalted butter into ten pieces. Put 3 medium egg yolks into a heatproof bowl with one piece of butter and a pinch of salt. Beat, then strain in the vinegar mixture. Place over a pan of hot water, making sure the base of the bowl doesn't touch the water. Whisk for 3 minutes until pale and starting to thicken. Add a piece of butter and beat until completely absorbed. Repeat with the remaining pieces of butter. Make sure the sauce doesn't get too hot during cooking. Season and add lemon juice to taste. Serves 6.

Try Something Different

Eggs Florentine: Cook 900g (2lb) washed spinach in a pan with a little salt until tender. Drain well, chop and reheat with 15g (½oz) butter. Melt 25g (1oz) butter, stir in 3 tbsp plain flour and cook gently for 1 minute, stirring. Remove from the heat and gradually stir in 300ml (½ pint) milk. Bring to the boil and cook, stirring, until thickened. Add 50g (2oz) grated Gruyère or Cheddar cheese and season. Do not allow to boil. Poach the eggs. Put the spinach in an ovenproof dish, arrange the eggs on top and pour the cheese sauce over them. Sprinkle with 25g (1oz) grated cheese and brown under the grill.

Serves 4	EASY		NUTRITIONAL INFORMATION
	Preparation Time 15 minutes	**Cooking Time** 10 minutes	**Per Serving** 402 calories, 33g fat (of which 18g saturates), 14g carbohydrate, 1.6g salt

Piperade

2 tbsp olive oil
1 medium onion, finely chopped
1 garlic clove, finely chopped
1 red pepper, seeded and chopped
375g (13oz) tomatoes, peeled, seeded and chopped
a pinch of cayenne pepper
8 large eggs
salt and ground black pepper
freshly chopped flat-leafed parsley to garnish
fresh bread to serve (optional)

1 Heat the oil in a heavy-based frying pan. Add the onion and garlic and cook gently for 5 minutes. Add the red pepper and cook for 10 minutes or until softened.

2 Add the tomatoes, increase the heat and cook until they are reduced to a thick pulp. Season well with cayenne pepper, salt and pepper.

3 Lightly whisk the eggs and add to the frying pan. Using a wooden spoon, stir gently until they've just begun to set but are still creamy. Garnish with parsley and serve with bread, if you like.

Serves 4	EASY		NUTRITIONAL INFORMATION	
	Preparation Time 20 minutes	**Cooking Time** 20 minutes	**Per Serving** 232 calories, 17g fat (of which 4g saturates), 7g carbohydrate, 0.4g salt	Vegetarian Dairy free

30 Minute Recipe

Baked Eggs with Spinach and Mushrooms

2 tbsp olive oil

125g (4oz) mushrooms, chopped

225g (8oz) fresh spinach, coarse stalks removed

2 medium eggs

2 tbsp single cream

salt and ground black pepper

1 Preheat the oven to 200°C (180°C fan oven) mark 6. Heat the oil in a large frying pan, add the mushrooms and stir-fry for 30 seconds. Add the spinach and stir-fry until wilted. Season to taste, then divide the mixture between two shallow ovenproof dishes.

2 Carefully break an egg into the centre of each dish, then spoon 1 tbsp single cream over it.

3 Cook in the oven for about 12 minutes or until just set – the eggs will continue to cook a little once they're out of the oven. Grind a little more pepper over the top, if you like, and serve.

EASY		NUTRITIONAL INFORMATION		Serves
Preparation Time 10 minutes	**Cooking Time** 15 minutes	**Per Serving** 238 calories, 21g fat (of which 5g saturates), 2g carbohydrate, 0.6g salt	Vegetarian Gluten free	**2**

Try Something Different

Blend 25g (1oz) mild goat's cheese with 1 tbsp crème fraîche; put in the centre of the omelette before folding.

30 Minute Recipe

Classic French Omelette

2–3 medium eggs

1 tbsp milk or water

25g (1oz) unsalted butter

salt and ground black pepper

sliced or grilled tomatoes and freshly chopped flat-leafed parsley to serve

1 Whisk the eggs in a bowl, just enough to break them down – over-beating spoils the texture of the omelette. Season with salt and pepper and add the milk or water.

2 Heat the butter in an 18cm (7in) omelette pan or non-stick frying pan until it is foaming, but not brown. Add the eggs and stir gently with a fork or wooden spatula, drawing the mixture from the sides to the centre as it sets and letting the liquid egg in the centre run to the sides. When set, stop stirring and cook for 30 seconds or until the omelette is golden brown underneath and still creamy on top: don't overcook. If you are making a filled omelette (see Try Something Different), add the filling at this point.

3 Tilt the pan away from you slightly and use a palette knife to fold over one-third of the omelette to the centre, then fold over the opposite third. Slide the omelette out on to a warmed plate, letting it flip over so that the folded sides are underneath. Serve immediately, with tomatoes sprinkled with parsley.

Serves 1	EASY		NUTRITIONAL INFORMATION	
	Preparation Time 5 minutes	**Cooking Time** 5 minutes	**Per Serving** 449 calories, 40g fat (of which 19g saturates), 1g carbohydrate, 1g salt	Vegetarian Gluten free

30
Minute
Recipe

Mushroom Soufflé Omelette

50g (2oz) small chestnut mushrooms, sliced

3 tbsp crème fraîche

2 medium eggs, separated

15g (½ oz) butter

5 fresh chives, roughly chopped

salt and ground black pepper

1 Heat a non-stick frying pan for 30 seconds. Add the mushrooms and cook, stirring, for 3 minutes to brown slightly, then stir in the crème fraîche and turn off the heat.

2 Lightly beat the egg yolks in a bowl, add 2 tbsp cold water and season with salt and pepper.

3 In a separate clean, grease-free bowl, whisk the egg whites until stiff but not dry, then gently fold into the egg yolks. Do not over-mix. Heat an 18cm (7in) non-stick frying pan over a medium heat. Add the butter, then the egg mixture, tilting the pan to cover the bottom. Cook for 3 minutes or until the underside is golden brown.

4 Meanwhile, preheat the grill. Gently reheat the mushrooms and add the chives. Put the omelette under the grill for 1 minute or until the surface is just firm and puffy. Tip the mushroom mixture on top. Run a spatula around and underneath the omelette to loosen it, then carefully fold it and turn out on to a warmed plate. Serve immediately.

EASY		NUTRITIONAL INFORMATION		Serves
Preparation Time 5 minutes	**Cooking Time** 7–10 minutes	**Per Serving** 440 calories, 42g fat (of which 23g saturates), 2g carbohydrate, 0.6g salt	Vegetarian Gluten free	**1**

Spanish Omelette

900g (2lb) potatoes, peeled and left whole

3–4 tbsp vegetable oil

1 onion, finely sliced

8 medium eggs

3 tbsp chopped flat-leafed parsley

3 streaky bacon rashers

salt and ground black pepper

green salad to serve

1 Add the potatoes to a pan of lightly salted cold water, bring to the boil and simmer for 15–20 minutes or until almost cooked. Drain and leave until cool enough to handle, then slice thickly.

2 Heat 1 tbsp oil in an 18cm (7in) non-stick frying pan (suitable for use under the grill). Add the onion and fry gently for 7–10 minutes until softened; remove and set aside.

3 Lightly beat the eggs in a bowl and season well with salt and pepper.

4 Heat the remaining oil in the frying pan, then layer the potato slices, onion and 2 tbsp chopped parsley in the pan. Pour in the beaten eggs and cook for 5–10 minutes until the omelette is firm underneath. Meanwhile, grill the bacon until golden and crisp, then break into pieces.

5 Put the omelette in the pan under the grill for 2–3 minutes until the top is just set. Scatter the bacon and remaining chopped parsley over the surface. Serve cut into wedges, with a green salad.

Serves 4	EASY		NUTRITIONAL INFORMATION	
	Preparation Time 15 minutes	**Cooking Time** 30–45 minutes	**Per Serving** 453 calories, 25g fat (of which 6g saturates), 38g carbohydrate, 1.6g salt	Gluten free Dairy free

rice and grains

Oven-baked Chilli Rice

3 tbsp olive oil

1 large red onion, thinly sliced

1 red chilli, seeded and thinly sliced (see Cook's Tips, page 10)

1 tbsp tamarind paste

1 tbsp light muscovado sugar

350g (12oz) mixed basmati and wild rice

a little oil or butter to grease

20g pack fresh mint, roughly chopped

100g bag baby leaf spinach

50g (2oz) flaked almonds, toasted

salt and ground black pepper

1 Heat the oil in a frying pan and fry the onion for 7–10 minutes over a medium heat until golden and soft. Add the chilli, tamarind paste and sugar. Cool, cover and chill.

2 Meanwhile, put the rice into a large pan. Add 800ml (1 pint 7fl oz) boiling water. Cover and bring to the boil, then reduce the heat to its lowest setting and cook according to the pack instructions. Spread on a baking sheet and leave to cool, then chill.

3 When ready to serve, preheat the oven to 200°C (180°C fan oven) mark 6. Tip the rice into a lightly greased, shallow ovenproof dish. Stir in the onion mixture and season with salt and pepper.

4 Reheat the rice in the oven for 20 minutes until piping hot. Stir in the mint, spinach and almonds and serve immediately.

Get Ahead

To prepare ahead Complete the recipe to the end of step 2, up to one day ahead. Cover and chill the rice and onions separately.
To use Complete the recipe.

Serves 8	EASY		NUTRITIONAL INFORMATION	
	Preparation Time 15 minutes, plus chilling	**Cooking Time** 40 minutes	**Per Serving** 265 calories, 8g fat (of which 1g saturates), 42g carbohydrate, 0.1g salt	Vegetarian Gluten Free • Dairy Free

Get Ahead

To prepare ahead Complete the recipe to the end of step 3. Cover and keep in a cool place for 1½ hours.
To use Complete the recipe.

Saffron Paella

½ tsp saffron threads

900ml–1.1 litres (1½–2 pints) hot chicken stock

5 tbsp olive oil

2 × 70g packs sliced chorizo sausage

6 boneless, skinless chicken thighs, each cut into three pieces

1 large onion, chopped

4 large garlic cloves, crushed

1 tsp paprika

2 red peppers, seeded and sliced

400g can chopped tomatoes in tomato juice

350g (12oz) long-grain rice

200ml (7fl oz) dry sherry

500g pack ready-cooked mussels

200g (7oz) cooked tiger prawns, drained

juice of ½ lemon

salt and ground black pepper

fresh flat-leafed parsley sprigs to garnish (optional)

lemon wedges to serve

1 Add the saffron to the hot stock and leave to infuse for 30 minutes. Meanwhile, heat half the oil in a large heavy-based frying pan. Add half the chorizo and fry for 3–4 minutes until crisp. Remove with a slotted spoon and drain on kitchen paper. Repeat with the remaining chorizo; put to one side.

2 Heat 1 tbsp oil in the pan, add half the chicken and cook for 3–5 minutes until pale golden brown. Remove from the pan and put to one side. Cook the remaining chicken and put to one side.

3 Reduce the heat slightly, heat the remaining oil and add the onion. Cook for 5 minutes or until soft. Add the garlic and paprika and cook for 1 minute. Put the chicken back into the pan, then add the peppers and the tomatoes.

4 Stir the rice into the pan, then add one-third of the stock and bring to the boil. Season with salt and pepper, reduce the heat and simmer, uncovered, stirring continuously until most of the liquid has been absorbed. Reheat the remaining stock.

5 Add the remaining stock, a little at a time, allowing the liquid to become absorbed after each addition (this should take about 25 minutes). Add the sherry and cook for a further 2 minutes.

6 Add the mussels and their juices to the pan with the prawns, lemon juice and reserved chorizo. Cook for 5 minutes to heat through. Adjust the seasoning, then garnish with the parsley, if you like, and serve with lemon wedges.

Serves 6	EASY		NUTRITIONAL INFORMATION	
	Preparation Time 5 minutes, plus infusing	**Cooking Time** 20 minutes	**Per Serving** 609 calories, 22g fat (of which 6g saturates), 59g carbohydrate, 1.5g salt	Dairy free

6 tbsp olive oil

2 shallots, finely chopped

2 garlic cloves, finely chopped

2 tsp freshly chopped thyme,
plus sprigs to garnish

1 tsp grated lemon zest

350g (12oz) arborio rice

150ml (¼ pint) dry white wine

900ml (1½ pints) vegetable stock

450g (1lb) mixed fresh mushrooms, such as oyster,
shiitake and cep, sliced if large

1 tbsp freshly chopped flat-leafed parsley

salt and ground black pepper

Wild Mushroom Risotto

1 Heat half the oil in a heavy-based pan. Add the shallots, garlic, chopped thyme and lemon zest, and fry gently for 5 minutes or until the shallots are softened. Add the rice and stir for 1 minute or until the grains are glossy. Add the wine, bring to the boil and let it bubble until almost totally evaporated. Heat the stock in a separate pan to a steady, low simmer.

2 Gradually add the stock to the rice, a ladleful at a time, stirring with each addition and allowing it to be absorbed before adding more. Continue adding the stock slowly until the rice is tender. This should take about 25 minutes.

3 About 5 minutes before the rice is ready, heat the remaining oil in a large frying pan and stir-fry the mushrooms over a high heat for 4–5 minutes. Add to the rice with the parsley. The risotto should still be moist: if necessary add a little more stock. Check the seasoning and serve at once, garnished with thyme.

EASY		NUTRITIONAL INFORMATION		Serves
Preparation Time 10 minutes	**Cooking Time** 30 minutes	**Per Serving** 347 calories, 12g fat (of which 2g saturates), 50g carbohydrate, 0.6g salt	Vegetarian Dairy free	**6**

Smoked Haddock Risotto with Poached Eggs

200g (7oz) smoked haddock

50g (2oz) butter

1 large leek, white part only, trimmed and finely sliced

150ml (¼ pint) dry white wine

300g (11oz) arborio rice

1.1 litres (2 pints) chicken stock

4 large eggs

salt and ground black pepper

1 tbsp freshly chopped parsley to garnish

1 Put the haddock into a dish, pour boiling water over, cover and leave for 10 minutes. Flake the fish into bite-size pieces, discarding the skin and the bones.

2 Melt half the butter in a heavy-based pan. Add the leek and cook gently, stirring occasionally, for 15 minutes or until softened. Add the wine and boil rapidly until it has almost evaporated. Add the rice and cook, for 1 minute, stirring to coat the grains.

3 Put the stock into a pan and bring to the boil, then keep at a gentle simmer. Add a ladleful of the hot stock to the rice. Simmer, stirring, until all the liquid has been absorbed. Continue adding the stock, a ladleful at a time, until the rice is al dente (just tender but with a little bite at the centre) – this will take about 25 minutes and you may not need to add all the stock.

4 Meanwhile, bring a wide shallow pan of water to the boil. Crack an egg into a cup, turn off the heat under the pan and slip in the egg close to the water. Repeat with the other eggs and cover the pan. Leave to stand for 3 minutes.

5 Before adding the last ladleful of stock, stir in the pieces of fish and the remaining butter and check the seasoning. Heat the risotto through, adding the remaining stock if necessary. Remove the eggs with a slotted spoon and trim. Top each serving of risotto with a poached egg and a sprinkling of parsley.

Serves	EASY		NUTRITIONAL INFORMATION
4	**Preparation Time** 15 minutes	**Cooking Time** about 40 minutes	**Per Serving** 508 calories, 17g fat (of which 8g saturates), 61g carbohydrate, 1.4g salt

Try Something Different

Fried Herb Polenta: Bring 900ml (1½ pints) water to the boil in a large pan with a good pinch of salt added. Sprinkle in 175g (6oz) coarse polenta, whisking constantly. Lower the heat and simmer, stirring frequently, for 20 minutes or until the polenta leaves the sides of the pan; it will be very thick. Stir in 2 tbsp freshly chopped sage and 1 tbsp freshly chopped rosemary and plenty of salt and pepper. Turn out on to a board and shape the polenta into a thick oblong mound. Leave for about 1 hour until set, then cut into slices. Melt the butter in a frying pan. When foaming, fry the polenta slices on both sides until golden. Serve with meat, poultry or vegetarian dishes.

Soft Herb Polenta: Serve the Fried Herb Polenta after you've stirred in the fresh sage and rosemary, as you would mashed potato.

Cheese Polenta with Tomato Sauce

Get Ahead

To prepare ahead Complete the recipe to the end of step 3. Cover and chill separately for up to two days.
To use Complete the recipe.

oil to grease

225g (8oz) polenta

4 tbsp freshly chopped herbs, such as oregano, chives and flat-leafed parsley

100g (3½oz) freshly grated Parmesan, plus fresh Parmesan shavings to serve (see Cook's Tip, page 26)

salt and ground black pepper

For the tomato and basil sauce

1 tbsp vegetable oil

3 garlic cloves, crushed

500g carton creamed tomatoes or passata

1 bay leaf

1 fresh thyme sprig

a large pinch of caster sugar

3 tbsp freshly chopped basil, plus extra to garnish

1 Lightly oil a 25.5 × 18cm (10 × 7in) dish. Bring 1.1 litres (2 pints) water and ¼ tsp salt to the boil in a large pan. Sprinkle in the polenta, whisking constantly. Reduce the heat and simmer, stirring frequently, for 10–15 minutes until the mixture leaves the sides of the pan.

2 Stir in the herbs and Parmesan and season to taste with salt and pepper. Turn into the prepared dish and leave to cool.

3 Next, make the tomato and basil sauce. Heat the oil in a pan and fry the garlic for 30 seconds (do not brown). Add the creamed tomatoes or passata, the bay leaf, thyme and sugar. Season with salt and pepper and bring to the boil, then reduce the heat and simmer, uncovered, for 5–10 minutes. Remove the bay leaf and thyme sprig and add the chopped basil.

4 To serve, cut the polenta into pieces and lightly brush with oil. Preheat a griddle and fry for 3–4 minutes on each side, or grill under a preheated grill for 7–8 minutes on each side. Serve with the tomato and basil sauce, fresh Parmesan shavings and chopped basil.

Serves 6	EASY		NUTRITIONAL INFORMATION	
	Preparation Time 15 minutes, plus cooling	**Cooking Time** 45 minutes	**Per Serving** 249 calories, 9g fat (of which 4g saturates), 31g carbohydrate, 0.9g salt	Vegetarian

Mediterranean Vegetable Couscous with Feta

2 red onions, roughly chopped

2 courgettes, roughly chopped

1 aubergine, roughly chopped

2 red peppers, seeded and roughly chopped

2 garlic cloves, sliced

4 tbsp olive oil

350g (12oz) tomatoes, quartered

225g (8oz) couscous

300ml (½ pint) hot vegetable stock

4 tbsp roughly chopped fresh flat-leafed parsley

2 tbsp balsamic vinegar

200g (7oz) feta cheese, cubed (see Cook's Tip, page 26)

salt and ground black pepper

1 Preheat the oven to 200°C (180°C fan oven) mark 6. Put the red onions, courgettes, aubergine, peppers and garlic into a roasting tin and drizzle with the olive oil. Season with salt and pepper, then toss together and roast for 30 minutes.

2 Add the tomatoes to the tin. Toss together and roast for a further 30 minutes.

3 Meanwhile, put the couscous into a large bowl. Pour in the hot stock, stir and cover. Set aside to soak for 10 minutes.

4 Fluff up the warm couscous with a fork, then add the chopped parsley, balsamic vinegar, and roasted vegetables. Toss together, then spoon into warmed bowls, scatter the feta cheese over and serve.

EASY		NUTRITIONAL INFORMATION		Serves
Preparation Time 20 minutes, plus soaking	**Cooking Time** 1 hour	**Per Serving** 580 calories, 25g fat (of which 8g saturates), 73g carbohydrate, 2.3g salt	Vegetarian	**4**

Chilli Bolognese

1 tbsp olive oil

1 large onion, finely chopped

½ large red chilli, seeded and thinly sliced (see Cook's Tips, page 10)

450g (1lb) minced beef or lamb

125g (4oz) smoked bacon, rind removed, cut into strips

3 roasted red peppers, drained and finely chopped

400g can chopped tomatoes

125ml (4fl oz) red wine

300g (11oz) spaghetti

25g (1oz) freshly grated Cheddar or Gruyère cheese, plus extra to garnish

2 tbsp freshly chopped flat-leafed parsley (optional), plus extra to garnish

salt and ground black pepper

1 Heat the oil in a large pan over a medium heat. Add the onion and chilli and fry for 5–10 minutes until soft and golden. Add the beef or lamb and the bacon strips and stir over the heat for 5–7 minutes until well browned.

2 Stir in the red peppers, tomatoes and wine. Season with salt and pepper and bring to the boil, then reduce the heat and simmer over a low heat for 15–20 minutes.

3 Meanwhile, cook the pasta in a large pan of lightly salted boiling water according to the pack instructions. Drain.

4 Just before serving, stir the grated cheese, parsley, if using, and the sauce into the spaghetti. Garnish with extra grated cheese and chopped parsley.

Serves 4	EASY		NUTRITIONAL INFORMATION
	Preparation Time 15 minutes	**Cooking Time** 30–40 minutes	**Per Serving** 756 calories, 33g fat (of which 13g saturates), 74g carbohydrate, 1.4g salt

300g (11oz) linguine pasta

2 tbsp olive oil

1 garlic clove, crushed

1 red chilli, seeded and finely chopped (see Cook's Tips page 10)

4 tomatoes, seeded and chopped

900g (2lb) clams in their shells, washed and scrubbed

150ml (¼ pint) light dry white wine

2 tbsp freshly chopped parsley

Linguine with Clams

1 Cook the linguine in lightly salted boiling water according to the pack instructions.

2 Meanwhile, heat the oil in a large pan. Add the garlic, chilli and tomatoes and fry for 4 minutes, stirring gently. Add the clams and wine. Cover the pan with a lid and cook over a high heat for 3–4 minutes until the clam shells spring open – discard any that remain closed.

3 Drain the pasta and return to the pan, then add the clams with the sauce and the parsley. Toss together gently and serve immediately.

EASY		NUTRITIONAL INFORMATION		Serves
Preparation Time 15 minutes	**Cooking Time** 10 minutes	**Per Serving** 405 calories, 8g fat (of which 1g saturates), 60g carbohydrate, 2.3g salt	Dairy free	**4**

Pasta with Anchovies, Tomatoes and Olives

50g can anchovy fillets in oil

2 garlic cloves, crushed

4 sun-dried tomatoes, drained and roughly chopped

400g can chopped tomatoes

500g (1lb 2oz) dried spaghetti

200g (7oz) pitted black olives, roughly chopped

2 tbsp capers, drained

2–3 tbsp freshly chopped flat-leafed parsley

salt and ground black pepper

1 Drain the oil from the anchovies into a large pan. Heat the oil, then add the garlic and cook for 1 minute. Add the anchovies and sun-dried tomatoes and cook, stirring, for a further 1 minute. Add the canned tomatoes and bring to the boil. Season well with salt and pepper and simmer for 10–15 minutes.

2 Meanwhile, cook the spaghetti in a large pan of lightly salted boiling water according to the pack instructions until al dente.

3 Stir the olives and capers into the tomato sauce. Drain the spaghetti thoroughly, reserving about 4 tbsp of the cooking water, then return to the pan.

4 Add the tomato sauce and chopped parsley to the pasta and toss well to mix, thinning the sauce with the reserved cooking water, if necessary. Serve at once.

Cook's Tip

Spaghetti takes its name from the Italian word *spago*, meaning string.

Serves	EASY		NUTRITIONAL INFORMATION	
4	**Preparation Time** 15 minutes	**Cooking Time** 20–25 minutes	**Per Serving** 620 calories, 12g fat (of which 2g saturates), 96g carbohydrate, 4.5g salt	Dairy free

Cook's Tip

Oil–water spray is far lower in calories than oil alone and, as it sprays on thinly and evenly, you'll use less. Fill one-eighth of a travel-sized spray bottle with oil such as sunflower, light olive or vegetable (rapeseed) oil, then top up with water. To use, shake well before spraying. Store in the fridge.

Italian Meatballs

50g (2oz) fresh breadcrumbs

450g (1lb) lean minced pork

1 tsp fennel seeds, crushed

¼ tsp dried chilli flakes, or to taste

3 garlic cloves, crushed

4 tbsp freshly chopped flat-leafed parsley

3 tbsp red wine

oil–water spray (see Cook's Tip)

spaghetti to serve

freshly chopped oregano to garnish

For the tomato sauce

oil–water spray

2 large shallots, finely chopped

3 pitted black olives, shredded

2 garlic cloves, crushed

2 pinches of dried chilli flakes

250ml (9fl oz) vegetable or chicken stock

500g carton passata

2 tbsp each freshly chopped flat-leafed parsley, basil and oregano

salt and ground black pepper

1 To make the tomato sauce, spray a pan with the oil–water spray and add the shallots. Cook gently for 5 minutes. Add the olives, garlic, chilli flakes and stock, and bring to the boil, then reduce the heat, cover and simmer for 3–4 minutes.

2 Uncover and simmer for 10 minutes or until the shallots and garlic are soft and the liquid syrupy. Stir in the passata and season with salt and pepper. Bring to the boil, then reduce the heat and simmer for 10–15 minutes. Stir in the herbs.

3 Meanwhile, put the breadcrumbs into a large bowl and add the pork, fennel seeds, chilli flakes, garlic, parsley and wine. Season and mix together, using your hands, until thoroughly combined. (If you wish to check the seasoning, fry a little mixture, taste and adjust if necessary.)

4 With wet hands, roll the mixture into balls. Line a grill pan with foil, shiny side up, and spray with the oil–water spray. Cook the meatballs under a preheated grill for 3–4 minutes on each side. Serve with the tomato sauce and spaghetti, garnished with oregano.

Serves 4	EASY		NUTRITIONAL INFORMATION	
	Preparation Time 15 minutes	**Cooking Time** 50 minutes	**Per Serving** 275 calories, 12g fat (of which 4g saturates), 16g carbohydrate, 1.8g salt	Dairy free

Tuna Pasta

225g can tuna steak in olive oil
1 onion, finely sliced
1 garlic clove, chopped
2 × 400g cans chopped tomatoes
500g (1lb 2oz) dried penne or other pasta
50g can anchovy fillets in oil, drained and chopped
2 tbsp small capers
2 tbsp basil leaves, roughly torn (optional)
salt and ground black pepper

1 Drain the oil from the tuna into a pan and put the tuna to one side.

2 Heat the tuna oil, add the onion and fry over a low heat for about 10 minutes or until softened. Add the garlic and cook for 1 minute.

3 Add the tomatoes and stir well. Season generously with salt and pepper, then simmer over a medium heat for 15 minutes to reduce and thicken the sauce.

4 Meanwhile, cook the pasta in a large pan of lightly salted boiling water according to the pack instructions until al dente.

5 Flake the tuna and add to the tomato sauce with the anchovies, capers and basil leaves, if using. Stir to mix well.

6 Drain the pasta well, return to the pan and add the tuna sauce. Toss everything together to mix and serve immediately in warmed bowls.

EASY		NUTRITIONAL INFORMATION		Serves
Preparation Time 10 minutes	**Cooking Time** 30 minutes	**Per Serving** 650 calories, 16g fat (of which 2g saturates), 102g carbohydrates, 2.3g salt	Dairy free	**4**

30 Minute Recipe

Creamy Parma Ham and Artichoke Tagliatelle

500g (1lb 2oz) tagliatelle
500ml (18fl oz) crème fraîche
280g jar roasted artichoke hearts, drained and each cut in half
80g pack Parma ham (6 slices), torn into strips
2 tbsp freshly chopped sage leaves, plus extra to garnish
salt and ground black pepper
40g (1½ oz) Parmesan shavings to serve (see Cook's Tip)

1 Cook the pasta in a large pan of lightly salted boiling water according to the pack instructions.

2 Drain the pasta well, leaving a ladleful of the cooking water in the pan, then put the pasta back into the pan.

3 Add the crème fraîche to the pan with the artichoke hearts, Parma ham and sage, then stir everything together. Season well.

4 Spoon the pasta into warmed bowls, sprinkle with the Parmesan shavings and garnish with sage. Serve immediately.

Cook's Tip

Make Parmesan shavings with a vegetable peeler. Hold the piece of cheese in one hand and pare off wafer-thin strips of cheese using the peeler.

EASY		NUTRITIONAL INFORMATION	Serves
Preparation Time 5 minutes	**Cooking Time** 12 minutes	**Per Serving** 972 calories, 56g fat (of which 36g saturates), 97g carbohydrate, 1.1g salt	**4**

Cook's Tip

If using 'no need to pre-cook' dried lasagne, add a little extra stock or water to the sauce.

Classic Lasagne

butter to grease

350g (12oz) fresh lasagne, or 225g (8oz) 'no need to pre-cook' lasagne (12–15 sheets, see Cook's Tip)

3 tbsp freshly grated Parmesan

For the Bolognese sauce

2 tbsp olive oil

1 onion, finely chopped

2 garlic cloves, crushed

450g (1lb) extra-lean minced beef

2 tbsp sun-dried tomato paste

300ml (½ pint) red wine

400g can chopped tomatoes

125g (4oz) chestnut mushrooms, sliced

2 tbsp Worcestershire sauce

salt and ground black pepper

For the béchamel sauce

300ml (½ pint) semi-skimmed milk

1 onion slice

6 peppercorns

1 mace blade

1 bay leaf

15g (½oz) butter

15g (½oz) plain flour

freshly grated nutmeg

salt and ground black pepper

1 To make the Bolognese sauce, heat the oil in a large pan, add the onion and fry over a medium heat for 10 minutes or until softened and golden. Add the garlic and cook for 1 minute. Add the beef and brown evenly, using a wooden spoon to break up the pieces. Stir in the tomato paste and wine, cover and bring to the boil. Add the tomatoes, mushrooms and Worcestershire sauce and season well with salt and pepper. Bring back to the boil, reduce the heat and simmer for 20 minutes.

2 To make the béchamel sauce, pour the milk into a pan and add the onion, peppercorns, mace and bay leaf. Bring almost to the boil, then remove from the heat, cover and leave to infuse for about 20 minutes. Strain. Melt the butter in a pan, stir in the flour and cook, stirring, for 1 minute or until cooked but not coloured. Remove from the heat and gradually pour in the milk, whisking constantly. Season lightly with nutmeg, salt and pepper. Return to the heat and cook, stirring constantly, until the sauce is thickened and smooth. Simmer gently for 2 minutes.

3 Preheat the oven to 180°C (160°C fan oven) mark 4. Spoon one-third of the Bolognese sauce over the base of a greased 2.3 litre (4 pint) ovenproof dish. Cover with a layer of lasagne sheets, then a layer of béchamel. Repeat these layers twice more, finishing with a layer of béchamel to cover the lasagne.

4 Sprinkle the Parmesan over the top and stand the dish on a baking sheet. Cook in the oven for 45 minutes or until well browned and bubbling.

Serves	EASY		NUTRITIONAL INFORMATION
6	**Preparation Time** 40 minutes	**Cooking Time** 45 minutes	**Per Serving** 367 calories, 14g fat (of which 5g sats) 36g carbohydrate, 1.9g salt

1 butternut squash

2 tbsp olive oil

1 medium onion, sliced

salt and ground black pepper

For the sauce

25g (1oz) butter

25g (1oz) plain flour

600ml (1 pint) milk

To assemble

225g bag baby leaf spinach

250g carton ricotta cheese

1 tsp freshly grated nutmeg

6 'no need to pre-cook' lasagne sheets, about 100g (3½oz)

50g (2oz) pecorino or Parmesan (see Cook's Tip, page 26), freshly grated

Butternut Squash and Spinach Lasagne

1 Preheat the oven to 200°C (180°C fan oven) mark 6. Peel, halve and seed the butternut squash, then cut into 3cm (1¼ in) cubes. Put into a large roasting tin with the olive oil, onion and 1 tbsp water. Toss everything together and season well with salt and ground black pepper. Roast for 25 minutes, tossing halfway through.

2 To make the sauce, melt the butter in a pan, then stir in the flour and cook over a medium heat for 1–2 minutes. Gradually add the milk over the heat, stirring constantly. Reduce the heat to a simmer and cook, stirring, for 5 minutes or until the sauce has thickened.

3 Heat 1 tbsp water in another pan. Add the spinach, cover and cook until the leaves are just wilted. Season generously.

4 Crumble the ricotta into the sauce and add the nutmeg. Mix together thoroughly and season with salt and pepper to taste.

5 Spoon the squash and onion mixture into a 1.7 litre (3 pint) ovenproof dish. Layer the spinach on top, then cover with a third of the sauce, then the lasagne. Spoon the remaining sauce on top, season and sprinkle with the grated cheese. Bake for 30–35 minutes until the cheese topping is golden and the pasta is cooked.

EASY		NUTRITIONAL INFORMATION		Serves
Preparation Time 30 minutes	**Cooking Time** 1 hour	**Per Serving** 320 calories, 17g fat (of which 8g saturates), 30g carbohydrate, 1g salt	Vegetarian	**6**

Spinach and Ricotta Cannelloni

1 tbsp olive oil, plus extra to grease

1 small onion, chopped

1 bay leaf

1 garlic clove, crushed

400g can chopped tomatoes

300g (11oz) spinach, coarse stalks removed

2 × 250g tubs ricotta cheese

1 large egg

25g (1oz) freshly grated Parmesan (see Cook's Tip, page 26)

freshly grated nutmeg

15 cannelloni tubes

125g mozzarella ball, roughly torn

salt and ground black pepper

fresh basil leaves to garnish

1 Heat the oil in a pan and gently fry the onion with the bay leaf for 10 minutes or until softened. Add the garlic and fry for 1 minute. Pour in the tomatoes along with half a can of cold water, bring to the boil, then simmer for 20 minutes or until slightly thickened.

2 Meanwhile, wash the spinach and put into a large pan set over a low heat. Cover the pan and cook the spinach for 2 minutes or until just wilted. Drain and cool under running water. When cool enough to handle, squeeze out the excess moisture and roughly chop.

3 Preheat the oven to 180°C (160°C fan oven) mark 4 and lightly oil a baking dish. Mix together the ricotta, egg, Parmesan and spinach with a grating of nutmeg and season with plenty of salt and ground black pepper. Spoon or pipe into the cannelloni tubes and put into the dish in one layer.

4 Pour the tomato sauce over the pasta, then dot with the mozzarella. Bake for 30–40 minutes until golden and bubbling. Scatter with the basil and serve.

Cook's Tip

Usually made from egg pasta, cannelloni are large, broad tubes designed to be stuffed, coated in sauce and baked.

Serves 4	EASY		NUTRITIONAL INFORMATION	
	Preparation Time 25 minutes	**Cooking Time** 1 hour 10 minutes	**Per Serving** 409 calories, 14g fat (of which 7g saturates), 53g carbohydrate, 1.5g salt	Vegetarian

one pot and
slow cook

One-pot Chicken

2 tbsp olive oil

1 large onion, cut into wedges

2 rindless streaky bacon rashers, chopped

1 chicken, about 1.6kg (3½ lb)

6 carrots

2 small turnips, cut into wedges

1 garlic clove, crushed

bouquet garni (see page 36)

600ml (1 pint) hot chicken stock

100ml (3½ fl oz) dry white wine

12 button mushrooms

3 tbsp freshly chopped flat-leafed parsley

salt and ground black pepper

mashed potatoes to serve (optional)

1 Heat the oil in a non-stick flameproof casserole. Add the onion and bacon and fry for 5 minutes or until golden. Remove and put to one side.

2 Add the whole chicken to the casserole and fry for 10 minutes, turning carefully to brown all over. Remove and put to one side.

3 Preheat the oven to 200°C (180°C fan oven) mark 6. Add the carrots, turnips and garlic to the casserole and fry for 5 minutes, then add the onion and bacon. Put the chicken back into the casserole, add the bouquet garni, hot stock and wine and season with salt and pepper. Bring to a simmer, then cover the pan and cook in the oven for 30 minutes.

4 Remove the casserole from the oven and add the mushrooms. Baste the chicken, then re-cover and cook for a further 50 minutes.

5 Lift out the chicken, then stir the parsley into the cooking liquid. Carve the chicken and serve with the vegetables and cooking liquid, and mashed potatoes, if you like.

Try Something Different

Use chicken pieces such as drumsticks or thighs, reducing the cooking time in step 4 to 20 minutes.

Chicken Cacciatore

2 tbsp olive oil
8 boneless, skinless chicken thighs
2 garlic cloves, crushed
1 tsp dried thyme
1 tsp dried tarragon
150ml (¼ pint) white wine
400g can chopped tomatoes
12 pitted black olives
12 capers, rinsed and drained
ground black pepper

1 Heat the oil in a flameproof casserole over a high heat. Add the chicken and brown all over. Reduce the heat and add the garlic, thyme, tarragon and wine to the casserole. Stir for 1 minute, then add the tomatoes and season with pepper.

2 Bring to the boil, then reduce the heat, cover the casserole and simmer for 20 minutes or until the chicken is tender.

3 Lift the chicken out of the casserole and put to one side. Bubble the sauce for 5 minutes or until thickened, add the olives and capers, stir well and cook for a further 2–3 minutes.

4 Put the chicken into the sauce. Serve with brown rice and broad beans or peas.

Serves 4	EASY		NUTRITIONAL INFORMATION	
	Preparation Time 5 minutes	**Cooking Time** 40 minutes	**Per Serving** 327 calories, 17g fat (of which 4g saturates), 3g carbohydrate, 1.3g salt	Gluten free Dairy free

Try Something Different

Use mixed beans instead of the butter beans.

Chicken with Chorizo and Beans

1 tbsp olive oil

12 chicken pieces (6 drumsticks and 6 thighs)

175g (6oz) chorizo sausage, cubed

1 onion, finely chopped

2 large garlic cloves, crushed

1 tsp mild chilli powder

3 red peppers, seeded and roughly chopped

400g (14oz) passata

2 tbsp tomato purée

150ml (¼ pint) hot chicken stock

2 × 400g cans butter beans, drained and rinsed

200g (7oz) new potatoes, quartered

1 small bunch of thyme

1 bay leaf

200g (7oz) baby leaf spinach

1 Heat the oil in a large pan over a medium heat. Add the chicken and fry until browned all over, then transfer to the slow cooker.

2 Add the chorizo to the pan and fry for 2–3 minutes until its oil starts to run. Add the onion, garlic and chilli powder and fry over a low heat for 5 minutes or until the onion is soft.

3 Add the red peppers and cook for 2–3 minutes until soft. Stir in the passata, tomato purée, hot stock, butter beans, potatoes, thyme sprigs and bay leaf. Bring to the boil, then add to the chicken. Cover and cook on Low for 4–5 hours until the chicken is cooked through.

4 Remove the thyme and bay leaf, then stir in the spinach until it wilts. Serve immediately.

EASY		NUTRITIONAL INFORMATION		Serves
Preparation Time 10 minutes	**Cooking Time** 4–5 hours on Low	**Per Serving** 690 calories, 41g fat (of which 12g saturates), 33g carbohydrate, 2.6g salt	Dairy free	**6**

Peppered Winter Stew

25g (1oz) plain flour

900g (2lb) stewing venison, beef or lamb, cut into 4cm (1½ in) cubes

5 tbsp oil

225g (8oz) button onions or shallots, peeled with root end intact

225g (8oz) onion, finely chopped

4 garlic cloves, crushed

2 tbsp tomato purée

125ml (4fl oz) red wine vinegar

75cl bottle red wine

2 tbsp redcurrant jelly

1 small bunch of fresh thyme, plus extra sprigs to garnish (optional)

4 bay leaves

6 cloves

900g (2lb) mixed root vegetables, such as carrots, parsnips, turnips and celeriac, cut into 4cm (1½ in) chunks; carrots cut a little smaller

600–900ml (1–1½ pints) beef stock

salt and ground black pepper

1 Preheat the oven to 180°C (160°C fan oven) mark 4. Put the flour into a plastic bag, season with salt and pepper, then toss the meat in it.

2 Heat 3 tbsp oil in a large flameproof casserole over a medium heat and brown the meat well in small batches. Remove and put to one side.

3 Heat the remaining oil and fry the button onions or shallots for 5 minutes or until golden. Add the chopped onion and the garlic and cook, stirring, until soft and golden. Add the tomato purée and cook for a further 2 minutes, then add the vinegar and wine and bring to the boil. Bubble for 10 minutes.

4 Add the redcurrant jelly, thyme, bay leaves, 1 tbsp coarsely ground black pepper, the cloves and meat to the pan, with the vegetables and enough stock to barely cover the meat and vegetables. Bring to the boil, then reduce the heat, cover the pan and cook in the oven for 1¾–2¼ hours until the meat is very tender. Serve hot, garnished with thyme sprigs, if you like.

Freezing Tip

To freeze Complete the recipe to the end of step 4, without the garnish. Cool quickly and put in a freezerproof container. Seal and freeze for up to one month.

To use Thaw overnight at cool room temperature. Preheat the oven to 180°C (160°C fan oven) mark 4. Put into a flameproof casserole and add an extra 150ml (¼ pint) beef stock. Bring to the boil. Cover and reheat for 30 minutes. Add the garnish and serve.

EASY		NUTRITIONAL INFORMATION		Serves
Preparation Time 20 minutes	**Cooking Time** 2¼–2¾ hours	**Per Serving** 540 calories, 24g fat (of which 7g saturates), 24g carbohydrate, 1.5g salt	Dairy free	**6**

Beef and Guinness Stew

1.4kg (3lb) shin of beef or braising steak, cut into 3cm (1¼ in) cubes

2 tbsp seasoned plain flour

4 tbsp vegetable oil

2 medium onions, sliced

4 medium carrots, cut into chunks

225ml (8fl oz) Guinness

300ml (½ pint) hot beef stock

2 bay leaves

700g (1½ lb) baby potatoes, halved if large

2 tbsp freshly chopped flat-leafed parsley

salt and ground black pepper

1 Toss the beef in the flour to coat and shake off any excess. Heat the oil in a large pan until hot. Add a handful of beef and cook until well browned. Remove with a slotted spoon, transfer to the slow cooker and repeat until all the meat is browned.

2 Add the onions and carrots to the pan and cook for 10 minutes or until browned. Add the Guinness, scraping the base to loosen the goodness, then stir in the hot stock. Add the bay leaves and potatoes and bring to the boil. Pour over the beef in the slow cooker, cover and cook on Low for 8–10 hours until the meat is tender.

3 Stir in the parsley, season to taste and serve.

Serves 6	EASY		NUTRITIONAL INFORMATION	
	Preparation Time 15 minutes	**Cooking Time** 8–10 hours on Low	**Per Serving** 526 calories, 29g fat (of which 10g saturates), 10g carbohydrate, 0.4g salt	Dairy free

Cook's Tips

Instead of a can of tomatoes with garlic, use a can of chopped tomatoes and 1 crushed garlic clove.
Adding a little dark chocolate to chilli con carne brings out the flavours of this tasty dish.

Mexican Chilli Con Carne

2 tbsp olive oil
450g (1lb) minced beef
1 large onion, finely chopped
$\frac{1}{2}$–1 tsp each hot chilli powder and ground cumin
3 tbsp tomato purée
150ml ($\frac{1}{4}$ pint) hot beef stock
400g can chopped tomatoes with garlic (see Cook's Tips)
25g (1oz) dark chocolate
400g can red kidney beans, drained and rinsed
2 × 20g packs coriander, chopped
salt and ground black pepper
guacamole, salsa, soured cream, grated cheese, tortilla chips and pickled chillies to serve

1 Heat 1 tbsp oil in a large pan and fry the beef for 10 minutes or until well browned, stirring to break up any lumps. Remove from the pan with a slotted spoon and transfer to the slow cooker.

2 Add the remaining oil to the pan, then fry the onion, stirring, for 10 minutes or until soft and golden.

3 Add the spices and fry for 1 minute, then add the tomato purée, hot stock and the tomatoes. Bring to the boil, then stir into the mince in the slow cooker. Cover and cook on Low for 4–5 hours.

4 Stir in the chocolate, kidney beans and coriander and season with salt and pepper, then leave to stand for 10 minutes.

5 Serve with guacamole, salsa, soured cream, grated cheese, tortilla chips and pickled chillies.

EASY		NUTRITIONAL INFORMATION		Serves
Preparation Time 5 minutes	**Cooking Time** 4–5 hours on Low	**Per Serving** 408 calories, 19g fat (of which 7g saturates), 28g carbohydrate, 1.1g salt	Gluten free Dairy free	**4**

Braised Lamb Shanks with Cannellini Beans

3 tbsp olive oil

6 lamb shanks

1 large onion, chopped

3 carrots, sliced

3 celery sticks, sliced

2 garlic cloves, crushed

2 × 400g cans chopped tomatoes

125ml (4fl oz) balsamic vinegar

2 bay leaves

2 × 400g cans cannellini beans, drained and rinsed

salt and ground black pepper

1 Preheat the oven to 170°C (150°C fan oven) mark 3. Heat the oil in a large flameproof casserole and brown the lamb shanks, in two batches, all over. Remove and set aside.

2 Add the onion, carrots, celery and garlic to the casserole and cook gently until softened and just beginning to colour.

3 Return the lamb to the casserole and add the chopped tomatoes and balsamic vinegar, giving the mixture a good stir. Season with salt and pepper and add the bay leaves. Bring to a simmer, cover and cook on the hob for 5 minutes.

4 Transfer to the oven and cook for 1½–2 hours until the lamb shanks are nearly tender.

5 Remove the casserole from the oven and add the cannellini beans. Cover and return to the oven for a further 30 minutes, then serve.

Serves 6	EASY		NUTRITIONAL INFORMATION	
	Preparation Time 15 minutes	**Cooking Time** 2½–3 hours	**Per Serving** 382 calories, 18g fat (of which 6g saturates), 29g carbohydrate, 1.2g salt	Gluten free Dairy free

Cook's Tip

To make clarified butter, heat butter in a pan without allowing it to colour. Skim off the foam; the solids will sink. Pour the clear butter into a bowl through a lined sieve. Leave for 10 minutes. Pour into a bowl, leaving any sediment behind. Cool. Store in a jar in the fridge for up to six months.

Lamb, Prune and Almond Tagine

2 tsp coriander seeds

2 tsp cumin seeds

2 tsp chilli powder

1 tbsp paprika

1 tbsp ground turmeric

5 garlic cloves, chopped

6 tbsp olive oil

1.4kg (3lb) lamb leg steaks

75g (3oz) ghee or clarified butter (see Cook's Tip)

2 large onions, finely chopped

1 carrot, roughly chopped

900ml (1½ pints) lamb stock

300g (11oz) ready-to-eat prunes

4 cinnamon sticks

4 bay leaves

50g (2oz) ground almonds

12 shallots

1 tbsp honey

salt and ground black pepper

toasted blanched almonds and freshly chopped flat-leafed parsley to garnish

couscous to serve

1 Using a pestle and mortar or a blender, combine the coriander and cumin seeds, chilli powder, paprika, turmeric, garlic and 4 tbsp oil. Coat the lamb with the paste, then cover and chill for at least 5 hours.

2 Preheat the oven to 170°C (150°C fan oven) mark 3. Melt 25g (1oz) ghee or butter in a large flameproof casserole. Add the onions and carrot and cook until soft. Remove and put to one side. Fry the paste-coated lamb on both sides in the remaining ghee or butter. Add a little of the stock and bring to the boil, scraping up the sediment from the bottom. Put the onions and carrot back in the casserole and add 100g (3½oz) prunes. Add the remaining stock with the cinnamon sticks, bay leaves and ground almonds. Season, cover and cook in the oven for 2 hours or until the meat is really tender.

3 Meanwhile, fry the shallots in the remaining oil and the honey until they turn a deep golden brown. Add to the casserole 30–40 minutes before the end of the cooking time.

4 Take the lamb out of the sauce and put to one side. Bring the sauce to the boil, then reduce to a thick consistency. Put the lamb back in the casserole, add the remaining prunes and bubble for 3–4 minutes. Garnish with the almonds and parsley. Serve hot with couscous.

Serves	EASY		NUTRITIONAL INFORMATION	
6	**Preparation Time** 20 minutes, plus marinating	**Cooking Time** 2½ hours	**Per Serving** 652 calories, 44g fat (of which 16g saturates), 31g carbohydrate, 0.6g salt	Gluten free

Cook's Tip

Massaman paste is a Thai curry paste. The ingredients include red chillies, roasted shallots, roasted garlic, galangal, lemongrass, roasted coriander seeds, roasted cumin, roasted cloves, white pepper, salt and shrimp paste. It's available in supermarkets or Asian food stores.

2 tbsp olive oil

1 medium onion, chopped

1 tbsp peeled and grated fresh root ginger

1.6kg (3½ lb) leg of lamb, diced

3–4 tbsp Massaman paste (see Cook's Tip)

1 tbsp fish sauce

2 tbsp peanut butter

100g (3½ oz) ground almonds

400ml can coconut milk

600ml (1 pint) hot chicken stock

1–2 tbsp dry sherry

500g (1lb 2oz) small potatoes, quartered

200g (7oz) green beans, trimmed

75g (3oz) toasted peanuts, roughly chopped, to garnish

20g pack coriander, finely chopped, to garnish

2 limes, quartered, and rice (optional) to serve

Lamb, Potato and Peanut Curry

1 Preheat the oven to 170°C (150°C fan oven) mark 3. Heat the oil in a large flameproof casserole. Add the onion and cook over a medium heat for 7–8 minutes until golden. Add the ginger and cook for 1 minute. Spoon the onion mixture out of the pan and set aside. Add the lamb and fry in batches until browned. Set aside.

2 Add the Massaman paste, fish sauce and peanut butter to the casserole dish and fry for 2–3 minutes, then add the reserved onion and ginger mixture and lamb pieces, the ground almonds, coconut milk, hot stock and sherry.

3 Bring to the boil, then cover with a lid and cook in the oven for 1 hour. Add the potatoes and cook for a further 40 minutes, uncovered, adding the green beans for the last 20 minutes. Garnish the curry with toasted peanuts and coriander. Serve with freshly cooked rice, if you like, and lime wedges to squeeze over the curry.

EASY		NUTRITIONAL INFORMATION		Serves
Preparation Time 20 minutes	**Cooking Time** about 2 hours	**Per Serving** 664 calories, 47g fat (of which 20g saturates), 19g carbohydrate, 0.5g salt	Gluten free Dairy free	**8**

One-pot Gammon Stew

1 tbsp olive oil

1.1kg (2½lb) smoked gammon joint

8 shallots, blanched in boiling water, drained, peeled and chopped into chunks

3 carrots, chopped into chunks

3 celery sticks, chopped into chunks

4 large Desirée potatoes, unpeeled

450ml (¾ pint) each apple juice and hot vegetable stock

½ small Savoy cabbage

25g (1oz) butter

1 Preheat the oven to 190°C (170°C fan oven) mark 5. Heat the oil in a large flameproof casserole. Add the gammon and cook for 5 minutes or until brown all over. Remove from the pan.

2 Add the shallots, carrots and celery to the pan and fry for 3–4 minutes until starting to soften.

3 Return the gammon to the pan. Chop the potatoes into quarters and add to the pan with the apple juice and hot stock. Cover and bring to the boil, then transfer to the oven and cook for 50 minutes or until the meat is cooked through and the vegetables are tender.

4 Remove from the oven and put the dish back on the hob over a low heat. Shred the cabbage and stir into the pan. Simmer for 2–3 minutes, then stir in the butter and serve.

Serves 4	EASY		NUTRITIONAL INFORMATION	
	Preparation Time 15 minutes	Cooking Time 1 hour 10 minutes	Per Serving 680 calories, 30g fat (of which 11g saturates), 41g carbohydrate, 6.3g salt	Gluten free

Try Something Different

Instead of pork, use the same quantity of lean lamb, such as leg, trimmed of excess fat and cut into cubes.

Warming Winter Casserole

2 tbsp olive oil

500g (1lb 2oz) pork fillet, cubed

1 onion, finely chopped

2 garlic cloves, finely chopped

1 tsp ground cinnamon

1 tbsp ground coriander

1 tsp ground cumin

2.5cm (1in) piece fresh root ginger, peeled and grated

400g can mixed beans or chickpeas, drained and rinsed

1 red pepper, seeded and sliced

50g (2oz) ready-to-eat dried apricots, roughly chopped

300ml (½ pint) chicken stock

25g (1oz) flaked almonds, toasted

salt and ground black pepper

freshly chopped flat-leafed parsley to garnish

brown basmati rice to serve

1 Heat 1 tbsp oil in a flameproof casserole, and fry the pork in batches, until brown all over. Remove and set aside. Add the remaining oil, then add the onion and cook for 10 minutes or until softened. Return the pork to the casserole, add the garlic, spices and ginger and cook for 2 minutes.

2 Add the mixed beans, red pepper, apricots and stock. Season well with salt and pepper, then stir and bring to the boil. Reduce the heat to the lowest setting and simmer, covered, for 40 minutes, adding a little extra stock if it begins to look dry.

3 Check the seasoning and sprinkle with the almonds, then garnish with the parsley and serve with brown basmati rice.

EASY		NUTRITIONAL INFORMATION		Serves
Preparation Time 20 minutes	**Cooking Time** 1 hour	**Per Serving** 407 calories, 16g fat (of which 3g saturates), 32g carbohydrate, 1g salt	Gluten free Dairy free	**4**

Fish Stew

2 tbsp olive oil

1 onion, chopped

1 leek, trimmed and chopped

2 tsp smoked paprika

2 tbsp tomato purée

450g (1lb) cod or haddock, roughly chopped

125g (4oz) basmati rice

175ml (6fl oz) white wine

450ml (¾ pint) hot fish stock

200g (7oz) cooked and peeled king prawns

a large handful of spinach leaves

crusty bread to serve

1 Heat the oil in a large pan. Add the onion and leek and fry for 8–10 minutes until they start to soften. Add the smoked paprika and tomato purée and cook for 1–2 minutes.

2 Add the fish, rice, wine and hot stock. Bring to the boil, then cover the pan, reduce the heat and simmer for 10 minutes or until the fish is cooked through and the rice is tender. Add the prawns and cook for 1 minute or until heated through. Stir in the spinach until it wilts, then serve with chunks of bread.

Healthy Tip

This dish is packed with body-building protein. The onions and leeks are rich in powerful sulphur-containing compounds, including the phytochemical quercetin, which helps keep the heart healthy.

Try Something Different

There are lots of alternatives to cod and haddock: try sea bass, gurnard, coley (saithe) or pollack.

EASY		NUTRITIONAL INFORMATION		Serves
Preparation Time 15 minutes	**Cooking Time** about 30 minutes	**Per Serving** 280 calories, 7g fat (of which 1g saturates) 34g carbohydrate, 0.3g salt	Gluten free Dairy free	**4**

fish and seafood

Cook's Tip

Gumbo is a traditional stew from the southern states of the USA, containing meat, vegetables and shellfish, and thickened with okra.

Seafood Gumbo

125g (4oz) butter

50g (2oz) plain flour

1–2 tbsp Cajun spice

1 onion, chopped

1 green pepper, seeded and chopped

5 spring onions, sliced

1 tbsp freshly chopped flat-leafed parsley

1 garlic clove, crushed

1 beef tomato, chopped

125g (4oz) garlic sausage, finely sliced

75g (3oz) American easy-cook rice

1.1 litres (2 pints) vegetable stock

250g (9oz) okra, sliced

1 bay leaf

1 fresh thyme sprig

2 tsp salt

$^1/_4$ tsp cayenne pepper

juice of $^1/_2$ lemon

4 cloves

175g (6oz) raw tiger prawns

175g (6oz) raw mussels in their shells, scrubbed, rinsed and beards removed (see Cook's Tips, page 39)

150g (5oz) squid tubes, sliced

ground black pepper

crusty bread to serve

1 Heat the butter in a 2.5 litre (4$^1/_4$–4$^1/_2$ pint) heavy-based pan over a low heat. Add the flour and Cajun spice and cook, stirring, for 1–2 minutes until golden brown. Add the onion, green pepper, spring onions, parsley and garlic, and cook for 5 minutes.

2 Add the tomato, garlic sausage and rice to the pan and stir well to coat. Add the stock, okra, bay leaf, thyme, salt, cayenne pepper, lemon juice and cloves. Season with black pepper. Bring to the boil and simmer, covered, for 12 minutes or until the rice is tender.

3 Add the seafood and cook for 3–4 minutes until the prawns are pink and the mussels have opened. Discard any mussels that are still closed. Serve the gumbo in deep bowls with bread.

Serves 4	EASY		NUTRITIONAL INFORMATION
	Preparation Time 10 minutes	**Cooking Time** 30 minutes	**Per Serving** 607 calories, 38g fat (of which 21g saturates), 42g carbohydrates, 1.6g salt

Healthy Tip

Squid is a good source of protein, and contains approximately 8g
(¹/₄oz) of fat per 100g (3¹/₂oz). It is rich in vitamin B6, selenium and
phosphorus. The haricot beans in this recipe add protein, complex
carbohydrate and iron.

Squid with Haricot Beans and Rocket

450g (1lb) prepared squid, cut into thick rings

3 tbsp extra virgin olive oil

1 rosemary sprig, cut into four pieces

1 chilli, seeded and finely chopped (see Cook's Tip, page 10)

zest and juice of 1 lemon

2 x 400g cans haricot beans, drained and rinsed

2 tbsp olive oil

6 slices sourdough bread (about 40g each slice)

55g pack rocket

salt and ground black pepper

lemon wedges to serve

1 Put the squid into a non-metallic bowl. Add 1 tbsp extra virgin olive oil, the rosemary, chilli and half the lemon zest. Season to taste with salt and pepper, then leave to marinate for 30 minutes.

2 Put the beans into a large bowl with the remaining lemon zest and extra virgin olive oil and the lemon juice. Season with salt and pepper, then use a potato masher to pound into a rough purée.

3 Heat the olive oil in a wok or a non-stick frying pan. Add the squid and cook for 1–2 minutes until opaque. Toast the bread.

4 Spread the bean purée over the toast. Top with the squid and rocket and serve with lemon wedges.

EASY		NUTRITIONAL INFORMATION	Serves
Preparation Time 20 minutes, plus marinating	**Cooking Time** about 2 minutes	**Per Serving** 308 calories 12g fat (of which 2g saturates) 33g carbohydrate, 0.8g salt — Dairy free	**6**

Moules Marinière

2kg (4½lb) fresh mussels, scrubbed, rinsed and beards removed (see Cook's Tips, page 39)

25g (1oz) butter

4 shallots, finely chopped

2 garlic cloves, crushed

200ml (7fl oz) dry white wine

2 tbsp freshly chopped flat-leafed parsley

100ml (3½fl oz) single cream

salt and ground black pepper

crusty bread to serve

1 Tap the mussels on the worksurface and discard any that do not close or have broken shells. Heat the butter in a large non-stick lidded frying pan and sauté the shallots over a medium-high heat for about 10 minutes or until soft.

2 Add the garlic, wine and half the parsley to the pan and bring to the boil. Tip in the mussels and reduce the heat a little. Cover and cook for about 5 minutes or until all the shells have opened; discard any mussels that are still closed.

3 Lift out the mussels with a slotted spoon and put into serving bowls, then cover with foil to keep warm. Add the cream to the pan, season with salt and pepper and cook for 1–2 minutes to heat through.

4 Pour a little sauce over the mussels and sprinkle with the rest of the parsley. Serve immediately with crusty bread.

Serves	EASY		NUTRITIONAL INFORMATION
4	**Preparation Time** 15 minutes	**Cooking Time** 20 minutes	**Per Serving** 262 calories, 13g fat (of which 7g saturates), 2g carbohydrates, 0.9g salt

30 Minute Recipe

Smoked Haddock Kedgeree

175g (6oz) long-grain rice
450g (1lb) smoked haddock fillets
2 medium eggs, hard-boiled and shelled
75g (3oz) butter
salt and cayenne pepper
freshly chopped parsley to garnish

1 Cook the rice in a pan of lightly salted fast-boiling water until tender. Drain well and rinse under cold water.

2 Meanwhile, put the haddock into a large frying pan with just enough water to cover. Bring to simmering point, then simmer for 10–15 minutes until tender. Drain, skin and flake the fish, discarding the bones.

3 Chop one egg and slice the other into rings. Melt the butter in a pan, add the cooked rice, fish, chopped egg, salt and cayenne pepper and stir over a medium heat for 5 minutes or until hot. Pile on to a warmed serving dish and garnish with parsley and the sliced egg.

EASY		NUTRITIONAL INFORMATION	Serves
Preparation Time 10 minutes	**Cooking Time** 20 minutes	**Per Serving** 429 calories, 20g fat (of which 11g saturates), 38g carbohydrates, 3.1g salt	**4**

Roasted Salmon

2 lemons, sliced, and the juice of ½ lemon, plus extra lemon slices to garnish

2 salmon sides, filleted, each 1.4kg (3lb), skin on, boned and trimmed

2 tbsp dry white wine

salt and ground black pepper

cucumber slices and 2 large bunches of watercress to garnish

For the dressing

500g carton crème fraîche

500g carton natural yogurt

2 tbsp horseradish sauce

3 tbsp freshly chopped tarragon

4 tbsp capers, roughly chopped, plus extra to garnish

¼ cucumber, seeded and finely chopped

1 Preheat the oven to 190°C (170°C fan oven) mark 5. Take two pieces of foil, each large enough to wrap one side of salmon, and put a piece of greaseproof paper on top. Divide the lemon slices between each piece of greaseproof paper and lay the salmon on top, skin side up. Season with salt and pepper, then pour the lemon juice and wine over.

2 Score the skin of each salmon fillet at 4cm (1½in) intervals to mark 10 portions. Scrunch the foil around each fillet, keeping it loose so the fish doesn't stick. Cook for 25 minutes until the flesh is just opaque. Unwrap the foil and cook for a further 5 minutes until the skin is crisp. Leave the fish to cool quickly in a cold place. Re-wrap and chill.

3 Put all the dressing ingredients into a bowl and season with salt and pepper. Mix well, then cover and chill.

4 Serve the salmon on a serving plate garnished with lemon, cucumber and watercress. Garnish the dressing with capers and chopped cucumber.

Get Ahead

To prepare ahead Complete the recipe to the end of step 3, then keep the salmon wrapped and chilled for up to one day.
To use Complete the recipe.

Cook's Tips

There'll be a lot of hot liquid in the parcel of salmon, so ask someone to help you lift it out of the oven.
To check the fish is cooked, ease a knife into one of the slashes in the skin. The flesh should look opaque and the knife should come out hot.

Serves 20	EASY		NUTRITIONAL INFORMATION	
	Preparation Time 20 minutes	**Cooking Time** about 30 minutes, plus cooling and chilling	**Per Serving** 347 calories, 25g fat (of which 9g saturates), 3g carbohydrates, 0.2g salt	Dairy free Gluten free

Healthy Tip

Fennel is packed with antioxidants that help protect the body from free radical damage. It is believed to help combat certain cancers. It is also a good source of fibre, vitamin C, folate, magnesium, calcium, iron and phosphorus, and helpful in easing digestive problems such as gas and bloating.

Cook's Tip

Ask your fishmonger to remove the scales from the cod's skin. When grilled, the skin will be crisp and delicious to eat.

Cod Steaks with Fennel

1 tbsp hoisin sauce

4 tbsp light soy sauce

4 tbsp dry vermouth

4 tbsp orange juice

½ tsp Chinese five-spice powder

½ tsp ground cumin

1 garlic clove, crushed

4 × 150g (5oz) thick cod fillets or steaks (see Cook's Tip)

1 tbsp vegetable oil

2 fennel bulbs, about 700g (1½lb), thinly sliced and tops put to one side

2 tsp sesame seeds

1 For the marinade, combine the hoisin sauce, soy sauce, vermouth, orange juice, five-spice powder, cumin and garlic. Put the cod into a shallow dish and pour the marinade over it. Cover and leave to marinate in a cool place for at least 1 hour.

2 Preheat the grill or a lightly oiled griddle. Remove the fish and put the marinade to one side. Cook the fish under the hot grill or on the hot griddle for 4 minutes, then turn over and cook for 3–4 minutes until cooked.

3 Heat the oil in a sauté pan. Add the fennel and cook briskly for 5–7 minutes until brown and beginning to soften. Add the marinade, bring to the boil and bubble until reduced and sticky.

4 Put the fish on a bed of fennel, spoon any pan juices around it and sprinkle with the sesame seeds. Garnish with the reserved fennel tops.

Serves 4	EASY		NUTRITIONAL INFORMATION	
	Preparation Time 10 minutes, plus marinating	**Cooking Time** 30 minutes	**Per Serving** 209 calories, 6g fat (of which 1g saturates) 6g carbohydrate, 1.4g salt	Dairy free

Cook's Tips

If the mackerel are large, make three shallow slashes on either side of the fish.
To test whether the fish is cooked, prise the flesh from the backbone with a knife: it should be opaque and come away easily.

30 Minute Recipe

Peppered Mackerel

4 tsp whole mixed peppercorns

4 fresh mackerel, gutted, about 250g (9oz) each

1 tbsp sunflower oil

200ml (7fl oz) crème fraîche

lemon wedges to garnish

asparagus and sugarsnap peas to serve

1 Lightly crush 2 tsp peppercorns using a pestle and mortar. Sprinkle one side of each mackerel with half the crushed peppercorns.

2 Heat the oil in a frying pan over a medium-high heat. Add the fish, peppered side down, and cook for 5–7 minutes. Sprinkle the mackerel with the remaining crushed peppercorns, turn the fish over and continue to fry for 5–7 minutes until cooked (see Cook's Tips). Remove and keep warm.

3 Wipe out the pan, add the crème fraîche and bring to the boil. Stir in the remaining whole peppercorns. (If the sauce becomes too thick, add some boiling water.)

4 To serve, spoon the sauce over the mackerel, garnish with lemon wedges and serve with asparagus and sugarsnap peas.

EASY		NUTRITIONAL INFORMATION		Serves
Preparation Time 10 minutes	**Cooking Time** 15 minutes	**Per Serving** 764 calories, 63g fat (of which 22g saturates), 1g carbohydrate, 0.4g salt	Gluten free	**4**

Sardines with Herbs

900g (2lb) sardines (at least 12), gutted

125ml (4fl oz) olive oil

3 tbsp lemon juice

2 tsp grated lemon zest

4 tbsp freshly chopped mixed herbs, such as parsley, chervil and thyme

salt and ground black pepper

crusty bread to serve

1 If you like, bone the sardines (see Cook's Tip), leaving the heads and tails intact. Rinse the sardines and pat dry with kitchen paper

2 In a bowl, mix together the olive oil, lemon juice, lemon zest, herbs and seasoning.

3 Lay the sardines on a grill rack, drizzle the herb dressing over them and grill under a medium-high heat for 5–7 minutes each side, basting frequently with the dressing. Serve hot or cold, with plenty of crusty bread.

Cook's Tip

To remove the backbones from small fish, such as sardines, make sure the cut along the belly (used for gutting) extends along to the tail. Put the fish, slit side down, on a board and open it out. Press firmly along the length of the backbone with your thumbs to loosen it from the flesh. Turn the fish over and pull out the backbone through the slit in the belly. Use scissors to snip the end of the backbone free inside the fish if necessary.

EASY		NUTRITIONAL INFORMATION		Serves
Preparation Time 10–20 minutes	**Cooking Time** 10 minutes	**Per Serving** 340 calories, 25g fat (of which 7g sats), 0g carbohydrates, 1.3g salt	Dairy free	**4**

Try Something Different

Replace the cod, haddock or coley with smoked haddock, herrings, canned tuna or salmon.

350g (12oz) fish, such as cod, haddock or coley, cooked and flaked

350g (12oz) potatoes, cooked and mashed

25g (1oz) butter

1 tbsp freshly chopped parsley

a few drops of anchovy essence (optional)

milk, if needed

1 medium egg, beaten

125g (4oz) fresh breadcrumbs

vegetable oil for shallow-frying

salt and ground black pepper

basil leaves to garnish

lemon wedges and salad to serve

Fishcakes

1 Mix the fish with the potatoes, butter, parsley, seasoning and anchovy essence, if using, binding if necessary with a little milk or beaten egg.

2 On a lightly floured board, form the mixture into a roll, then cut into eight slices and shape into flat cakes. Coat them with egg and breadcrumbs.

3 Heat the oil in a frying pan, add the fishcakes and fry, turning once, until crisp and golden. Drain well on kitchen paper. Garnish with basil and serve with lemon wedges and salad.

Serves	EASY		NUTRITIONAL INFORMATION
4	**Preparation Time** 15 minutes	**Cooking Time** 20 minutes	**Per Serving** 412 calories, 19g fat (of which 5g saturates), 39g carbohydrates, 1.5g salt

Red Mullet with Cherry Tomatoes and Basil Oil

450g (1lb) cherry tomatoes, mixture of red and yellow
2 tbsp green peppercorns in brine, drained
8 garlic cloves, bruised not peeled
zest and juice of 1 small lemon
75ml (2½fl oz) basil oil
12 × 50g (2oz) red mullet fillets, descaled
a small handful of fresh basil leaves
salt and ground black pepper
steamed new potatoes to serve

1 Preheat the oven to 180°C (160°C fan oven) mark 4. Halve the larger tomatoes, then put them all into a shallow roasting tin. Add the peppercorns, garlic and lemon zest, drizzle with half the oil and bake for 20 minutes.

2 Add the fish to the tin and drizzle with the remaining oil. Cook for a further 15–20 minutes until golden and cooked through.

3 Pour the lemon juice over the fish and sprinkle with basil leaves, salt and pepper. Serve with steamed new potatoes.

EASY		NUTRITIONAL INFORMATION		Serves
Preparation Time 40 minutes	**Cooking Time** 10 minutes	**Per Serving** 282 calories, 17g fat (of which 2g saturates), 4g carbohydrates, 0.4g salt	Gluten free Dairy free	**4**

Traditional Kippers

2 kippers

butter, freshly chopped parsley and toast to serve

1 Grill the kippers for 5 minutes. Alternatively, put into a jug of boiling water and leave in a warm place for 5–10 minutes. You can also wrap them in foil and bake them in the oven at 190°C (170°C fan oven) mark 5 for 10–15 minutes.

2 Serve with butter, parsley and toast.

Cook's Tip

Kippers are whole herrings that have been split and opened out flat. They are lightly brined, then cold-smoked, which gives them a rich flavour.

Serves	EASY	NUTRITIONAL INFORMATION	
2	**Cooking Time** 5–15 minutes	**Per Serving** 331 calories, 25g fat (of which 4g saturates), 38g carbohydrates, 3.1g salt	Dairy free

chicken and other birds

Cook's Tip

Beurre Manié: A beurre manié is a mixture of equal parts of softened butter and flour that has been kneaded together to form a paste. It is used to thicken sauces and stews and is whisked in towards the end of cooking, then boiled briefly to allow it to thicken.

Roast Chicken with Stuffing and Gravy

1.4kg (3lb) chicken

2 garlic cloves

1 onion, cut into wedges

2 tsp sea salt

2 tsp ground black pepper

4 fresh parsley sprigs

4 fresh tarragon sprigs

2 bay leaves

50g (2oz) butter, cut into cubes

salt and ground black pepper

For the stuffing

40g (1½oz) butter

1 small onion, chopped

1 garlic clove, crushed

75g (3oz) fresh white breadcrumbs

finely grated zest and juice of 1 small lemon, halves reserved for the chicken

2 tbsp each freshly chopped flat-leafed parsley and tarragon

1 medium egg yolk

For the gravy

200ml (7fl oz) white wine

1 tbsp Dijon mustard

450ml (¾ pint) hot chicken stock

25g (1oz) butter, mixed with 25g (1oz) plain flour (beurre manié, see Cook's Tip)

1 Preheat the oven to 190°C (170°C fan oven) mark 5. To make the stuffing, melt the butter in a pan, add the onion and garlic, and fry for 5–10 minutes until soft. Cool, then add the remaining ingredients, stirring in the egg yolk last. Season well with salt and pepper.

2 Put the chicken on a board, breast upwards, then put the garlic, onion, reserved lemon halves and half the salt, pepper and herb sprigs into the body cavity.

3 Lift the loose skin at the neck and fill the cavity with stuffing. Turn the bird on to its breast and pull the neck flap over the opening to cover the stuffing. Rest the wing tips across it and truss the chicken. Weigh the stuffed bird to calculate the cooking time, and allow 20 minutes per 450g (1lb), plus an extra 20 minutes.

4 Put the chicken on a rack in a roasting tin. Season with the remaining salt and pepper, then top with the remaining herbs and the bay leaves. Dot with the butter and roast, basting halfway through, until cooked and the juices run clear when the thickest part of the thigh is pierced with a skewer.

5 Put the chicken on a serving dish and cover with foil. Leave to rest while you make the gravy. Pour off all but about 3 tbsp fat from the tin, put the tin over a high heat, add the wine and boil for 2 minutes. Add the mustard and hot stock and bring back to the boil. Gradually whisk in knobs of the butter mixture until smooth, then season with salt and pepper. Carve the chicken and serve with the stuffing and gravy.

Serves 5	EASY		NUTRITIONAL INFORMATION
	Preparation Time 30 minutes	**Cooking Time** 1 hour 20 minutes, plus resting	**Per Serving** 682 calories, 49g fat (of which 21g saturates), 17g carbohydrate, 1g salt

Roast Chicken with Lemon and Garlic

1 chicken, about 1.8kg (4lb)

25g (1oz) butter, softened

2 tbsp olive oil

1½ lemons, cut in half

1 small head of garlic, cut in half horizontally

salt and ground black pepper

potatoes and seasonal vegetables to serve

1 Preheat the oven to 220°C (200°C fan oven) mark 7. Put the chicken into a roasting tin just large enough to hold it comfortably. Spread the butter all over the chicken, then drizzle with the oil and season with salt and pepper.

2 Squeeze lemon juice over the chicken, then put one lemon half inside the chicken. Put the other halves and the garlic into the roasting tin.

3 Roast the chicken in the oven for 15 minutes, then reduce the oven temperature to 190°C (170°C fan oven) mark 5 and roast for a further 45 minutes–1 hour until the juices run clear when the thickest part of the thigh is pierced with a skewer. While the bird is cooking, baste from time to time with the pan juices. Add a splash of water to the tin if the juices dry out.

4 Put the chicken on a warmed plate, cover with foil and leave for 15 minutes, so that the juices that have risen to the surface can soak back into the meat. This will make it more moist and easier to slice. Mash some of the garlic into the pan juices and serve the gravy with the chicken. Serve with potatoes and seasonal vegetables.

EASY		NUTRITIONAL INFORMATION		Serves
Preparation Time 5 minutes	**Cooking Time** 1 hour–1¼ hours, plus resting	**Per Serving** 639 calories, 46g fat (of which 13g saturates), 0g carbohydrate, 0.6g salt	Gluten free	**4**

Sticky Chicken Thighs

1 garlic clove, crushed
1 tbsp clear honey
1 tbsp Thai sweet chilli sauce
4 chicken thighs
rice (optional) and green salad to serve

1 Preheat the oven to 200°C (180°C fan oven) mark 6. Put the garlic into a bowl with the honey and chilli sauce and stir to mix. Add the chicken thighs and toss to coat.

2 Put the chicken into a roasting tin and roast in the oven for 15–20 minutes until golden and cooked through and the juices run clear when the thighs are pierced with a skewer. Serve with rice, if you like, and a crisp green salad.

Try Something Different

Try this with sausages instead of the chicken, if you like.

Italian Marinade: Mix 1 crushed garlic clove with 4 tbsp olive oil, the juice of 1 lemon and 1 tsp dried oregano. If you like, leave to marinate for 1–2 hours before cooking.

Oriental Marinade: Mix together 2 tbsp soy sauce, 1 tsp demerara sugar, 2 tbsp dry sherry or apple juice, 1 tsp finely chopped fresh root ginger and 1 crushed garlic clove.

Honey and Mustard Marinade: Mix together 2 tbsp grain mustard, 3 tbsp clear honey and the grated zest and juice of 1 lemon.

Serves	EASY		NUTRITIONAL INFORMATION	
4	**Preparation Time** 5 minutes	**Cooking Time** 20 minutes	**Per Serving** 218 calories, 12g fat (of which 3g saturates), 5g carbohydrate, 0.4g salt	Gluten free Dairy free

Cook's Tip

Sage has a strong, pungent taste, so you need only a little to flavour the chicken. Don't be tempted to add more than just one leaf to each chicken breast or it will overpower the finished dish.

30 Minute Recipe

Stuffed Chicken Breasts

vegetable oil to oil

150g (5oz) ball mozzarella

4 skinless chicken breasts, about 125g (4oz) each

4 sage leaves

8 slices Parma ham

ground black pepper

new potatoes and spinach to serve

1 Preheat the oven to 200°C (180°C fan oven) mark 6. Lightly oil a baking sheet. Slice the mozzarella into eight, then put two slices on each chicken piece. Top each with a sage leaf.

2 Wrap each piece of chicken in two slices of Parma ham, covering the mozzarella. Season with pepper.

3 Put on the prepared baking sheet and cook in the oven for 20 minutes or until the chicken is cooked through. Serve with new potatoes and spinach.

Serves 4	EASY		NUTRITIONAL INFORMATION	
	Preparation Time 5 minutes	**Cooking Time** 20 minutes	**Per Serving** 297 calories, 13g fat (of which 7g saturates), trace carbohydrate, 1.4g salt	Gluten free

Try Something Different

Spicy Chicken Kiev: To make a spicy butter filling, sauté
1 finely chopped shallot with 2 tsp cayenne pepper in 1 tbsp
butter until soft but not brown. Stir in 1 tbsp freshly chopped
parsley. Combine with 175g (6oz) softened butter and season.
Form into a roll, cover and chill for at least 1 hour as step 1, then
continue with the recipe.

Chicken Kiev

175g (6oz) butter, softened

grated zest of ¹/₂ lemon

1 tbsp lemon juice

1 tbsp freshly chopped parsley

1 garlic clove, crushed

6 large boneless, skinless chicken breasts

25g (1oz) seasoned flour

1 medium egg, beaten

125g (4oz) fresh breadcrumbs

vegetable oil for deep-frying

salt and ground black pepper

potato wedges and peas to serve

1 Put the butter, lemon zest and juice, parsley, garlic and salt
and pepper to taste into a bowl and beat well to combine.
(Alternatively, whiz in a food processor.) Form into a roll,
cover and chill for at least 1 hour.

2 Put the chicken breasts on a flat surface and, using a meat
mallet or rolling pin, pound them to an even thickness. Cut
the butter into six pieces and put one piece on the centre of
each chicken breast. Roll up, folding the ends in to enclose the
butter completely. Secure the rolls with wooden cocktail sticks.

3 Put the seasoned flour, beaten egg and breadcrumbs in three
separate flat dishes. Coat each chicken roll with the flour,
then turn them in the beaten egg and coat them with
breadcrumbs, patting the crumbs firmly on to the chicken.

4 Put the rolls on to a baking sheet, cover lightly with non-
stick or greaseproof paper and chill in the fridge for 2 hours
or until required, to allow the coating to dry.

5 Heat the oil in a deep-fryer to 160°C (test by frying a small
cube of bread; it should brown in 60 seconds). Put two
chicken rolls into a frying basket and lower into the oil. Fry
for 15 minutes – the chicken is cooked when it is browned
and firm when pressed with a fork. Do not pierce.

6 Remove the rolls from the fryer, drain on kitchen paper and
keep them warm while you cook the remaining chicken.
Remove the cocktail sticks before serving.

7 Serve with potato wedges and peas.

EASY		NUTRITIONAL INFORMATION	Serves
Preparation Time 15 minutes, plus chilling	**Cooking Time** 45 minutes	**Per Serving** 594 calories, 41g fat (of which 19g saturates), 20g carbohydrate, 1.2g salt	**6**

Chicken with Wine and Capers

1 tbsp olive oil

15g (1/2 oz) butter

4 small skinless chicken breasts

lemon wedges to garnish

rice to serve

For the wine and caper sauce

125ml (4fl oz) white wine

3 tbsp capers, rinsed and drained

juice of 1 lemon

15g (1/2 oz) butter

1 tbsp freshly chopped flat-leafed parsley

1 Heat the oil and butter in a large frying pan over a medium heat. Add the chicken breasts and fry for about 10–12 minutes on each side until cooked through. Transfer to a warmed plate, then cover and keep warm.

2 To make the sauce, add the wine and capers to the same pan. Bring to the boil, then reduce the heat and simmer for 2–3 minutes until the wine is reduced by half. Add the lemon juice and butter and stir in the parsley.

3 Divide the chicken among four warmed plates, pour the sauce over the chicken, garnish each serving with a lemon wedge and serve immediately with cooked rice.

EASY		NUTRITIONAL INFORMATION		Serves
Preparation Time 5 minutes	**Cooking Time** 25 minutes	**Per Serving** 234 calories, 10g fat (of which 5g saturates), trace carbohydrate, 0.3g salt	Gluten free	**4**

Tarragon Chicken with Fennel

1 tbsp olive oil

4 chicken thighs

1 onion, finely chopped

1 fennel bulb, finely chopped

juice of ½ lemon

200ml (7fl oz) hot chicken stock

200ml (7fl oz) crème fraîche

1 small bunch of tarragon, roughly chopped

salt and ground black pepper

new potatoes and broccoli to serve

1 Preheat the oven to 200°C (180°C fan oven) mark 6. Heat the oil in a large flameproof casserole over a medium-high heat. Add the chicken thighs and fry for 5 minutes or until browned, then remove and put them to one side to keep warm.

2 Add the onion to the casserole and fry for 5 minutes, then add the fennel and cook for 5–10 minutes until softened.

3 Add the lemon juice to the casserole, followed by the hot stock. Bring to a simmer and cook until the sauce is reduced by half.

4 Stir in the crème fraîche and put the chicken back into the casserole. Stir once to mix, then cover and cook in the oven for 25–30 minutes. Stir the tarragon into the sauce, season with salt and pepper and serve with potatoes and broccoli.

Serves	EASY		NUTRITIONAL INFORMATION	
4	**Preparation Time** 10 minutes	**Cooking Time** 45–55 minutes	**Per Serving** 334 calories, 26g fat (of which 15g saturates), 3g carbohydrate, 0.5g salt	Gluten free

Freezing Tip

To freeze the paste, at the end of step 1, put two of the portions of tandoori paste into separate freezer bags and freeze. They will keep for up to three months.

To use the frozen paste, put the paste in a microwave and cook on Defrost for 1 minute 20 seconds (based on a 900W oven), or thaw at a cool room temperature for 1 hour.

4 tbsp groundnut oil, plus extra to grease

3 x 150g cartons natural yogurt

juice of ½ lemon

4 boneless, skinless chicken breasts, about 600g (1lb 5oz), cut into finger-width pieces

½ cucumber

salt and ground black pepper

fresh mint leaves to garnish

For the tandoori paste

24 garlic cloves, about 125g (4oz), crushed

5cm (2in) piece fresh root ginger, peeled and chopped

3 tbsp each coriander seeds, cumin seeds, ground fenugreek and paprika

3 red chillies, seeded and chopped (see Cook's Tip, page 10)

3 tsp English mustard

2 tbsp tomato purée

1 tsp salt

Tandoori Chicken with Cucumber Raita

1 Put all the ingredients for the tandoori paste into a food processor or blender with 8 tbsp water and blend to a paste. Divide the paste into three equal portions, freeze two (see Freezing Tip) and put the other in a large bowl.

2 To make the tandoori chicken, add 2 tbsp oil, 2 cartons of yogurt and the lemon juice to the tandoori paste. Add the chicken and stir well to coat. Cover the bowl, chill and leave to marinate for at least 4 hours.

3 Preheat the oven to 220°C (200°C fan oven) mark 7. Oil a roasting tin. Put the chicken in it, drizzle the remaining oil over the chicken and roast in the oven for 20 minutes or until cooked through.

4 Meanwhile, prepare the raita. Whisk the remaining carton of yogurt. Using a vegetable peeler, scrape the cucumber into very thin strips. Put the strips in a bowl and pour the whisked yogurt over them. Season, then chill until ready to serve. Garnish the cucumber raita with mint. Sprinkle the chicken with mint and serve with the raita.

EASY		NUTRITIONAL INFORMATION		Serves
Preparation Time 45 minutes, plus marinating	**Cooking Time** 20 minutes	**Per Serving** 399 calories, 20g fat (of which 4g saturates), 15g carbohydrate, 2g salt	Gluten free	**4**

Chicken and Coconut Curry

2 garlic cloves, peeled

1 onion, quartered

1 lemongrass stalk, trimmed and halved

2.5cm (1in) piece fresh root ginger, peeled and halved

2 small hot chillies (see Cook's Tips, page 10)

a small handful of fresh coriander

1 tsp ground coriander

grated zest and juice of 1 lime

2 tbsp vegetable oil

6 boneless, skinless chicken breasts, each cut into three pieces

2 large tomatoes, peeled and chopped

2 tbsp Thai fish sauce

900ml (1½ pints) coconut milk

salt and ground black pepper

finely sliced red chilli to garnish

basmati rice to serve

1 Put the garlic, onion, lemongrass, ginger, chillies, fresh coriander, ground coriander and lime zest and juice into a food processor and whiz to a paste. Add a little water if the mixture gets stuck under the blades.

2 Heat the oil in a wok or large frying pan. Add the spice paste and cook over a fairly high heat for 3–4 minutes, stirring constantly. Add the chicken and cook for 5 minutes, stirring to coat in the spice mixture.

3 Add the tomatoes, fish sauce and coconut milk. Cover and simmer for about 25 minutes or until the chicken is cooked. Season with salt and pepper, garnish with red chilli and serve with basmati rice.

Serves 6	EASY		NUTRITIONAL INFORMATION	
	Preparation Time 15 minutes	**Cooking Time** 35 minutes	**Per Serving** 204 calories, 6g fat (of which 1g saturates), 10g carbohydrate, 1.5g salt	Gluten free Dairy free

Roast Turkey with Parsley, Sage and Thyme

6.3kg (14lb) turkey
2 small red onions, cut into wedges
2 lemons, cut into wedges
6 whole garlic cloves
8 fresh thyme sprigs
8 fresh sage leaves
8 fresh flat-leafed parsley sprigs
250ml (8fl oz) olive oil
roast vegetables to serve

For the seasoning
1 tbsp whole pink peppercorns
2 tsp sea salt
2 tbsp paprika
2 tbsp celery salt

For the stuffing
4 tbsp olive oil
2 large onions, finely chopped
4 garlic cloves, crushed
150g (5oz) fresh white breadcrumbs
75g (3oz) medium cornmeal or polenta
100g (3½ oz) hazelnuts, toasted and chopped
finely grated zest of 2 lemons and juice of 1 lemon
4 tbsp freshly chopped flat-leafed parsley
4 tbsp freshly chopped sage
2 medium eggs, lightly beaten
salt and ground black pepper

1 To make the stuffing, heat the oil in a pan. Add the onions and garlic and fry gently for 10 minutes to soften but not brown. Tip into a bowl to cool. Meanwhile, put the breadcrumbs, cornmeal or polenta, hazelnuts, lemon zest, parsley, sage and eggs into a large bowl and squeeze the lemon juice over. Add the cooled onion and garlic, and season with salt and pepper. Stir to bind together and leave to cool.

2 To make the seasoning, put the peppercorns, sea salt, paprika and celery salt into a pestle and mortar and pound to crush, or whiz in a mini processor. Stand the turkey upright on a board, with the parson's nose (the rear end) facing upwards. Sprinkle the inside cavity with 1 tbsp of the peppercorn seasoning, then pack the cavity with half the onions and lemon wedges, garlic cloves, thyme and sage and all the parsley sprigs.

3 Sit the turkey with the parson's nose facing away from you. Lift up the loose skin at the neck end with one hand and, using the other, fill the cavity with handfuls of cold stuffing. Turn the turkey over on to its breast, then lift the neck flap up and over the stuffing to cover and bring the wing tips round on top.

4 Thread a trussing needle with 2m (6ft) fine string and sew the neck flap to the turkey. Push the skewer firmly through the wings, twist the string around the ends and pull to tighten so that both wings are snug against the breast. Turn the turkey over, tuck in the parson's nose, cross the legs together, then bring the string up and over the legs and wrap around tightly, finishing with a double knot to secure. Cut off any excess.

5 Pour the olive oil into a large roasting tin. Immerse a piece of muslin, about 60cm (24in), in it to coat completely, then stretch it out, with the edges overhanging the tin. Sit the turkey on top and sprinkle with the remaining peppercorn seasoning. Scatter over the remaining thyme and sage, then arrange the remaining lemon and onion wedges and the garlic cloves around the bird. Bring the muslin up and over the turkey to wrap completely, then turn it over so that it's breast side down in the tin. Over-wrap with clingfilm and leave to chill overnight in the bottom of the fridge. Remember to take it out 30 minutes before cooking so that it has time to come to room temperature.

6 Remove the muslin and keep the turkey breast side down. Preheat the oven to 180°C (160°C fan oven) mark 4. Roast the turkey for about 3¾ hours, basting occasionally to keep the flesh moist. Turn the turkey over after cooking for 1 hour 50 minutes. To check that the turkey is cooked, pierce the thickest part of the thigh with a skewer; the juices should run clear. Serve with roasted vegetables.

EASY		NUTRITIONAL INFORMATION		Serves
Preparation Time 40 minutes, plus chilling	**Cooking Time** 3¾ hours	**Per Serving** 280 calories, 10g fat (of which 2g saturates), 11g carbohydrate, 2.2g salt	Dairy free	**16**

Cook's Tip

Giblet Stock: Put the turkey giblets, 1 onion, quartered, 1 carrot, halved, 1 celery stick, halved, 6 black peppercorns and 1 bay leaf into a large pan and add 1.4 litres (2¹/₂ pints) cold water. Cover and bring to the boil, then reduce the heat and simmer for 30 minutes–1 hour, skimming occasionally. Strain through a sieve into a bowl and cool quickly. This can be made in advance: cover and chill for up to two days. Makes 1.3 litres (2¹/₄ pints).

6 small red onions, halved

7 small red eating apples, unpeeled, halved

5kg (11lb) oven-ready goose, washed, dried and seasoned inside and out

1 small bunch of fresh sage

1 small bunch of fresh rosemary

1 bay leaf

salt and ground black pepper

For the gravy

1 tbsp plain flour

300ml (¹/₂ pint) red wine

200ml (7fl oz) Giblet Stock (see Cook's Tip)

Goose with Roasted Apples

1 Preheat the oven to 230°C (210°C fan oven) mark 8. Put half an onion and half an apple inside the goose with half the sage and rosemary and the bay leaf. Tie the legs together with string. Push a long skewer through the wings to tuck them in. Put the goose, breast side up, on a rack in a roasting tin. Prick the breast all over and season with salt and pepper. Put the remaining onions around the bird, then cover with foil.

2 Roast for 30 minutes, then take the goose out of the oven and baste with the fat that has run off. Remove and reserve any excess fat. Reduce the oven temperature to 190°C (170°C fan oven) mark 5.

3 Put the goose back in the oven and roast for a further 1¹/₂ hours, removing any excess fat every 20–30 minutes. Remove the foil. Remove excess fat, then add the remaining apples. Sprinkle the goose with the remaining herbs and roast for a further 1 hour. Transfer to a warmed serving plate, cover with foil and leave to rest for 30 minutes. Remove the apples and onions and keep warm.

4 To make the gravy, pour out all but 1 tbsp of the fat from the tin, stir in the flour, then add the wine and stock. Bring to the boil and cook, stirring all the time, for 5 minutes. Carve the goose, cut the roast apples into wedges and serve with the goose, onions and gravy.

Serves 8	EASY		NUTRITIONAL INFORMATION	
	Preparation Time 30 minutes	**Cooking Time** about 3 hours, plus resting	**Per Serving** 646 calories, 41g fat (of which 12g saturates), 11g carbohydrate, 1g salt	Dairy free

Cook's Tips

Some fat may be in the cavity of the duck, and should be pulled out before cooking. Most of the fat is under the skin and will melt out during cooking. Save it and use for roasting root vegetables.

Whole ducks look large because they have a large cavity and carcass. They don't feed as many people as the size might suggest.

Glazed Oranges: Preheat the grill. Quarter the oranges or cut into wedges. Dust with a little caster sugar and grill until caramelised.

Roast Duck with Orange

2 large oranges

2 large fresh thyme sprigs

2.3kg (5lb) duck, with giblets if possible

4 tbsp vegetable oil

2 shallots, chopped

1 tsp plain flour

600ml (1 pint) chicken stock

25g (1oz) caster sugar

2 tbsp red wine vinegar

100ml (3½fl oz) fresh orange juice

100ml (3½fl oz) fruity German white wine

2 tbsp orange liqueur, such as Grand Marnier (optional)

1 tbsp lemon juice

salt and ground black pepper

Glazed Oranges (see Cook's Tip) to garnish

mangetouts and broccoli to serve

1 Preheat the oven to 200°C (180°C fan oven) mark 6. Using a zester, remove strips of zest from the oranges. Put half the zest into a pan of cold water, bring to the boil, then drain and put to one side. Remove the pith from both oranges and cut the flesh into segments.

2 Put the thyme and unblanched orange zest inside the duck and season. Rub the skin with 2 tbsp oil, sprinkle with salt and put, breast side up, on a rack over a roasting tin. Roast, basting every 20 minutes, for 1¼–1½ hours until just cooked and the juices run clear when the thickest part of the thigh is pierced with a skewer. After 30 minutes, turn breast side down, then breast side up for the last 10 minutes.

3 Meanwhile, cut the gizzard, heart and neck into pieces. Heat the remaining 2 tbsp oil in a heavy-based pan. Add the giblets and fry until dark brown. Add the chopped shallots and flour, and cook for 1 minute. Pour in the stock, bring to the boil and bubble until reduced by half, then strain.

4 Put the sugar and vinegar into a heavy-based pan over a low heat until the sugar dissolves. Turn up the heat and cook until it forms a dark caramel. Pour in the orange juice and stir. Cool, cover and put to one side.

5 Lift the duck off the rack and keep warm. Skim all the fat off the juices to leave about 3 tbsp sediment. Stir the wine into the sediment, bring to the boil and bubble for 5 minutes or until syrupy. Add the stock mixture and orange mixture. Bring back to the boil and bubble until syrupy, skimming if necessary. To serve the sauce, add the blanched orange zest and segments. Add Grand Marnier, if using, and lemon juice to taste.

6 Carve the duck and garnish with the glazed orange wedges. Serve with the orange sauce, and steamed mangetouts and broccoli.

EASY		NUTRITIONAL INFORMATION		Serves
Preparation Time 50 minutes	**Cooking Time** 1 hour 40 minutes, plus resting	**Per Serving** 561 calories, 38g fat (of which 9g saturates), 20g carbohydrate, 0.5g salt	Dairy free	**4**

Marinated Duck with Prunes

4 duck breasts
8 fat garlic cloves, unpeeled
8 ready-to-eat prunes
25g (1oz) butter
1 tsp plain flour
mashed potato to serve

For the marinade
1 carrot, finely chopped
2 shallots, finely chopped
1 fresh parsley sprig
1 fresh thyme sprig, plus extra to garnish
1 bay leaf
1 tsp black peppercorns
250ml (9fl oz) prune juice
125ml (4fl oz) red wine
4 tbsp brandy
4 tbsp olive oil
1/2 tsp salt

For the red cabbage
1 tbsp olive oil
1 red onion, halved and sliced
2 garlic cloves, crushed
1 large red cabbage, about 1kg (2 1/4 lb), shredded
2 tbsp light muscovado sugar
2 tbsp red wine vinegar
8 juniper berries
1/4 tsp allspice
300ml (1/2 pint) vegetable stock
2 pears, cored and sliced
salt and ground black pepper

1 Combine the marinade ingredients (putting half of the prune juice to one side) in a dish large enough to hold the duck breasts in a single layer, then add the duck. Cover, chill and leave to marinate overnight, turning occasionally.

2 Soak four small wooden skewers in water for 20 minutes. To make the red cabbage, heat the oil in a large pan. Add the onion and fry for 5 minutes. Add the remaining ingredients except the pears. Season, bring to the boil, then cover, reduce the heat and simmer for 30 minutes. Add the pears and cook for 15 minutes or until nearly all the liquid has evaporated and the cabbage is tender.

3 Boil the garlic for 10 minutes. Drain, peel and put to one side.

4 Remove the duck from the marinade and dry on kitchen paper. In a pan, bring the marinade to the boil, then reduce by half. Strain and keep warm. Push the prunes and garlic on to the soaked skewers.

5 Melt the butter in a large frying pan. Fry the duck, skin side down, for 8 minutes or until golden. Turn and cook for 3–4 minutes. Remove from the pan and leave to rest for 10 minutes. Cook the skewers in the pan, turning, until the garlic colours. Remove from the pan and put to one side.

6 Add the flour to the pan and cook, stirring, for 2–3 seconds. Add the marinade and remaining prune juice and simmer, stirring, until it thickens and becomes glossy. Serve the duck and skewers with the red cabbage and mashed potato and garnished with thyme.

Serves 4	EASY		NUTRITIONAL INFORMATION
	Preparation Time 30 minutes, plus marinating and soaking	**Cooking Time** 1 1/4 hours, plus resting	**Per Serving** 654 calories, 51g fat (of which 14g saturates), 38g carbohydrate, 0.6g salt

Try Something Different

Instead of the pheasants, use oven-ready poussins, small corn-fed chickens or small guinea fowl; put an onion wedge inside each bird before browning to impart extra flavour.

Pot-roasted Pheasant with Red Cabbage

25g (1oz) butter

1 tbsp oil

2 oven-ready young pheasants, halved

2 onions, peeled and sliced

450g (1lb) red cabbage, cored and finely shredded

1 tsp cornflour

250ml (9fl oz) red wine

2 tbsp redcurrant jelly

1 tbsp balsamic vinegar

4 rindless smoked streaky bacon rashers, halved

salt and ground black pepper

1 Preheat the oven to 200°C (180°C fan oven) mark 6. Melt the butter with the oil in a large flameproof casserole over a medium to high heat. Add the pheasant halves and brown on all sides, then remove and put to one side. Add the onions and cabbage to the casserole and fry for 5 minutes, stirring frequently, until softened.

2 Blend the cornflour with a little water to make a paste. Add to the casserole with the wine, redcurrant jelly and vinegar. Season with salt and pepper, and bring to the boil, stirring.

3 Arrange the pheasant halves, skin side up, on the cabbage. Put the halved bacon rashers on top. Cover the casserole and cook in the oven for 30 minutes or until the birds are tender (older pheasants will take an extra 10–20 minutes).

4 Serve the pot-roasted pheasants and red cabbage with the cooking juices spooned over them.

Serves	EASY		NUTRITIONAL INFORMATION
4	**Preparation Time** 15 minutes	**Cooking Time** 1 hour	**Per Serving** 659 calories, 21g fat (of which 12g saturates), 11g carbohydrate, 1.4g salt

Get Ahead

To prepare ahead Complete the recipe to the end of step 3, then cool and chill for up to two days.
To use Preheat the oven to 180°C (160°C fan oven) mark 4. Bring to the boil on the hob, then reheat in the oven for about 30–40 minutes or until hot.

Cook's Tip

If you can't find guinea fowl, use corn-fed chicken joints instead.

Fruity Guinea Fowl

225g (8oz) onion, roughly chopped

125g (4oz) carrot, roughly chopped

125g (4oz) celery, roughly chopped

6–8 guinea fowl joints, 2kg (4½ lb) total weight

750ml (1¼ pints) red wine

1 tsp black peppercorns, crushed

1 tbsp freshly chopped thyme

2 bay leaves

175g (6oz) ready-to-eat dried prunes

3 tbsp vegetable oil

3 garlic cloves, crushed

1 tsp harissa paste

1 tbsp tomato purée

2 tbsp plain flour

300ml (½ pint) chicken stock

225g (8oz) streaky bacon, cut into strips

2 apples, cored and sliced

salt and ground black pepper

mashed potato to serve

1 Put the onion, carrot, celery, guinea fowl, 600ml (1 pint) wine, the peppercorns, thyme and bay leaves into a large bowl. Cover, chill and leave to marinate for at least 3–4 hours. Soak the prunes in the remaining wine for 3–4 hours.

2 Preheat the oven to 170°C (150°C fan oven) mark 3. Drain and pat the joints dry (put the vegetables and wine to one side). Heat 2 tbsp oil in a large flameproof casserole over a medium heat. Cook the joints in batches until browned on both sides. Remove from the pan and put to one side.

3 Add the marinated vegetables to the same pan (keep the marinade to one side) and stir-fry for 5 minutes. Add the garlic, harissa and tomato purée and cook for 1 minute. Mix in the flour and cook for 1 minute. Pour in the reserved marinade and stock. Bring to the boil, stirring. Put the joints back into the casserole, with the legs at the bottom. Bring to the boil, season, cover and cook in the oven for 40 minutes.

4 Heat the remaining oil in a pan. Add the bacon and cook, stirring, for 5 minutes or until golden brown. Remove from the pan and put to one side. Cook the apples for 2–3 minutes on each side until golden. Put to one side. Remove the joints from the casserole. Strain the sauce and put back into the pan with the joints. Add the prunes and any juices, the bacon and apples. Heat through in the oven for 10 minutes. Serve with mashed potato.

EASY		NUTRITIONAL INFORMATION		Serves
Preparation Time 40 minutes, plus marinating	Cooking Time 1½ hours	Per Serving 811 calories, 49g fat (of which 14g saturates), 24g carbohydrate, 1.7g salt	Dairy free	6

meat

Classic Roast Beef with Yorkshire Puddings

1 boned and rolled rib, sirloin, rump or topside of beef, about 1.8kg (4lb)

1 tbsp plain flour

1 tbsp mustard powder

salt and ground black pepper

fresh thyme sprigs to garnish

vegetables to serve

For the Yorkshire pudding

125g (4oz) plain flour

½ tsp salt

300ml (½ pint) milk

2 eggs

For the gravy

150ml (¼ pint) red wine

600ml (1 pint) beef stock

1 Preheat the oven to 230°C (210°C fan oven) mark 8. Put the beef in a roasting tin, thickest part of the fat uppermost. Mix the flour with the mustard powder and salt and pepper. Rub the mixture over the beef.

2 Roast the beef in the centre of the oven for 30 minutes.

3 Baste the beef and reduce the oven temperature to 190°C (170°C fan oven) mark 5. Cook for a further 1 hour, basting occasionally.

4 Meanwhile, prepare the Yorkshire pudding batter. Sift the flour and salt into a bowl. Mix in half the milk, then add the eggs and season with pepper. Beat until smooth, then whisk in the remaining milk.

5 Put the beef on a warmed carving dish, cover loosely with foil and leave to rest in a warm place. Increase the oven temperature to 220°C (200°C fan oven) mark 7.

6 Pour off about 3 tbsp fat from the roasting tin and use to grease 8–12 individual Yorkshire pudding tins. Heat in the oven for 5 minutes or until the fat is almost smoking. Pour the Yorkshire batter into the tins. Bake for 15–20 minutes until well risen, golden and crisp.

7 Meanwhile, make the gravy. Skim off any remaining fat from the roasting tin. Put the tin on the hob, add the wine and boil until syrupy. Pour in the stock and, again, boil until syrupy – there should be about 450ml (¾ pint) gravy. Taste and adjust the seasoning.

8 Carve the beef into slices. Garnish with thyme, serve with the gravy, Yorkshire puddings and vegetables of your choice.

Serves 8	EASY		NUTRITIONAL INFORMATION
	Preparation Time 20 minutes	**Cooking Time** about 1½ hours, plus resting	**Per Serving** 510 calories, 24g fat (of which 9g saturates), 16g carbohydrate, 0.5g salt

Stuffed Topside of Beef

1.4kg (3lb) topside or top rump of beef
1 tbsp balsamic vinegar
2 tbsp white wine vinegar
3 tbsp olive oil
3 tbsp freshly chopped marjoram or thyme
2 red peppers, cored, seeded and quartered
75g (3oz) fresh spinach, cooked and well drained
75g (3oz) pitted black olives, chopped
50g (2oz) smoked ham, chopped
75g (3oz) raisins or sultanas
salt and ground black pepper
roast potatoes and vegetables to serve

1 Make a deep cut along the beef to create a pocket and put the joint into a dish. Combine the vinegars, oil, marjoram or thyme and some black pepper. Pour over the beef and into the pocket. Marinate in a cool place for 4–6 hours, or overnight.

2 Grill the peppers, skin side up, under a hot grill until the skins are charred. Cool in a covered bowl, then remove the skins.

3 Squeeze the excess water from the spinach, then chop and put into a bowl with the olives, ham and raisins or sultanas. Mix well and season with salt and pepper.

4 Preheat the oven to 190°C (170°C fan oven) mark 5. Line the pocket of the beef with the peppers, keeping back two pepper quarters for the gravy. Spoon the spinach mixture into the pocket and spread evenly. Reshape the meat and tie at intervals with string. Put the beef into a roasting tin just large enough to hold it and pour the marinade over it.

5 Roast for 1 hour for rare beef, or 1¼ hours for medium-rare, basting from time to time. Put the beef on a board, cover with foil and leave to rest in a warm place while you make the gravy.

6 Skim off the excess fat from the roasting tin. Put the tin on the hob and bring the pan juices to the boil. Add 125ml (4fl oz) water and bubble for 2–3 minutes. Finely chop the remaining pepper pieces and add to the gravy.

7 Carve the beef and serve with the gravy, roast potatoes and vegetables of your choice.

Serves	EASY		NUTRITIONAL INFORMATION	
6	**Preparation Time** 35 minutes, plus marinating	**Cooking Time** 1–1¼ hours, plus resting	**Per Serving** 535 calories, 29g fat (of which 10g saturates), 13g carbohydrate, 1.4g salt	Gluten free Dairy free

Steak and Chips

2 large potatoes, cut into chips

2 tbsp olive oil

4 sirloin steaks, 125g (4oz) each, fat trimmed

25g (1oz) Roquefort cheese, cut into four small pieces

salt and ground black pepper

watercress to garnish

1 Preheat the oven to 220°C (200°C fan oven) mark 7. Put the potato chips into a pan of lightly salted water. Bring to the boil, then reduce the heat and simmer for 4–5 minutes. Drain well.

2 Put the chips into a roasting tin, toss with 1 tbsp oil and cook in the oven, turning once, for 30–40 minutes until cooked through and golden.

3 When the chips are nearly done, heat a non-stick frying pan until really hot. Brush the remaining oil over the steaks and season with salt and pepper. Add to the pan and fry for 3 minutes on each side for medium-rare, or 2 minutes more if you prefer the meat well done. Put on to warmed plates, top each steak with a small piece of Roquefort while still hot and serve with the chips. Garnish with watercress.

EASY		NUTRITIONAL INFORMATION		Serves
Preparation Time 10 minutes	**Cooking Time** 35–45 minutes	**Per Serving** 318 calories, 13g fat (of which 5g saturates), 18g carbohydrate, 0.4g salt	Gluten free	**4**

Fillet of Beef en Croûte

1–1.4kg (2¼–3lb) fillet of beef, trimmed
50g (2oz) butter
2 shallots, chopped
15g (½oz) dried porcini mushrooms, soaked in
100ml (3½fl oz) boiling water
2 garlic cloves, chopped
225g (8oz) flat mushrooms, finely chopped
2 tsp freshly chopped thyme, plus extra sprigs to garnish
175g (6oz) chicken liver pâté
175g (6oz) thinly sliced Parma ham
375g ready-rolled puff pastry
plain flour to dust
1 medium egg, beaten
salt and ground black pepper
Rich Red Wine Sauce (see Cook's Tip) to serve

1 Season the beef with salt and pepper. Melt 25g (1oz) butter in a large frying pan and, when foaming, add the beef and cook for 4–5 minutes to brown all over. Transfer to a plate and leave to cool.

2 Melt the remaining butter in a pan, add the shallots and cook for 1 minute. Drain the porcini mushrooms, saving the liquid, and chop them. Add them to the pan with the garlic, the reserved liquid and the fresh mushrooms. Increase the heat and cook until the liquid has evaporated, then season with salt and pepper and add the thyme. Leave to cool.

3 Put the pâté into a bowl and beat until smooth. Add the mushroom mixture and stir well until thoroughly combined. Check the seasoning. Spread half the mushroom mixture evenly over one side of the beef. Lay half the Parma ham on a length of clingfilm, overlapping the slices. Invert the mushroom-topped beef on to the ham. Spread the remaining mushroom mixture on the other side of the beef, then lay the remaining Parma ham, also overlapping, on top of the mushroom mixture. Wrap the beef in the clingfilm to form a firm sausage shape and chill for 30 minutes. Preheat the oven to 220°C (200°C fan oven) mark 7.

4 Cut off one-third of the pastry and roll out on a lightly floured surface to 3mm (⅛in) thick and 2.5cm (1in) larger all around than the beef. Prick all over with a fork. Transfer to a baking sheet and bake for 12–15 minutes until brown and crisp. Cool on a wire rack, then trim to the size of the beef and place on a baking sheet. Remove the clingfilm from the beef, brush with the egg and place on the cooked pastry.

5 Roll out the remaining pastry to a 25.5 × 30.5cm (10 × 12in) rectangle. Roll a lattice pastry cutter over it and gently ease the lattice open. Cover the beef with the lattice, tuck the ends under and seal the edges. Brush with the beaten egg, then cook for 40 minutes for rare to medium-rare, 45 minutes for medium. Leave to rest for 10 minutes before carving. Garnish with thyme and serve with Red Wine Sauce.

Cook's Tip

Rich Red Wine Sauce: Soften 350g (12oz) finely chopped shallots in 2 tbsp olive oil for 5 minutes. Add 3 chopped garlic cloves and 3 tbsp tomato purée and cook for 1 minute, then add 2 tbsp balsamic vinegar. Simmer briskly until reduced to almost nothing, then add 200ml (7fl oz) red wine and reduce by half. Pour in 600ml (1 pint) beef stock and simmer until reduced by one-third.

EASY		NUTRITIONAL INFORMATION	Serves
Preparation Time 1 hour, plus soaking and chilling	**Cooking Time** about 1 hour 20 minutes, plus resting	**Per Serving** 802 calories, 53g fat (of which 15g saturates), 27g carbohydrate, 2.4g salt	**6**

Try Something Different

For a more sophisticated burger, replace the cheese and gherkins with thick slices of ripe avocado and use a generous handful of fresh rocket instead of the lettuce.

1kg (2¼lb) extra-lean minced beef

2 tsp salt

2 tbsp steak seasoning

sunflower oil to brush

6 large soft rolls, halved

6 thin-cut slices havarti or raclette cheese

4 small cocktail gherkins, sliced lengthways

6 tbsp mustard mayonnaise

6 lettuce leaves, such as frisée

4 large vine-ripened tomatoes, sliced thickly

2 large shallots, sliced into thin rings

ground black pepper

Hamburgers

1 Put the minced beef into a large bowl and add the salt, steak seasoning and plenty of pepper. Use your hands to mix the ingredients together thoroughly. Lightly oil the inside of six 10cm (4in) rosti rings and put on a foil-lined baking sheet. Press the meat firmly into the rings, or use your hands to shape the mixture into six even-sized patties. Cover with clingfilm and chill for at least 1 hour.

2 Heat a large griddle pan until it's really hot. Put the rolls, cut sides down, on the griddle and toast.

3 Lightly oil the griddle, ease the burgers out of the moulds and brush with oil. Griddle over a medium heat for about 3 minutes, then turn the burgers over carefully. Put a slice of cheese and a few slices of gherkin on top of each and cook for another 3 minutes. While the burgers are cooking, spread the mustard mayonnaise on the toasted side of the rolls. Add the lettuce, tomato and shallots. Put the burgers on top and sandwich with the other half rolls.

Serves	EASY		NUTRITIONAL INFORMATION
6	**Preparation Time** 20 minutes, plus chilling	**Cooking Time** 10 minutes	**Per Serving** 645 calories, 45g fat (of which 17g saturates), 19g carbohydrate, 2.3g salt

Freezing Tip

To freeze Complete the recipe, transfer to a freezerproof container, cool, label and freeze for up to three months.
To use Thaw overnight in the fridge. Put in a pan, cover and bring to the boil; reduce the heat to low and simmer until piping hot.

30 Minute Recipe

Beef Stroganoff

700g (1½lb) rump or fillet steak, trimmed
50g (2oz) unsalted butter or 4 tbsp olive oil
1 onion, thinly sliced
225g (8oz) brown-cap mushrooms, sliced
3 tbsp brandy
1 tsp French mustard
200ml (7fl oz) crème fraîche
100ml (3½fl oz) double cream
3 tbsp freshly chopped flat-leafed parsley
salt and ground black pepper
rice or noodles to serve

1 Cut the steak into strips about 5mm (¼in) wide and 5cm (2in) long.

2 Heat half the butter or oil in a large heavy frying pan over a medium heat. Add the onion and cook gently for 10 minutes or until soft and golden. Remove with a slotted spoon and put to one side. Add the mushrooms to the pan and cook, stirring, for 2–3 minutes until golden brown; remove and put to one side.

3 Increase the heat and add the remaining butter or oil to the pan. Quickly fry the meat, in two or three batches, for 2–3 minutes, stirring constantly to ensure even browning. Remove from the pan. Add the brandy to the pan and allow it to bubble to reduce.

4 Put all the meat, onion and mushrooms back into the pan. Reduce the heat and stir in the mustard, crème fraîche and cream. Heat through, stir in most of the parsley and season with salt and pepper. Serve with rice or noodles, with the remaining parsley scattered over the top.

EASY		NUTRITIONAL INFORMATION	Serves
Preparation Time 10 minutes	**Cooking Time** about 20 minutes	**Per Serving** 750 calories, 60g fat (of which 35g saturates), 3g carbohydrate, 0.5g salt	**4**

Braised Beef with Bacon and Mushrooms

175g (6oz) smoked pancetta or smoked streaky bacon, cut into cubes

2 medium leeks, trimmed and thickly sliced

1 tbsp olive oil

450g (1lb) braising steak, cut into 5cm (2in) pieces

1 large onion, finely chopped

2 carrots and 2 parsnips, thickly sliced

1 tbsp plain flour

300ml (½ pint) red wine

1–2 tbsp redcurrant jelly

125g (4oz) chestnut mushrooms, halved

salt and ground black pepper

freshly chopped flat-leafed parsley to garnish

1 Preheat the oven to 170°C (150°C fan oven) mark 3. Fry the pancetta or bacon in a shallow flameproof casserole for 2–3 minutes until golden. Add the leeks and cook for 2 minutes or until the leeks are just beginning to colour. Remove with a slotted spoon and put to one side.

2 Heat the oil in the casserole and fry the beef in batches for 2–3 minutes until a rich golden colour on all sides. Remove from the casserole and put to one side. Add the onion and fry over a gentle heat for 5 minutes or until golden. Stir in the carrots and parsnips and fry for 1–2 minutes.

3 Put the beef back into the casserole and stir in the flour to soak up the juices. Gradually add the red wine and 300ml (½ pint) water, then stir in the redcurrant jelly. Season with pepper and bring to the boil. Cover with a tight-fitting lid and cook in the oven for 2 hours.

4 Stir in the fried leeks, pancetta and mushrooms, re-cover and cook for a further 1 hour or until everything is tender. Serve scattered with chopped flat-leafed parsley.

Freezing Tip

To freeze Put into a freezerproof container, cool and freeze for up to three months.
To use Thaw overnight at cool room temperature. Preheat the oven to 180°C (160°C fan oven) mark 4. Bring to the boil on the hob, cover tightly and reheat in the oven for 30 minutes or until piping hot.

Cook's Tip

Leeks can trap a lot of fine soil, so need to be washed thoroughly: trim the ends of the leaves, then cut a cross about 7.5cm (3in) into the white part and hold under cold running water.

Serves 4	EASY		NUTRITIONAL INFORMATION	
	Preparation Time 20 minutes	**Cooking Time** about 3½ hours	**Per Serving** 535 calories, 25g fat (of which 9g saturates), 29g carbohydrate, 1.6g salt	Dairy free

Roast Pork Loin with Rosemary and Mustard

2 tbsp freshly chopped rosemary

4 tbsp Dijon mustard

50ml (2fl oz) lemon juice

50g (2oz) light muscovado sugar

175g (6oz) honey

1 tbsp soy sauce

1.4kg (3lb) loin of pork, chine bone (backbone) removed, rib bones cut off and separated into individual ribs (ask the butcher to do this for you)

lemon wedges and rosemary sprigs to serve

1 Preheat the oven to 200°C (180°C) mark 6. Mix together the rosemary, mustard, lemon juice, sugar, honey and soy sauce and put to one side.

2 Put the loin into a roasting tin and cook in the oven for 40 minutes.

3 Add the ribs to the roasting tin and cook the pork for a further 40 minutes.

4 Drain off any fat and brush the pork with the mustard glaze. Put back in the oven for about 15 minutes, basting occasionally with the glaze or until well browned and tender. Serve hot or cold, garnished with rosemary and lemon.

Cook's Tip

The sweetness of buttered parsnips makes them an ideal accompaniment to pork. Cut about 700g (1½ lb) scrubbed, unpeeled parsnips into chunky lengths from the stalk to the root end. Melt 50g (2oz) butter in a deep frying pan and add the parsnips. Stir over the heat for 5–7 minutes, shaking the pan occasionally, until the parsnips are tender and have a wonderful sticky glaze.

Serves 8	EASY		NUTRITIONAL INFORMATION	
	Preparation Time 5 minutes	**Cooking Time** 1 hour 35 minutes	**Per Serving** 354 calories, 13g fat (of which 4g saturates), 24g carbohydrate, 1.1g salt	Dairy free

Cook's Tip

The best cut of belly pork is the thicker part of the belly, as it is leaner and sometimes more tender.

Belly of Pork with Cider

2kg (4½lb) piece pork belly roast, on the bone

500ml bottle medium cider

600ml (1 pint) hot chicken stock

6–8 fresh rosemary sprigs

3 fat garlic cloves, halved

2 tbsp olive oil

grated zest and juice of 1 large orange and 1 lemon

3 tbsp light muscovado sugar

25g (1oz) softened butter, mixed with 1 tbsp plain flour as beurre manié (see Cook's Tip page 116)

salt and ground black pepper

mixed vegetables to serve

1 Preheat the oven to 150°C (130°C fan oven) mark 2. Put the pork, skin side up, in a roasting tin just large enough to hold it. Add the cider, hot stock and half the rosemary. Bring to the boil on the hob, then cover with foil and cook in the oven for 4 hours. Leave to cool in the cooking liquid.

2 Strip the leaves from the remaining rosemary and chop. Put into a pestle and mortar with the garlic, oil, orange and lemon zest, 1 tsp salt and 1 tbsp sugar. Pound for 3–4 minutes to make a rough paste.

3 Remove the pork from the tin (keep the cooking liquid) and slice off the rind from the top layer of fat. Set aside. Score the fat into a diamond pattern and rub in the rosemary paste. Cover loosely with clingfilm and chill until required.

4 Pat the rind dry with kitchen paper and put it fat side up on a foil-lined baking sheet. Cook under a hot grill, about 10cm (4in) away from the heat, for 5 minutes. Turn over, sprinkle lightly with salt, then grill for 7–10 minutes until crisp. Cool, then cut the crackling into rough pieces.

5 Make the gravy. Strain the cooking liquid into a pan. Add the orange and lemon juice and the remaining 2 tbsp sugar, bring to the boil and bubble until reduced by half. Whisk the butter mixture into the liquid and boil for 4–5 minutes until thickened. Set aside.

6 When almost ready to serve, preheat the oven to 220°C (200°C fan oven) mark 7. Cook the pork, uncovered, in a roasting tin for 20 minutes or until piping hot. Wrap the crackling in foil and warm in the oven for the last 5 minutes of the cooking time. Heat the gravy on the hob. Carve the pork into slices and serve with the crackling, gravy and vegetables.

EASY		NUTRITIONAL INFORMATION	Serves
Preparation Time 30 minutes, plus cooling and chilling	**Cooking Time** about 4½ hours	**Per Serving** 694 calories, 52g fat (of which 19g saturates), 9g carbohydrate, 0.5g salt	**8**

Honey Pork with Roast Potatoes and Apples

1kg (2¼lb) loin of pork, with skin and four bones

4 tbsp olive oil

25g (1oz) butter

700g (1½lb) Charlotte potatoes, scrubbed and halved

1 large onion, cut into eight wedges

1 tbsp clear honey mixed with 1 tbsp wholegrain mustard

2 Cox's Orange Pippin apples, cored and each cut into six wedges

12 fresh sage leaves

175ml (6fl oz) dry cider

salt and ground black pepper

1 Preheat the oven to 240°C (220°C fan oven) mark 9. Put the pork on a board and use a paring knife to score the skin into thin strips, cutting about halfway into the fat underneath. Rub 1 tsp salt and 2 tbsp oil over the skin and season well with pepper. Put the meat on a rack, skin side up, over a large roasting tin (or just put the pork in the tin). Roast for 25 minutes. Reduce the oven temperature to 190°C (170°C fan oven) mark 5 and continue to roast for 15 minutes.

2 Add the remaining oil and the butter to the roasting tin. Scatter the potatoes and onion around the meat, season and continue to roast for 45 minutes.

3 Brush the meat with the honey and mustard mixture. Add the apples and sage leaves to the tin and roast for a further 15 minutes or until the pork is cooked.

4 Remove the pork from the tin and wrap completely with foil, then leave to rest for 10 minutes. Put the potatoes, onions and apples into a warmed serving dish and put back in the oven to keep warm.

5 Put the roasting tin on the hob, add the cider and stir well to make a thin gravy. Season.

6 Cut between each bone and cut the meat away from the bone. Pull the crackling away from the meat and cut into strips. Carve the joint, giving each person some crackling, and a bone to chew. Serve with the gravy and potatoes, onion and apples.

EASY		NUTRITIONAL INFORMATION		Serves
Preparation Time 20 minutes	**Cooking Time** 1 hour 40 minutes, plus resting	**Per Serving** 830 calories, 55g fat (of which 19g saturates), 40g carbohydrate, 0.4g salt	Gluten free	**4**

American Sticky Ribs

900g (2lb) lean pork spare ribs

125g (4oz) hoisin sauce

2 tbsp mild clear honey

2 tsp English mustard

3 tsp white wine or cider vinegar

4 tbsp tomato ketchup

2 garlic cloves, crushed

4 tbsp fresh apple or orange juice

coleslaw, onion rings and orange wedges to serve

1 Preheat the oven to 200°C (180°C fan oven) mark 6. Line a large tin with a double layer of foil and spread the ribs over the base.

2 Whisk together the remaining ingredients in a bowl, then spoon over the pork – it may look as though there isn't enough liquid but the ribs will release plenty of juices as they cook.

3 Cover with foil and cook for 20 minutes. Turn the ribs over, then put back in the oven, uncovered. Cook for 40–45 minutes, basting occasionally, until they are dark golden and sticky, and most of the liquid has gone. Serve hot, with coleslaw, onion rings and orange wedges.

Serves	EASY		NUTRITIONAL INFORMATION	
4	**Preparation Time** 10 minutes	**Cooking Time** about 1 hour	**Per Serving** 485 calories, 30g fat (of which 12g saturates), 12g carbohydrate, 1.3g salt	Dairy free

Cumberland Glazed Gammon

4.5kg (10lb) smoked gammon joint, on the bone
2 celery sticks, roughly chopped
1 onion, quartered
1 carrot, roughly chopped
1 tsp black peppercorns
1 tbsp cloves
75g (3oz) redcurrant sprigs

For the Cumberland glaze
grated zest and juice of ½ lemon and ½ orange
4 tbsp redcurrant jelly
1 tsp Dijon mustard
2 tbsp port
salt and ground black pepper

1 Put the gammon into a large pan. Add the celery, onion, carrot and peppercorns. Cover the meat and vegetables with cold water and bring to the boil. Simmer, covered, for 2¾ hours–3½ hours, or allowing 15–20 minutes per 450g (1lb) plus 15 minutes. Lift the gammon out of the pan. Preheat the oven to 200°C (180°C fan oven) mark 6.

2 Meanwhile, make the glaze. Heat the lemon and orange zests and juices, redcurrant jelly, mustard and port in a pan to dissolve the jelly. Bring to the boil and bubble for 5 minutes or until syrupy. Season with salt and pepper to taste.

3 Remove the gammon rind and score the fat in a diamond pattern. Put the gammon into a roasting tin, then stud the fat with cloves. Spoon the glaze evenly over the gammon joint.

4 Roast the gammon for 40 minutes, basting the meat with any juices. Add the redcurrant sprigs 10 minutes before the end of the cooking time. Serve the gammon hot or cold, carved into thin slices.

EASY		NUTRITIONAL INFORMATION		Serves
Preparation Time 30 minutes	**Cooking Time** 3½–4¼ hours	**Per Serving** 406 calories, 21g fat (of which 7g saturates), 4g carbohydrate, 6.3g salt	Gluten free Dairy free	**16**

Roast Leg of Lamb with Rosemary

2.5kg (5½lb) leg of lamb
4 rosemary sprigs
½ tbsp oil
4 garlic cloves, cut into slivers
4 anchovy fillets, roughly chopped
4 oregano sprigs
1 large onion, thickly sliced
1 lemon, cut into 6 wedges
salt and ground black pepper
vegetables to serve

For the gravy
2 tbsp plain flour
150ml (5fl oz) white wine
500ml (17fl oz) lamb or chicken stock

1 Take the lamb out of the fridge an hour before roasting. Pat the skin dry with kitchen paper.

2 Preheat the oven to 220°C (200°C fan) mark 7. Cut the rosemary into smaller sprigs. Rub the oil over the lamb. Cut small slits all over the meat and insert the garlic slivers, rosemary sprigs, anchovy pieces and the leaves from two oregano sprigs into the gaps. Season well.

3 Put the onion slices into the base of a roasting tin just large enough to hold the lamb. Top with the remaining oregano, then put in the meat, fat side up (the onions must be covered to prevent them burning). Tuck lemon wedges around the meat.

4 Put the lamb into the oven and reduce the oven temperature to 190°C (170°C fan) mark 5. Roast for 15 minutes per 450lb (1lb) for pink meat, or longer if you like it more cooked.

5 Transfer the lamb to a board and cover with foil, reserving the roasting tin and its contents. Rest for 30 minutes before carving.

6 To make the gravy, put the roasting tin over a medium hob heat. Stir in the flour and cook for 1 minute. Gradually add the wine, stirring all the time, and leave to cook for 1 minute. Stir in the stock and leave to bubble gently, stirring occasionally, for 5 minutes.

7 Strain the gravy into a jug and check the seasoning. Serve with the lamb and vegetables.

Cook's Tip

Buy the best meat you can to ensure great flavour and texture. The lamb is served pink here, but allow an extra 20–30 minutes if you prefer your meat more cooked.

Get Ahead

To prepare ahead, the lamb to the end of step 3 up to 2 hours ahead.
To use, complete the recipe.

Serves 8	EASY		NUTRITIONAL INFORMATION	
	Preparation Time 15 minutes	**Cooking Time** 1½ hours, plus resting	**Per Serving** 601 calories, 39g fat (of which 17g saturates), 1g carbohydrate, 1.3g salt	Gluten free Dairy free

Rack of Lamb with Balsamic Gravy

4 fat garlic cloves, crushed

2 tbsp Herbes de Provence

6 tbsp balsamic vinegar

12 tbsp olive oil

4 trimmed racks of lamb, each with about 6 bones

salt and ground black pepper

1 Preheat the oven to 220°C (200°C fan oven) mark 7. Put the garlic into a bowl along with the herbs, 2 tbsp vinegar and 4 tbsp oil. Season with salt and pepper.

2 Put the racks in a large flameproof roasting tin and rub the garlic mixture into both the fat and meat.

3 Roast for 25–30 minutes if you like your meat pink, or cook for a further 5–10 minutes if you like it well done. Lift the racks from the roasting tin and put to one side on a warm serving dish. Cover with foil and leave to rest.

4 Put the roasting tin on the hob over a medium heat and whisk in the remaining vinegar and oil, scraping up any sediment as the liquid bubbles. Season if needed. Pour into a small heatproof jug.

5 Serve the lamb in cutlets with the hot gravy.

EASY		NUTRITIONAL INFORMATION		Serves
Preparation Time 5 minutes	**Cooking Time** 30–45 minutes	**Per Serving** 532 calories, 48g fat (of which 18g saturates), 0.2g carbohydrate, 0.2g salt	Gluten free Dairy free	**8**

Lamb Chops with Crispy Garlic Potatoes

2 tbsp Mint Sauce (see Cook's Tips)
8 small lamb chops
3 medium potatoes, cut into 5mm (¼in) slices
2 tbsp Garlic-infused Olive Oil (see Cook's Tips)
1 tbsp olive oil
salt and ground black pepper
steamed green beans to serve

1 Spread the mint sauce over the lamb chops and leave to marinate while you prepare the potatoes.

2 Boil the potatoes in a pan of lightly salted water for 2 minutes or until just starting to soften. Drain, tip back into the pan and season, then add the garlic oil and toss to combine.

3 Meanwhile, heat the olive oil in a large frying pan and fry the chops for 4–5 minutes on each side until just cooked, adding a splash of boiling water to the pan to make a sauce. Remove the chops and sauce from the pan and keep warm.

4 Add the potatoes to the pan. Fry over a medium heat for 10–12 minutes until crisp and golden. Divide the potatoes, chops and sauce among four warmed plates and serve with green beans.

Cook's Tips

Mint Sauce: Finely chop 20g (¾oz) fresh mint and mix with 1 tbsp each olive oil and white wine vinegar.
Garlic-infused Olive Oil: Gently heat 2 tbsp olive oil with a peeled sliced garlic clove for 5 minutes and use immediately. Do not store.

Serves	EASY		NUTRITIONAL INFORMATION	
4	**Preparation Time** 10 minutes	**Cooking Time** 20 minutes	**Per Serving** 835 calories, 45g fat (of which 19g saturates), 22g carbohydrate, 0.7g salt	Gluten free Dairy free

30
Minute
Recipe

Calf's Liver
with Sage
and Balsamic

15g (½oz) butter plus a little olive oil for frying

12 sage leaves

4 thin slices calf's liver

1–2 tbsp balsamic vinegar

rice, with freshly chopped parsley stirred through,
or grilled polenta to serve

1 Preheat the oven to a low setting. Melt the butter with a little oil in a heavy-based frying pan and when hot add the sage leaves. Cook briefly for 1 minute or so until crisp. Remove, put in a single layer in a shallow dish and keep hot in the oven.

2 Add a little extra oil to the pan, put in two slices of calf's liver and cook quickly for 30 seconds on each side over a high heat. Remove and place on a plate while you quickly cook the remaining two slices.

3 Return all four slices to the pan, splash the balsamic vinegar over the top and cook for another minute or so. Serve immediately with rice or grilled polenta.

Serves	EASY		NUTRITIONAL INFORMATION
4	**Preparation Time** 5 minutes	**Cooking Time** 5 minutes	**Per Serving** 88 calories, 6g fat (of which 3g saturates), trace carbohydrate, 0.1g salt

8 lamb's kidneys, membrane removed

225g (8oz) baby onions, peeled

25g (1oz) unsalted butter

3 tbsp balsamic vinegar

1 tbsp plain flour

300ml (½ pint) well-flavoured lamb stock

3 tbsp Madeira

salt and ground black pepper

freshly chopped parsley to garnish

rice to serve

Sautéed Lamb's Kidneys and Baby Onions

1 Halve the lamb's kidneys lengthways and snip out the white cores with kitchen scissors. Add the baby onions to a pan of boiling water and blanch for 3–5 minutes; drain well.

2 Melt the butter in a sauté pan, add the onions and cook gently for 10–15 minutes until soft and browned. Increase the heat and add the lamb's kidneys, stirring and turning them for about 2 minutes or until browned. Lift out the kidneys and onions and put on to a plate.

3 Deglaze the pan with the balsamic vinegar, scraping up any sediment from the bottom of the pan, and allow almost all of the liquid to evaporate. Sprinkle in the flour and cook, stirring, over a medium heat until it begins to colour. Whisk in the stock and Madeira. Bring the sauce to the boil, then turn down the heat and simmer until reduced and slightly syrupy. Check the seasoning.

4 Return the kidneys and baby onions to the sauce and reheat gently for 5 minutes. Scatter with plenty of chopped parsley and serve with rice.

EASY		NUTRITIONAL INFORMATION	Serves
Preparation Time 10 minutes	**Cooking Time** 30 minutes	**Per Serving** 180 calories, 8g fat (of which 4g saturates), 8g carbohydrate, 1.6g salt	**4**

stir-fries and noodles

30 Minute Recipe

Chicken Chow Mein

250g (9oz) medium egg noodles

1 tbsp toasted sesame oil

2 boneless, skinless chicken breasts, about 125g (4oz) each, cut into thin strips

1 bunch of spring onions, thinly sliced diagonally

150g (5oz) mangetouts, thickly sliced diagonally

125g (4oz) bean sprouts

100g (3½ oz) cooked ham, finely shredded

120g sachet chow mein sauce

salt and ground black pepper

light soy sauce to serve

1 Cook the noodles in boiling water for 4 minutes or according to the pack instructions. Drain, rinse thoroughly in cold water, drain again and put to one side.

2 Meanwhile, heat a wok or large frying pan until hot, then add the oil. Add the chicken and stir-fry over a high heat for 3–4 minutes until browned all over. Add the spring onions and mangetouts and stir-fry for 2 minutes. Stir in the bean sprouts and ham and cook for a further 2 minutes.

3 Add the drained noodles, then pour the chow mein sauce into the pan and toss together to coat evenly. Stir-fry for 2 minutes or until piping hot. Season with salt and pepper and serve immediately with light soy sauce to drizzle over the chow mein.

Serves 4	EASY		NUTRITIONAL INFORMATION	
	Preparation Time 10 minutes	**Cooking Time** 10 minutes	**Per Serving** 451 calories, 11g fat (of which 2g saturates), 59g carbohydrate, 1.3g salt	Dairy free

Cook's Tip

Coconut milk gives a thick creaminess to stir-fries, soups and curries.

Chilli-fried Chicken with Coconut Noodles

2 tbsp plain flour

1 tsp mild chilli powder

1 tsp ground ginger

$\frac{1}{2}$ tsp salt

1 tsp caster sugar

6 boneless, skinless chicken breasts, about 150g (5oz) each, cut diagonally into three

250g (9oz) thread egg noodles

3 tbsp groundnut oil

1 large bunch of spring onions, sliced

1$\frac{1}{2}$ tsp Thai red curry paste or tandoori paste

150g (5oz) salted roasted peanuts, finely chopped

6 tbsp coconut milk

1 Mix the flour, chilli powder, ground ginger, salt and sugar in a bowl. Dip the chicken into the spiced flour and coat well.

2 Cook the noodles in boiling water according to the pack instructions, then drain.

3 Heat the oil in a frying pan. Add the chicken and fry for 5 minutes or until cooked. Put to one side, cover and keep warm. Add the spring onions to the pan and fry for 1 minute. Put to one side and keep warm.

4 Add the curry paste to the pan with 75g (3oz) peanuts and fry for 1 minute. Add the noodles and fry for 1 minute. Stir in the coconut milk and toss the noodles over a high heat for 30 seconds.

5 Put the chicken and spring onions on the coconut noodles. Scatter with the remaining peanuts and serve.

EASY		NUTRITIONAL INFORMATION		Serves
Preparation Time 15–20 minutes	**Cooking Time** 15 minutes	**Per Serving** 567 calories, 26g fat (of which 5g saturates), 40g carbohydrate, 0.6g salt	Dairy free	**6**

Turkey and Sesame Stir-fry with Noodles

300g (11oz) turkey breast fillets, cut into thin strips

3 tbsp teriyaki marinade

3 tbsp clear honey

500g (1lb 2oz) medium egg noodles

about 1 tbsp sesame oil, plus extra for the noodles

300g (11oz) ready-prepared mixed stir-fry vegetables, such as carrots, broccoli, red cabbage, mangetouts, bean sprouts and purple spring onions

2 tbsp sesame seeds, lightly toasted in a dry wok or heavy-based pan

1 Put the turkey strips into a large bowl with the teriyaki marinade and honey and stir to coat. Cover and put to one side for 5 minutes.

2 Cook the noodles in boiling water for about 4 minutes or according to the pack instructions. Drain well, then toss in a little oil.

3 Heat 1 tbsp oil in a wok or large frying pan and add the turkey, reserving the marinade. Stir-fry over a very high heat for 2–3 minutes until cooked through and beginning to brown. Add a drop more oil, if needed, then add the vegetables and reserved marinade. Continue to cook over a high heat, stirring, until the vegetables have started to soften and the sauce is warmed through.

4 Scatter with the sesame seeds and serve immediately with the noodles.

Serves 4	EASY		NUTRITIONAL INFORMATION	
	Preparation Time 10 minutes	**Cooking Time** 10 minutes	**Per Serving** 672 calories, 18g fat (of which 4g saturates), 97g carbohydrate, 0.7g salt	Dairy free

2 tsp dark soy sauce

4 tsp dry sherry

1 tsp cornflour

1 tsp sugar

1 tbsp sesame oil

225g (8oz) rump steak, cut into thin
strips about 7.5cm (3in) long

175g (6oz) egg noodles

3 tbsp vegetable oil

1 bunch of spring onions, sliced

3 garlic cloves, crushed

1 large green chilli, seeded and sliced (see Cook's Tips, page 10)

125g (4oz) Chinese leaves, or cabbage, sliced

50g (2oz) bean sprouts

salt and ground black pepper

Beef Chow Mein

1 Put the soy sauce, sherry, cornflour, sugar and 1 tsp sesame oil into a bowl and whisk together. Pour this mixture over the beef, then cover, chill and leave to marinate for at least 1 hour or overnight.

2 Cook the noodles in boiling water for 4 minutes or according to the pack instructions. Rinse in cold water and drain.

3 Drain the beef, reserving the marinade. Heat the vegetable oil in a wok or large non-stick frying pan and fry the beef over a high heat until well browned. Remove with a slotted spoon and put to one side.

4 Add the spring onions, garlic, chilli, Chinese leaves or cabbage and the bean sprouts to the pan and stir-fry for 2–3 minutes. Return the beef to the pan with the noodles and reserved marinade. Bring to the boil, stirring all the time, and bubble for 2–3 minutes. Sprinkle the remaining sesame oil over it, season with salt and pepper and serve immediately.

Serves 4	EASY		NUTRITIONAL INFORMATION	
	Preparation Time 15 minutes, plus marinating	Cooking Time 15 minutes	Per Serving 408 calories, 20g fat (of which 5g saturates), 38g carbohydrate, 1.2g salt	Dairy free

Try Something Different

Use pork fillet instead of beef, trimmed of fat and cut into thin slices.

30
Minute
Recipe

Sweet Chilli Beef Stir-fry

1 tsp chilli oil

1 tbsp each tamari (wheat-free Japanese soy sauce) and runny honey

1 garlic clove, crushed

1 large red chilli, seeded and chopped (see Cook's Tips, page 10)

400g (14oz) lean beef, cut into strips

1 tsp sunflower oil

1 broccoli head, thinly sliced

200g (7oz) mangetouts, halved

1 red pepper, halved, seeded and cut into strips

rice to serve

1. Pour the chilli oil into a medium-sized shallow bowl. Add the tamari, honey, garlic and chilli and stir well. Add the strips of beef and toss in the marinade.

2. Heat the sunflower oil in a wok over a high heat until it is very hot. Cook the strips of beef in two batches, for 3–4 minutes until just cooked through, then remove from the wok and put to one side. Wipe the wok with kitchen paper to remove any residue.

3. Add the broccoli, mangetouts, red pepper and 2 tbsp water and stir-fry for 5–6 minutes until starting to soften. Return the beef to the wok to heat through. Serve with rice.

EASY		NUTRITIONAL INFORMATION		Serves
Preparation Time 10 minutes	**Cooking Time** 10–15 minutes	**Per Serving** 273 calories, 13g fat (of which 5g saturates), 8g carbohydrate, 0.2g salt	Gluten free Dairy free	**4**

Try Something Different

Use 400g (14oz) pork escalope cut into strips instead of beef. Cook for 5 minutes before removing from the pan at step 2.

30
Minute
Recipe

Sesame Beef

2 tbsp soy sauce
2 tbsp Worcestershire sauce
2 tsp tomato purée
juice of ½ lemon
1 tbsp sesame seeds
1 garlic clove, crushed
400g (14oz) rump steak, sliced
1 tbsp vegetable oil
3 small pak choi, chopped
1 bunch of spring onions, sliced
egg noodles or tagliatelle to serve

1 Put the soy and Worcestershire sauces, tomato purée, lemon juice, sesame seeds and garlic into a bowl and mix well. Add the steak and toss to coat.

2 Heat the oil in a large wok or non-stick frying pan until hot. Add the steak and sear well. Remove from the wok and put to one side.

3 Add any sauce from the bowl to the wok and heat for 1 minute. Add the pak choi, spring onions and steak and stir-fry for 5 minutes. Add freshly cooked and drained noodles, toss and serve immediately.

Serves	EASY		NUTRITIONAL INFORMATION	
4	**Preparation Time** 20 minutes	**Cooking Time** 10 minutes	**Per Serving** 207 calories, 10g fat (of which 3g saturates), 4g carbohydrate, 2g salt	Dairy free

Get Ahead

To prepare ahead Complete the recipe to the end of step 3, then cool, wrap and chill the pork and vegetables separately for up to four hours.

To use Complete the recipe. Make sure the pork is piping hot.

.

Stir-fried Pork with Chinese Greens

200g (7oz) pork tenderloin or fillet, cut into strips

2 tbsp finely chopped fresh root ginger

3 tbsp soy sauce

2 garlic cloves, crushed

700g (1½ lb) mixed vegetables, such as pak choi, broccoli, carrots, bean sprouts and sugarsnap peas

3 tbsp vegetable oil

5 spring onions, cut into four lengthways

1 red chilli, seeded and sliced (see Cook's Tips, page 10)

1 tbsp sesame oil

2 tbsp dry sherry

2 tbsp oyster sauce

salt and ground black pepper

1 Put the pork into a non-metallic dish with the ginger, 2 tbsp soy sauce and the garlic. Put to one side to marinate for at least 30 minutes.

2 Meanwhile, prepare the vegetables. Cut the pak choi into quarters, separate the broccoli into florets and cut the carrot into ribbons, using a vegetable peeler.

3 Heat a wok or large frying pan over a high heat and add the vegetable oil. Stir-fry the pork in two batches, cooking each batch for 2–3 minutes until the meat is browned. Season the pork with salt and pepper, then put to one side and keep warm.

4 Add the spring onions and chilli to the pan and cook for 30 seconds. Add all the vegetables and stir-fry for 4–5 minutes. Return the pork to the pan. Add the remaining soy sauce, the sesame oil, sherry and oyster sauce and stir-fry for 2 minutes or until the sauce is syrupy. Serve immediately.

EASY		NUTRITIONAL INFORMATION		Serves
Preparation Time 15 minutes, plus marinating	**Cooking Time** 15 minutes	**Per Serving** 234 calories, 15g fat (of which 2g saturates), 6g carbohydrate, 1.8g salt	Dairy free	**4**

Pork Stir-fry with Chilli and Mango

75g (3oz) medium egg noodles

1 tsp groundnut oil

½ red chilli, seeded and finely chopped
(see Cook's Tip and page 10)

125g (4oz) pork stir-fry strips

1 head pak choi, roughly chopped

1 tbsp soy sauce

½ ripe mango, peeled, stoned and sliced

1 Cook the egg noodles in boiling water according to the pack instructions. Drain, then plunge into cold water and put to one side.

2 Meanwhile, put the oil into a wok or large frying pan and heat until very hot. Add the chilli and pork and stir-fry for 3–4 minutes. Add the pak choi and soy sauce and cook for a further 2–3 minutes. Add the mango and toss to combine.

3 Drain the noodles and add to the pan. Toss well and cook for 1–2 minutes until heated through. Serve immediately.

Cook's Tip

The smaller the chilli, the hotter it is.

.

EASY		NUTRITIONAL INFORMATION		Serves
Preparation Time 5 minutes	**Cooking Time** 10 minutes	**Per Serving** 550 calories, 15g fat (of which 4g saturates), 67g carbohydrate, 3.1g salt	Dairy free	**1**

Cook's Tip

Ready-prepared stir-fry vegetables make this extra-quick, but if you can't find them, try a mixture of three or four of the following: strips of red, orange or yellow peppers, baby sweetcorn, mangetouts or sugarsnaps, carrots cut into matchsticks, or bean sprouts.

30 Minute Recipe

Prawn and Peanut Noodles

300g (11oz) straight-to-wok noodles

360g pack stir-fry vegetables

4 tbsp coconut cream

4 tbsp smooth peanut butter

1 tbsp Thai red or green curry paste

juice of $\frac{1}{2}$ lime

225g (8oz) cooked and peeled king prawns

a small handful of freshly chopped coriander

25g (1oz) peanuts, chopped

1 Put the noodles and stir-fry vegetables into a large bowl or wok and cover with boiling water. Cover with clingfilm and leave for 5 minutes.

2 Meanwhile, mix the coconut cream with the peanut butter, curry paste and lime juice in a bowl.

3 Drain the noodles and vegetables in a colander. Put back into the bowl and toss with the prawns, coriander and half the dressing. Sprinkle with the peanuts and serve with the remaining dressing.

Serves 4	EASY		NUTRITIONAL INFORMATION	
	Preparation Time 10 minutes, plus soaking		**Per Serving** 579 calories, 24g fat (of which 7g saturates), 67g carbohydrate, 0.7g salt	Dairy free

Stir-fried Salmon and Broccoli

2 tsp sesame oil

1 red pepper, seeded and thinly sliced

½ red chilli, seeded and thinly sliced (see Cook's Tips, page 10)

1 garlic clove, crushed

125g (4oz) broccoli florets

2 spring onions, sliced

2 salmon fillets, about 125g (4oz) each, cut into strips

1 tsp Thai fish sauce

2 tsp soy sauce

wholewheat noodles to serve

1 Heat the oil in a wok or large frying pan. Add the red pepper, chilli, garlic, broccoli and spring onions and stir-fry over a high heat for 3–4 minutes.

2 Add the salmon, fish sauce and soy sauce and cook for 2 minutes, stirring gently. Serve immediately with wholewheat noodles.

EASY		NUTRITIONAL INFORMATION		Serves
Preparation Time 10 minutes	**Cooking Time** 5–6 minutes	**Per Serving** 90 calories, 4g fat (of which 1g saturates), 9g carbohydrate, 2.7g salt	Dairy free	**2**

Teriyaki Tuna with Sesame Noodles

2 tuna steaks

2 nests medium egg noodles

75g (3oz) green beans, trimmed and halved

1 tsp toasted sesame oil

4 spring onions, sliced

1 tbsp freshly chopped coriander

2 tsp sesame seeds

lime wedges to serve

For the marinade

1 small garlic clove, crushed

2.5cm (1in) piece fresh root ginger, peeled and freshly grated

3 tbsp teriyaki sauce

1 tbsp clear honey

1 tsp oil

1 Mix together the marinade ingredients in a non-metallic dish and add the tuna steaks. Leave to marinate in the fridge for 2 hours.

2 Preheat the grill to high. Cook the egg noodles according to the pack instructions with the green beans. Drain and cool under running water.

3 Meanwhile, put the tuna on a grill rack and cook for 3 minutes per side, brushing with the marinade, until firm but still moist.

4 Gently heat the sesame oil in a pan and toss in the noodles and green beans to reheat. Add the spring onions, coriander and sesame seeds.

5 To serve, divide the noodles between two plates, top with the tuna and garnish with lime wedges.

Serves 2	EASY		NUTRITIONAL INFORMATION	
	Preparation Time 20 minutes, plus marinating	**Cooking Time** 10 minutes	**Per Serving** 508 calories, 17g fat (of which 9g saturates), 48g carbohydrate, 5.1g salt	Dairy free

Healthy Tip

Chickpeas are an excellent low-fat source of protein and complex carbohydrate. Being high in both soluble and insoluble fibre and with a low GI, chickpeas can help you to feel fuller for longer, thereby helping to control appetite and manage weight. Eaten regularly they can also help to reduce the risk of chronic diseases such as obesity, diabetes, heart disease and also certain cancers.

30 Minute Recipe

Chickpea and Chilli Stir-fry

2 tbsp olive oil

1 tsp ground cumin

1 red onion, sliced

2 garlic cloves, finely chopped

1 red chilli, seeded and finely chopped (see Cook's Tips, page 10)

2 × 400g cans chickpeas, drained and rinsed

400g (14oz) cherry tomatoes

125g (4oz) baby spinach leaves

salt and ground black pepper

rice or pasta to serve

1 Heat the oil in a wok or large frying pan. Add the cumin and fry for 1–2 minutes. Add the onion and stir-fry for 5–7 minutes.

2 Add the garlic and chilli and stir-fry for 2 minutes.

3 Add the chickpeas to the wok with the tomatoes. Reduce the heat and simmer until the chickpeas are hot. Season with salt and pepper. Add the spinach and cook for 1–2 minutes until the leaves have wilted. Serve with rice or pasta.

Serves 4	EASY		NUTRITIONAL INFORMATION	
	Preparation Time 10 minutes	**Cooking Time** 15–20 minutes	**Per Serving** 258 calories, 11g fat (of which 1g saturates), 30g carbohydrate, 1g salt	Vegetarian Dairy free

Cook's Tip

Check the ingredients in the Thai curry paste: some contain shrimp and are therefore not suitable for vegetarians.

2 tbsp sesame oil

2 green chillies, seeded and finely chopped (see Cook's Tips, page 10)

2.5cm (1in) piece fresh root ginger, peeled and finely grated

2 garlic cloves, crushed

1 tbsp Thai green curry paste

125g (4oz) carrots, cut into fine matchsticks

125g (4oz) baby sweetcorn, halved

125g (4oz) mangetouts, halved on the diagonal

2 large red peppers, seeded and finely sliced

2 small pak choi, quartered

4 spring onions, finely chopped

300ml (½ pint) coconut milk

2 tbsp peanut satay sauce

1 tbsp light soy sauce

1 tsp soft brown sugar

4 tbsp freshly chopped coriander, plus extra sprigs to garnish

ground black pepper

25g (1oz) roasted peanuts to garnish

rice or noodles to serve

Chilli Vegetable and Coconut Stir-fry

1 Heat the oil in a wok or large non-stick frying pan over a medium heat. Add the chillies, ginger and garlic and stir-fry for 1 minute. Add the curry paste and fry for a further 30 seconds.

2 Add the carrots, sweetcorn, mangetouts and red peppers. Stir-fry over a high heat for 3–4 minutes, then add the pak choi and spring onions. Cook, stirring, for a further 1–2 minutes.

3 Pour in the coconut milk, satay sauce, soy sauce and sugar. Season with pepper, bring to the boil and cook for 1–2 minutes, then add the chopped coriander. Garnish with the peanuts and coriander sprigs and serve with rice or noodles.

EASY		NUTRITIONAL INFORMATION		Serves
Preparation Time 25 minutes	**Cooking Time** 10 minutes	**Per Serving** 191 calories, 11g fat (of which 2g saturates), 18g carbohydrate, 1.3g salt	Vegetarian Dairy free	**4**

Thai Egg Noodles

1 lemongrass stalk, inner leaves only, finely chopped

100g (3½ oz) medium egg noodles

100g (3½ oz) sugarsnap peas, halved diagonally

4 tbsp vegetable oil

4 garlic cloves, crushed

3 large eggs, beaten

juice of 2 lemons

3 tbsp Thai fish sauce

2 tbsp light soy sauce

½ tsp caster sugar

50g (2oz) roasted salted peanuts

½ tsp chilli powder

12 spring onions, roughly chopped

150g (5oz) bean sprouts

2 tbsp freshly chopped coriander, plus extra to garnish

salt and ground black pepper

1 Put the lemongrass into a heatproof bowl with the noodles. Pour in 600ml (1 pint) boiling water and put to one side for 20 minutes, stirring from time to time.

2 Cook the sugarsnap peas in lightly salted boiling water for 1 minute, then drain and plunge them into ice-cold water.

3 Heat the oil in a wok or large frying pan, add the garlic and fry for 30 seconds. Add the beaten eggs and cook gently until lightly scrambled. Add the lemon juice, fish sauce, soy sauce, sugar, peanuts, chilli powder, spring onions and bean sprouts to the eggs. Pour the noodles, lemongrass and soaking liquid into the pan. Bring to the boil and bubble for 4–5 minutes, stirring from time to time.

4 Drain the sugarsnap peas, then add them to the noodle mixture with the chopped coriander. Heat through and season with salt and pepper. Garnish with coriander and serve immediately.

EASY		NUTRITIONAL INFORMATION		Serves
Preparation Time 15 minutes, plus soaking	**Cooking Time** 12–15 minutes	**Per Serving** 289 calories, 18g fat (of which 3g saturates), 24g carbohydrate, 2.9g salt	Dairy free	**4**

bbqs and grills

Chicken Tarragon Burgers

225g (8oz) minced chicken

2 shallots, finely chopped

1 tbsp freshly chopped tarragon

25g (1oz) fresh breadcrumbs

1 large egg yolk

vegetable oil to oil

salt and ground black pepper

1 Put the chicken into a bowl with the shallots, tarragon, breadcrumbs and egg yolk. Mix well, then beat in about 75ml (2½ fl oz) cold water and season with salt and pepper.

2 Lightly oil a foil-lined baking sheet. Divide the chicken mixture into two or four portions (depending on how large you want the burgers) and put on the foil. Using the back of a wet spoon, flatten each portion to a thickness of 2.5cm (1in). Cover and chill for 30 minutes.

3 Preheat the barbecue or grill. If cooking on the barbecue, lift the burgers straight on to the grill rack; if cooking under the grill, slide the baking sheet under the grill. Cook the burgers for 5–6 minutes on each side until cooked through, then serve in a toasted burger bun with a dollop of mayonnaise or Greek yogurt, a few salad leaves and tomato salad.

Try Something Different

Pork and Apricot Burgers: Replace the chicken with minced pork, use freshly chopped sage instead of the tarragon, and add 100g (3½ oz) chopped ready-to-eat dried apricots to the mixture before shaping into burgers.

Serves 2	EASY		NUTRITIONAL INFORMATION	
	Preparation Time 30 minutes, plus chilling	**Cooking Time** 12 minutes	**Per Serving** 205 calories, 4g fat (of which 1g saturates), 12g carbohydrate, 0.4g salt	Dairy free

Chicken Kebabs with Tabbouleh

1 tbsp balsamic vinegar

6 tbsp olive oil

grated zest of 1 lime and juice of 2 limes

2 garlic cloves, crushed

4 large skinless chicken breasts, about 700g (1½ lb), cut into 2.5cm (1in) cubes

75g (3oz) bulgur wheat

½ cucumber, halved lengthways, seeded and diced

4 plum tomatoes, seeded and diced

1 small red onion, finely chopped

4 tbsp freshly chopped mint

4 tbsp freshly chopped flat-leafed parsley

ground black pepper

lime wedges and mint sprigs to garnish

1 Whisk the balsamic vinegar, 3 tbsp oil, the zest and juice of 1 lime and 1 garlic clove together in a large bowl. Add the chicken, mix well, then cover, chill and leave to marinate for at least 2 hours, preferably overnight.

2 To make the tabbouleh, put the bulgur wheat into a bowl, cover with double its volume of boiling water and leave to soak for 15 minutes. Drain the bulgur wheat, squeeze out the liquid and put back into the bowl. Stir in the cucumber, tomatoes, onion and herbs and season with pepper.

3 Whisk the remaining oil, lime juice and garlic together in a small bowl. Add to the bulgur wheat and mix gently but thoroughly until the bulgur is well coated. Cover and chill in the fridge.

4 Preheat the barbecue, grill or griddle. Soak eight wooden skewers in water for 20 minutes. Remove the chicken from the marinade, thread on to the skewers and cook for 10–12 minutes, turning every now and then, or until cooked through. Serve with the tabbouleh, garnished with lime wedges and mint sprigs.

Serves 4	EASY		NUTRITIONAL INFORMATION	
	Preparation Time 35 minutes, plus marinating and soaking	**Cooking Time** 12 minutes	**Per Serving** 330 calories, 8g fat (of which 1g saturates), 19g carbohydrate, 0.3g salt	Dairy free

Cook's Tip

Salt-baked New Potatoes: Toss 550g (1¼ lb) par-boiled new potatoes with 2 tbsp olive oil and 1 tbsp sea salt flakes. Cook at 200°C (180°C fan oven) mark 6 for 40 minutes until tender.

1 garlic clove, crushed

1 tbsp olive oil

2 tbsp mixed peppercorns, crushed

2 tbsp Dijon mustard

4 x 150g (5oz) sirloin steaks

Salt-baked New Potatoes (see Cook's Tip) and cherry tomatoes to serve

fresh oregano sprigs to garnish

For the aïoli

2 garlic cloves, crushed

200ml (7fl oz) mayonnaise

2 tbsp lemon juice

salt and ground black pepper

30 Minute Recipe

Peppercorn Steaks with Aïoli

1 Mix together the garlic, oil, crushed peppercorns and mustard. Spread the mixture on both sides of the steaks and leave to marinate for at least 15 minutes or overnight.

2 To make the aïoli, mix the garlic with the mayonnaise, lemon juice and salt and pepper. Cover and chill until ready to serve.

3 Preheat the barbecue, grill or griddle. Cook the steaks for 3–4 minutes on each side. Allow to rest in a warm place for 5 minutes before serving. Serve with salt-baked new potatoes and cherry tomatoes, and garnish with oregano sprigs. Serve the aïoli in a separate bowl.

EASY		NUTRITIONAL INFORMATION		Serves
Preparation Time 15 minutes, plus marinating	**Cooking Time** 8 minutes	**Per Serving** 607 calories, 51g fat (of which 9g saturates), 2g carbohydrate, 0.8g salt	Gluten free Dairy free	**4**

Barbecued Lamb Steaks

small bunch each of flat-leafed parsley and fresh mint – or any other herbs – roughly chopped

3 garlic cloves, sliced

1 tbsp Dijon or wholegrain mustard

juice of 2 small lemons

4 tbsp olive oil

4 thick lamb leg steaks

lemon wedges, rocket and crusty bread or couscous to serve

1 Put the herbs into a small bowl. Add the garlic, mustard, lemon juice and oil, and mix well. Put the lamb into a glass dish and spoon the herb mixture over. Cover the dish and marinate for at least 10 minutes.

2 Preheat the barbecue or griddle. Cook the lamb steaks for about 4 minutes on each side (or 5–6 minutes if you like them well done) until golden and crusted. Serve hot, with lemon wedges, rocket and bread or couscous.

Serves 4	EASY		NUTRITIONAL INFORMATION	
	Preparation Time 15 minutes, plus marinating	**Cooking Time** 8–12 minutes	**Per Serving** 322 calories, 23g fat (of which 9g saturates), trace carbohydrate, 0.3g salt	Gluten free Dairy free

Freezing Tip

To freeze, complete the recipe to the end of step 1, place the patties on a tray to freeze, then wrap, label and freeze for up to one month.

To use, thaw at cool room temperature for four hours. Complete the recipe.

Spiced Lamb in Pitta

1 small green pepper, seeded and chopped

½ small onion, chopped

3 garlic cloves

2 tsp ground cumin

3 tbsp olive oil

1 tbsp freshly chopped mint

550g (1¼ lb) lean minced lamb

450g (1lb) very ripe tomatoes, chopped

2 tbsp freshly chopped flat-leafed parsley

4 large pitta breads

salt and ground black pepper

Greek yogurt to serve

mint sprigs to garnish

1 Put the chopped pepper and onion in a food processor with the garlic, cumin and oil, and pulse to form a coarse paste. Add the chopped mint. Mix together the paste and the minced lamb, season with salt and pepper and shape into 16 patties. Chill for 30 minutes or overnight.

2 Put the tomatoes into a bowl, stir in the parsley and season with salt and pepper.

3 Preheat the barbecue, griddle or grill. Cook the lamb patties for 4–5 minutes on each side. Warm the pitta breads, wrap into a cone and secure with a cocktail stick. Fill each with four lamb patties and spoon on a drizzle of yogurt. Serve with the tomatoes and garnish with mint sprigs.

EASY		NUTRITIONAL INFORMATION	Serves
Preparation Time 20 minutes, plus chilling	**Cooking Time** 8–10 minutes	**Per Serving** 550 calories, 20g fat (of which 9g saturates), 60g carbohydrate, 1.3g salt	**4**

Lemon Tuna

3 large lemons
2 garlic cloves, crushed
100ml (3½ fl oz) extra virgin olive oil
900g (2lb) fresh tuna in one piece
3 tbsp freshly chopped flat-leafed parsley
ground black pepper
flatbread to serve

1 Finely grate the zest from one lemon and squeeze the juice from the grated lemon and one other lemon. Mix the zest and juice with the garlic and oil and season well with pepper.

2 Cut the tuna in half lengthways, then cut into strips about 2cm (¾ in) thick. Lay the strips in a shallow dish, pour the marinade over them, then turn the fish to coat. Cover and leave to marinate for at least 30 minutes.

3 Preheat the barbecue or grill. Soak eight bamboo skewers in water for 20 minutes.

4 Fold the strips of tuna and thread on to the soaked skewers. Cut the remaining lemon into eight wedges and push one on to each skewer. Drizzle with any remaining marinade and sprinkle with the chopped parsley.

5 Lay the skewers on the barbecue or grill and cook for 2–3 minutes on each side. Serve immediately with warmed flatbread.

EASY		NUTRITIONAL INFORMATION		Serves
Preparation Time 15–20 minutes, plus marinating	**Cooking Time** 4–6 minutes	**Per Serving** 180 calories, 8g fat (of which 2g saturates), trace carbohydrate, 0.1g salt	Gluten fre Dairy free	**8**

Saffron and Lime Prawns

finely grated zest and juice of 1 lime

a large pinch of saffron

1 garlic clove, crushed

2 small red chillies, seeded and very
finely chopped (see Cook's Tips, page 10)

75ml (3fl oz) extra virgin olive oil

32 raw tiger prawns, deveined and peeled

salad and pitta bread or griddle garlic bread to serve

1 Put the lime zest and juice into a small pan and heat gently. Add the saffron and leave to soak for 5 minutes. Stir in the garlic and chillies and add the oil. Pour into a screwtopped jar, secure the lid tightly and shake well.

2 Put the prawns into a shallow dish, add the marinade, cover and leave for at least 1 hour.

3 Preheat the barbecue or grill. Soak eight bamboo skewers in water for 20 minutes.

4 Thread four prawns on each skewer. Lay the skewers on the barbecue or grill and cook for about 2 minutes on each side until they've just turned pink. Serve immediately, with salad and warm pitta bread or griddled garlic bread.

Serves 8	EASY		NUTRITIONAL INFORMATION	
	Preparation Time 10 minutes, plus marinating	**Cooking Time** 4 minutes	**Per Serving** 37 calories, 2g fat (of which trace saturates), 0g carbohydrate, 0.2g salt	Gluten free Dairy free

Cook's Tip

Herbes de Provence, an aromatic dried mixture made up of rosemary, thyme, basil, bay and savory, is a wonderful complement to barbecued or grilled food.

Grilled Sweet Potatoes with Feta and Olives

1 large sweet potato, weighing about 500g (1lb 2oz)

4 tbsp olive oil, plus extra to brush

200g (7oz) feta cheese (see Cook's Tip, page 26)

2 tsp dried Herbes de Provence (see Cook's Tip)

50g (2oz) pitted black olives, chopped

1 garlic clove, crushed

salt and ground black pepper

flat-leafed parsley sprigs to garnish

1 Preheat the barbecue or griddle. Peel the sweet potato and cut lengthways into eight wedges. Put them into a pan of boiling water and bring back to the boil, then simmer for 3 minutes. Drain and refresh in cold water. Drain, dry well on kitchen paper, then brush lightly with oil. Season with salt and pepper, then barbecue or grill for 10–15 minutes until well browned and cooked through.

2 Meanwhile, mash the cheese, herbs, olives, garlic and 4 tbsp oil together. Serve the sweet potato with the feta cheese mixture, garnished with flat-leafed parsley.

EASY		NUTRITIONAL INFORMATION		Serves
Preparation Time 15 minutes	**Cooking Time** 15–20 minutes	**Per Serving** 324 calories, 23g fat (of which 9g saturates), 21g carbohydrate, 2.5g salt	Vegetarian Gluten free	**4**

Aubergine, Feta and Tomato Stacks

200g (7oz) feta cheese, crumbled (see Cook's Tip, page 26)

2 tbsp olive oil, plus extra to brush

1 garlic clove, crushed, plus 1 garlic clove for rubbing

2 plump aubergines, cut into 1cm (½ in) thick slices

a handful of fresh basil leaves, torn

3 large vine-ripened tomatoes, each sliced into four

salt and ground black pepper

rocket and toasted ciabatta to serve

1 Preheat the barbecue or grill. Put the feta into a bowl, stir in the oil and garlic, season with salt and pepper and set aside.

2 Brush each aubergine slice with a little oil and barbecue or grill for about 6 minutes, turning occasionally, or until softened and golden. Remove from the heat.

3 Sprinkle a little of the feta mixture on six of the aubergine slices and put some torn basil leaves on top, then a slice of tomato on each. Season well. Repeat with the feta mixture, basil leaves, aubergine and tomato. Finish with a third aubergine slice and press down firmly.

4 Secure each stack with a cocktail stick. Either use a hinged grill rack, well oiled, or wrap the stacks in foil and barbecue for 2–3 minutes on each side. Serve with rocket leaves and toasted ciabatta rubbed with a garlic clove.

Serves 4	EASY		NUTRITIONAL INFORMATION	
	Preparation Time 10 minutes	**Cooking Time** 12 minutes	**Per Serving** 138 calories, 11g fat (of which 5g saturates), 4g carbohydrate, 1.2g salt	Vegetarian Gluten free

family favourites

Welsh Rarebit

225g (8oz) Cheddar cheese, grated (see Cook's Tip, page 26)

25g (1oz) butter

1 tsp English mustard

4 tbsp brown ale

4 slices white bread, crusts removed

salt and ground black pepper

1 Preheat the grill. Put the cheese, butter, mustard and ale into a heavy-based pan over a low heat and stir occasionally until the cheese is melted and the mixture is smooth and creamy. Season with salt and pepper to taste.

2 Toast the bread under the grill on one side only. Turn the slices over and spread the cheese mixture on the untoasted side. Put under the grill for 1 minute or until golden and bubbling, then serve.

Serves	EASY		NUTRITIONAL INFORMATION	
4	**Preparation Time** 5 minutes	**Cooking Time** 6–8 minutes	**Per Serving** 380 calories, 25g fat (of which 15g saturates), 21g carbohydrate, 1.9g salt	Vegetarian

Try Something Different

Add 1 hot red chilli, seeded and finely chopped (see Cook's Tips, page 10), 1 tbsp freshly grated ginger and a handful of freshly chopped coriander leaves to the pork sausage meat.

Sausage Rolls

450g (1lb) puff pastry, thawed if frozen

flour to dust

450g (1lb) pork sausage meat

milk to brush

beaten egg to glaze

1 Preheat the oven to 220°C (200°C fan oven) mark 7. Roll out half the puff pastry on a lightly floured surface to a 40.5 × 20.5cm (16 × 8in) rectangle; cut lengthways into two strips.

2 Divide the sausage meat into four, dust with flour and form two portions into rolls, the length of the pastry. Lay a sausage-meat roll on each strip of pastry. Brush the pastry edges with a little milk, fold one side of the pastry over and press the long edges together to seal. Repeat with the remaining pastry and sausage meat. Trim the ends.

3 Brush the pastry with beaten egg to glaze and cut each roll into 5cm (2in) lengths. Make two or three slits in the top of each one.

4 Transfer to a baking sheet and cook for 15 minutes. Reduce the oven temperature to 180°C (160°C fan oven) mark 4 and cook for a further 15 minutes. Transfer to a wire rack. Serve hot or cold.

Makes 28	EASY		NUTRITIONAL INFORMATION
	Preparation Time 25 minutes	**Cooking Time** 30 minutes	**Per Serving** 119 calories, 9g fat (of which 2g saturates), 8g carbohydrate, 0.4g salt

Try Something Different

To use leftover chicken or turkey, don't fry the meat at step 2. Add it to the pan with the crème fraîche at step 3. Cook the leeks in 2 tsp olive oil.

For a different flavour, make the mash with 2 large potatoes and a small celeriac, that has been peeled, cut into chunks and cooked with the potato.

Chicken and Leek Pie

5 large potatoes, chopped into chunks

200g (7oz) crème fraîche

3 boneless chicken breasts, with skin on, about 125g (4oz) each

3 large leeks, trimmed and chopped into chunks

about 10 fresh tarragon leaves, finely chopped

salt and ground black pepper

1 Preheat the oven to 200°C (180°C fan oven) mark 6. Put the potatoes into a pan of lightly salted cold water. Cover the pan and bring to the boil, then reduce the heat and simmer for 10–12 minutes until soft. Drain and put back into the pan. Add 1 tbsp crème fraîche, season with salt and pepper and mash well.

2 Meanwhile, heat a frying pan, add the chicken, skin side down, and fry gently for 5 minutes or until the skin is golden. Turn the chicken over and fry for 6–8 minutes. Remove the chicken from the pan and put on to a board. Tip the leeks into the pan and cook in the juices over a low heat for 5 minutes to soften.

3 Discard the chicken skin and cut the flesh into bite-size pieces (don't worry if it is not quite cooked through). Put the chicken back into the pan, stir in the remaining crème fraîche and heat for 2–3 minutes until bubbling. Stir in the tarragon and season with salt and pepper, then spoon into a 1.7 litre (3 pint) ovenproof dish and spread the mash on top.

4 Cook in the oven for 20–25 minutes until golden and heated through. Serve hot.

EASY		NUTRITIONAL INFORMATION		Serves
Preparation Time 15 minutes	**Cooking Time** 40–45 minutes	**Per Serving** 591 calories, 23g fat (of which 15g saturates), 54g carbohydrate, 0.3g salt	Gluten free	**4**

700g (1½ lb) middle neck lamb cutlets, fat trimmed

2 onions, thinly sliced

450g (1lb) potatoes, thinly sliced

1 tbsp freshly chopped parsley, plus extra to garnish

1 tbsp dried thyme

300ml (½ pint) lamb stock

Irish Stew

1 Preheat the oven to 170°C (150°C fan oven) mark 3. Layer the meat, onions and potatoes in a deep casserole dish, sprinkling some herbs and seasoning between each layer. Finish with a layer of potato, overlapping the slices neatly.

2 Pour the stock over the potatoes, then cover with greaseproof paper and a lid. Cook for about 2 hours or until the meat is tender.

3 Preheat the grill. Take the lid off the casserole and remove the paper. Put under the grill and brown the top. Sprinkle with parsley and serve immediately.

Serves 4	EASY		NUTRITIONAL INFORMATION	
	Preparation Time 15 minutes	**Cooking Time** 2 hours	**Per Serving** 419 calories, 20g fat (of which 9g saturates), 24g carbohydrate, 0.6g salt	Dairy free

Cook's Tip

As well as ground meat, sausages also contain some type of fat, herbs, spices, seasoning and cereal. The meat-to-fat ratio varies hugely between varieties of sausage, and from region to region, but a pork sausage should contain a minimum of 42 per cent pork meat. Sausages are usually sold twisted into links. There are endless varieties of sausage, but the most famous of the pork-based are:

Cumberland: Traditionally sold in a coil, rather than twisted into links. With a chunky texture and peppery flavour, they are a great all-round sausage.

Lincolnshire: These have a chunky and open texture. Flavoured with thyme and sage.

Chipolatas: Famous for being wrapped in bacon and served with the Christmas turkey. Slender sausages which are usually grilled rather than pan-fried or oven-roasted.

Chorizo: A distinctive red Spanish sausage, strongly flavoured with paprika. It has a coarse texture and hot, spicy flavour. Available both raw and cooked, smoked and unsmoked.

Frankfurters: Lightly smoked German sausages with a fine texture. They are the classic hot dog sausage.

Toulouse: A pungent coarse sausage flavoured with wine, garlic and seasoning. Great in hot-pots or cassoulets.

Toad in the Hole

125g (4oz) plain flour, sifted
2 large eggs, lightly beaten
150ml (¼ pint) semi-skimmed milk
2 tbsp oil
4 pork sausages
salt and ground black pepper
steamed carrots and broccoli or green beans to serve

1 Preheat the oven to 220°C (200°C fan oven) mark 7. Put the flour into a bowl, make a well in the centre and pour in the eggs and milk. Whisk the batter thoroughly and season it well with salt and pepper.

2 Divide the oil and sausages between two 600ml (1 pint) shallow ovenproof dishes and cook in the oven for 10 minutes, turning once or twice.

3 Divide the batter between the dishes and continue to cook for 15–20 minutes until the batter is puffy and a rich golden colour all over. Serve immediately, with steamed carrots and broccoli or green beans.

EASY		NUTRITIONAL INFORMATION	Serves
Preparation Time 10 minutes	**Cooking Time** 25–30 minutes	**Per Serving** 571 calories, 31g fat (of which 8g saturates), 57g carbohydrate, 2.6g salt	2

Sausages with Red Onion Marmalade

12 gluten-free (100% meat) venison sausages

6 tsp redcurrant jelly

Colcannon (see Cook's Tip) or mashed potatoes to serve

For the red onion marmalade

400g (14oz) red onions, chopped

2 tbsp olive oil

4 tbsp red wine vinegar

2 tbsp demerara sugar

1 tsp juniper berries, crushed

1 Preheat the oven to 220°C (200°C fan oven) mark 7. Put the sausages into a small roasting tin. Roast in the oven for 35 minutes, turning once (after 25 minutes, spoon the redcurrant jelly over them and continue to cook).

2 Meanwhile, make the red onion marmalade. Gently fry the onions in the oil for 15–20 minutes. Add the vinegar, sugar and juniper berries and cook for a further 5 minutes or until the onions are very tender. Serve the sausages with the red onion marmalade and colcannon.

Cook's Tip

Colcannon: Cook 1.1kg (2½ lb) floury potatoes in lightly salted boiling water until tender. Drain in a colander. Add 25g (1oz) butter to the pan and gently fry 1 chopped leek or 100g (3½ oz) shredded cabbage until soft. Return the potato to the pan with another 25g (1oz) butter and a handful of chopped herbs such as parsley, chives and thyme. Heat through gently.

EASY		NUTRITIONAL INFORMATION		Serves
Preparation Time 15 minutes	**Cooking Time** 35 minutes	**Per Serving** 390 calories, 25g fat (of which 10g saturates), 14g carbohydrate, 0.3g salt	Gluten free Dairy free	**6**

Shepherd's Pie

2 tbsp sunflower oil

450g (1lb) lamb mince

1 large onion, chopped

50g (2oz) mushrooms, sliced

2 carrots, chopped

2 tbsp plain flour

1 tbsp tomato purée

1 bay leaf

300ml (½ pint) lamb stock

700g (1½ lb) potatoes, cut into large chunks

25g (1oz) butter

75ml (2½ fl oz) milk

50g (2oz) Lancashire cheese or Cheddar, crumbled (optional)

salt and ground black pepper

green vegetables to serve

1 Heat half the oil in a large pan and brown the mince over a medium to high heat – do this in batches, otherwise the meat will steam rather than fry. Remove with a slotted spoon and put to one side.

2 Turn the heat to low and add the remaining oil. Gently fry the onion, mushrooms and carrots for 10 minutes or until softened. Stir in the flour and tomato purée and cook for 1 minute. Return the meat to the pan and add the bay leaf. Pour in the stock and bring to the boil, then cover the pan, reduce the heat and simmer for 25 minutes.

3 Preheat the oven to 200°C (180°C fan oven) mark 6. Cook the potatoes in lightly salted boiling water for 20 minutes or until tender. Drain and leave to stand in the colander for 2 minutes to steam dry. Melt the butter with the milk in the potato pan and add the cooked potatoes. Mash until smooth.

4 Spoon the lamb mixture into a 1.7 litre (3 pint) ovenproof casserole dish. Remove the bay leaf and check the seasoning. Cover with the mashed potato and sprinkle the cheese over it, if using. Bake for 15–20 minutes until bubbling and golden. Serve immediately with green vegetables.

Serves 4	EASY		NUTRITIONAL INFORMATION
	Preparation Time 20 minutes	**Cooking Time** about 55 minutes	**Per Serving** 513 calories, 27g fat (of which 11g saturates), 44g carbohydrate, 0.6g salt

Try Something Different

Instead of garlic mayonnaise, serve with one of the following.
Simple Tartare Sauce: Mix 8 tbsp mayonnaise with 1 tbsp each chopped capers and gherkins, 1 tbsp freshly chopped tarragon or chives and 2 tsp lemon juice.
Herby Lemon Mayonnaise: Fold 2 tbsp finely chopped parsley, grated zest of ½ lemon and 2 tsp lemon juice into 8 tbsp mayonnaise.

900g (2lb) Desiree, Maris Piper or King Edward potatoes, peeled

2–3 tbsp olive oil

sea salt flakes

sunflower oil to deep-fry

2 × 128g packs batter mix

1 tsp baking powder

¼ tsp salt

330ml bottle of lager

4 plaice fillets, about 225g (8oz) each, with skin on, trimmed and cut in half

plain flour to dust

salt and ground black pepper

lemon wedges and chives to garnish

For the garlic mayonnaise

2 garlic cloves, crushed

8 tbsp mayonnaise

1 tsp lemon juice

Fish and Chips

1 Preheat the oven to 240°C (220°C fan oven) mark 9. Cut the potatoes into chips. Put them in a pan of lightly salted boiling water, cover and bring to the boil. Boil for 2 minutes, then drain well and turn on to kitchen paper to remove the excess moisture. Tip into a large non-stick roasting tin, toss with the olive oil and season with sea salt. Roast for 40–50 minutes until golden and cooked, turning from time to time.

2 Meanwhile, half-fill a deep-fat fryer with sunflower oil and heat to 190°C. Put the batter mix into a bowl with the baking powder and salt and gradually whisk in the lager. Season the plaice and lightly dust with flour. Dip two of the fillets into the batter and deep-fry in the hot oil until golden. Transfer to a warmed plate and cover lightly with foil to keep warm while you deep-fry the remaining plaice fillets.

3 Mix the garlic, mayonnaise and lemon juice together in a bowl and season well. Serve the garlic mayonnaise with the plaice and chips, garnished with lemon wedges and chives.

EASY		NUTRITIONAL INFORMATION		Serves
Preparation Time 30 minutes	**Cooking Time** 40–50 minutes	**Per Serving** 993 calories, 67g fat (of which 9g saturates), 64g carbohydrate, 1.6g salt	Dairy free	**4**

Old-fashioned Fish Pie

450g (1lb) haddock, cod or coley fillets

300ml (½ pint) milk

1 bay leaf

6 black peppercorns

2 onion slices for flavouring

65g (2½oz) butter

3 tbsp flour

150ml (¼ pint) single cream

2 medium eggs, hard-boiled, shelled and chopped

2 tbsp freshly chopped parsley

6 tbsp milk

900g (2lb) potatoes, cooked and mashed

1 medium egg

salt and ground black pepper

1 Put the fish in a frying pan, pour the milk over and add the bay leaf, peppercorns, onion slices and a good pinch of salt. Bring slowly to the boil, cover and simmer for 8–10 minutes until the fish flakes when tested with a fork.

2 Lift the fish out of the pan using a fish slice and put on a plate. Flake the fish, discarding the skin and bone. Strain and put the milk to one side. Preheat the oven to 200°C (180°C fan oven) mark 6.

3 Melt 40g (1½oz) butter in a pan, stir in the flour and cook gently for 1 minute, stirring. Remove the pan from the heat and gradually stir in the reserved milk. Bring to the boil slowly and continue to cook, stirring until the sauce thickens. Season.

4 Stir in the cream and fish, together with any juices. Add the chopped eggs and parsley, and adjust the seasoning. Spoon the mixture into a 1.1 litre (2 pint) pie dish or similar ovenproof dish.

5 Heat the milk and remaining butter in a pan, then beat into the potatoes. Season and leave to cool slightly.

6 Spoon the cooled potato into a large piping bag fitted with a large star nozzle. Pipe shell-shaped lines of potato across the fish mixture. Alternatively, spoon potato on top and roughen the surface with a fork.

7 Put the dish on a baking sheet and cook in the oven for 10–15 minutes until the potato is set.

8 Beat the egg with a good pinch of salt, then brush over the pie. Return to the oven for 15 minutes or until golden brown.

Try Something Different

Stir 125g (4oz) grated Cheddar cheese into the sauce.

Beat 125g (4oz) grated Cheddar or Red Leicester cheese into the mashed potatoes.

Stir 175g (6oz) canned sweetcorn, drained, and ¼ tsp cayenne pepper into the fish mixture.

Fry 125g (4oz) sliced button mushrooms in 25g (1oz) butter for 3 minutes. Stir into the fish mixture.

Sprinkle the potato topping with 50g (2oz) mixed grated Parmesan and fresh breadcrumbs after the first 10–15 minutes.

Cover the pie with puff pastry instead of the potatoes.

Serves 4	EASY		NUTRITIONAL INFORMATION
	Preparation Time 20 minutes	**Cooking Time** 50 minutes	**Per Serving** 610 calories, 28g fat (of which 15g saturates), 56g carbohydrate, 1.4g salt

meat-free meals

Cook's Tip

The root vegetables take longest to cook through, while the asparagus and leeks only need a short time under the grill.

Grilled Vegetables with Walnut Sauce

2 large carrots, peeled
1 fennel bulb
225g (8oz) sweet potatoes
225g (8oz) Jerusalem artichokes, scrubbed
225g (8oz) thick asparagus spears
8 baby leeks
4–6 tbsp olive oil
salt and ground black pepper

For the walnut sauce

50g (2oz) day-old bread, crusts removed
75g (3oz) walnuts, toasted
2 garlic cloves, chopped
1 tbsp red wine vinegar
2 tbsp chopped parsley
90ml (3fl oz) olive oil
50ml (2fl oz) walnut oil

1 First make the walnut sauce. Crumble the bread into a bowl, add 2 tbsp water, then squeeze dry. Put the bread into a food processor with the toasted walnuts, garlic, vinegar and parsley and whiz until fairly smooth. Add the olive and walnut oils and whiz briefly to form a thick sauce. Season with salt and pepper and transfer to a serving dish.

2 Preheat the grill to medium-high. Prepare the vegetables. Cut the carrots into 5mm (¼ in) slices; thinly slice the fennel lengthways; peel and thinly slice the sweet potatoes; thinly slice the Jerusalem artichokes. Trim the asparagus and leeks, but leave whole.

3 Baste the vegetables with the oil and grill in batches, turning once, for 2–6 minutes on each side until charred and tender (see Cook's Tip); keep warm in a low oven while grilling the rest.

4 Transfer all the grilled vegetables to a warmed serving plate and season with a little salt and pepper. Serve accompanied by the walnut sauce.

Serves 4	EASY		NUTRITIONAL INFORMATION	
	Preparation Time 25 minutes	**Cooking Time** 15–20 minutes	**Per Serving** 598 calories, 48g fat (of which 6g saturates), 35g carbohydrate, 0.3g salt	Vegetarian Dairy free

Freezing Tip

To freeze Complete the recipe, then cool, wrap and freeze for up to one month.
To use Thaw overnight at room temperature, then reheat at 200°C (180°C fan oven) mark 6 for 20 minutes in an ovenproof dish with 200ml (7fl oz) hot stock.

Spicy Roasted Roots

3 carrots, sliced lengthways

3 parsnips, sliced lengthways

3 tbsp olive oil

1 butternut squash, chopped

2 red onions, cut into wedges

2 leeks, sliced

3 garlic cloves, roughly chopped

2 tbsp mild curry paste

salt and ground black pepper

1 Preheat the oven to 200°C (180°C fan oven) mark 6. Put the carrots and parsnips into a large roasting tin, drizzle with 1 tbsp oil and cook for 40 minutes.

2 Add the butternut squash, onions, leeks and garlic to the roasting tin. Season with salt and pepper, then drizzle with the remaining 2 tbsp oil.

3 Roast for 45 minutes or until the vegetables are tender and golden. Stir in the curry paste and return to the oven for a further 10 minutes. Serve immediately.

EASY		NUTRITIONAL INFORMATION		Serves
Preparation Time 25 minutes	**Cooking Time** about 1½ hours	**Per Serving** 134 calories, 8g fat (of which 1g saturates), 14g carbohydrate, 0.1g salt	Vegetarian Gluten free • Dairy free	**8**

Ratatouille

4 tbsp olive oil

2 onions, thinly sliced

1 large garlic clove, crushed

350g (12oz) small aubergine, thinly sliced

450g (1lb) small courgettes, thinly sliced

450g (1lb) tomatoes, skinned, seeded and roughly chopped

1 green and 1 red pepper, each cored, seeded and sliced

1 tbsp chopped basil

2 tsp chopped thyme

2 tbsp chopped flat-leafed parsley

2 tbsp sun-dried tomato paste

salt and ground black pepper

1 Heat the oil in a large pan, add the onions and garlic and fry gently for 10 minutes or until softened and golden.

2 Add the aubergine, courgettes, tomatoes, sliced peppers, herbs, tomato paste and seasoning. Fry, stirring, for 2–3 minutes.

3 Cover the pan tightly and simmer for 30 minutes or until all the vegetables are just tender. If necessary, uncover towards the end of the cooking time to evaporate some of the liquid.

4 Taste and adjust the seasoning. Serve the ratatouille hot or cold.

Serves 6	EASY		NUTRITIONAL INFORMATION	
	Preparation Time 20 minutes	**Cooking Time** about 45 minutes	**Per Serving** 150 calories, 10g fat (of which 4g saturates), 12g carbohydrate, 1.2g salt	Vegetarian Gluten free • Dairy free

Try Something Different

Use sliced courgettes instead of aubergine.

Leek and Broccoli Bake

2 tbsp olive oil

1 large red onion, cut into wedges

1 aubergine, chopped

2 leeks, trimmed and cut into chunks

1 broccoli head, cut into florets and stalks chopped

3 large flat mushrooms, chopped

2 x 400g cans cherry tomatoes

3 rosemary sprigs, chopped

50g (2oz) Parmesan, freshly grated (see Cook's Tip, page 26)

salt and ground black pepper

1 Preheat the oven to 200°C (180°C fan oven) mark 6. Heat the oil in a large flameproof dish, add the onion, aubergine and leeks and cook for 10–12 minutes until golden and softened.

2 Add the broccoli, mushrooms, cherry tomatoes, half the rosemary and 300ml (½ pint) boiling water. Season with salt and pepper. Stir well, then cover and cook in the oven for 30 minutes.

3 Meanwhile, put the Parmesan into a bowl. Add the remaining rosemary and season with pepper. When the vegetables are cooked, remove the lid and sprinkle the Parmesan mixture on top. Cook, uncovered, in the oven for a further 5–10 minutes until the topping is golden.

Serves 4	EASY		NUTRITIONAL INFORMATION	
	Preparation Time 20 minutes	**Cooking Time** 45–55 minutes	**Per Serving** 245 calories, 13g fat (of which 4g saturates), 18g carbohydrate, 0.4g salt	Vegetarian Gluten free

Tomato and Butter Bean Stew

2 tbsp olive oil
1 onion, finely sliced
2 garlic cloves, finely chopped
2 large leeks, trimmed and sliced
2 x 400g cans cherry tomatoes
2x 400g cans butter beans, drained and rinsed
150ml (¼ pint) hot vegetable stock
1–2 tbsp balsamic vinegar
salt and ground black pepper

1 Preheat the oven to 180°C (160°C fan oven) mark 4. Heat the oil in a flameproof casserole over a medium heat. Add the onion and garlic and cook for 10 minutes or until golden and soft. Add the leeks and cook, covered, for 5 minutes.

2 Add the tomatoes, beans and hot stock and season well with salt and pepper. Bring to the boil, then cover and cook in the oven for 35–40 minutes until the sauce has thickened. Remove from the oven, stir in the vinegar and spoon into warmed bowls.

EASY		NUTRITIONAL INFORMATION		Serves
Preparation Time 10 minutes	**Cooking Time** 50–55 minutes	**Per Serving** 286 calories, 8g fat (of which 1g saturates), 41g carbohydrate, 1.8g salt	Vegetarian Dairy free	**4**

Spring Vegetable Stew

225g (8oz) new potatoes, scrubbed

75g (3oz) unsalted butter

4 shallots, blanched in boiling water, drained, peeled and thinly sliced

1 garlic clove, crushed

2 tsp freshly chopped thyme

1 tsp grated lime zest

6 baby leeks, trimmed and sliced into 5cm (2in) lengths

125g (4oz) baby carrots, scrubbed

125g (4oz) podded peas

125g (4oz) podded broad beans

300ml (½ pint) vegetable stock

1 Little Gem lettuce, shredded

4 tbsp freshly chopped herbs, such as chervil, chives, mint and parsley

salt and ground black pepper

1 Put the potatoes into a pan of lightly salted water. Bring to the boil, cover and par-boil for 5 minutes. Drain and refresh under cold water.

2 Meanwhile, melt half the butter in a large sauté pan, add the shallots, garlic, thyme and lime zest and fry gently for 5 minutes or until softened and lightly golden. Add the leeks and carrots and sauté for a further 5 minutes. Stir in the potatoes, peas and broad beans, then pour in the stock and bring to the boil. Reduce the heat, cover the pan and simmer gently for 10 minutes. Remove the lid and cook, uncovered, for a further 5–8 minutes until all the vegetables are tender.

3 Add the shredded lettuce to the stew with the chopped herbs and remaining butter. Heat through until the butter is melted. Check the seasoning and serve at once.

Serves 4	EASY		NUTRITIONAL INFORMATION	
	Preparation Time 20 minutes	**Cooking Time** 30–35 minutes	**Per Serving** 270 calories, 17g fat (of which 10g saturates), 23g carbohydrate, 0.6g salt	Vegetarian Gluten free • Dairy free

Try Something Different

Replace carrots and/or broccoli with alternative vegetables – try baby sweetcorn, sugarsnap peas or mangetouts and simmer for only 5 minutes until tender.

30 Minute Recipe

Thai Vegetable Curry

2–3 tbsp red Thai curry paste (see Cook's Tip, page 179)

2.5cm (1in) piece fresh root ginger, peeled and finely chopped

50g (2oz) cashew nuts

400ml can coconut milk

3 carrots, cut into thin batons

1 broccoli head, cut into florets

20g (3/4oz) fresh coriander, roughly chopped

zest and juice of 1 lime

2 large handfuls of spinach leaves

basmati rice to serve

1 Put the curry paste into a large pan, add the ginger and cashew nuts and stir-fry over a medium heat for 2–3 minutes.

2 Add the coconut milk, cover and bring to the boil. Stir the carrots into the pan, then reduce the heat and simmer for 5 minutes. Add the broccoli florets and simmer for a further 5 minutes or until tender.

3 Stir the coriander and lime zest into the pan with the spinach. Squeeze the lime juice over and serve with basmati rice.

EASY		NUTRITIONAL INFORMATION		Serves
Preparation Time 10 minutes	**Cooking Time** 15 minutes	**Per Serving** 200 calories, 10g fat (of which 2g saturates), 19g carbohydrate, 0.7g salt	Vegetarian Gluten free • Dairy free	**4**

Cook's Tip

This is an ideal accompaniment to a vegetarian frittata.

Baked Tomatoes and Fennel

900g (2lb) fennel, trimmed and cut into quarters
75ml (2½ fl oz) white wine
5 thyme sprigs
75ml (2½ fl oz) olive oil
900g (2lb) ripe beef or plum tomatoes

1 Preheat the oven to 200°C (180°C fan oven) mark 6. Put the fennel into a roasting tin and pour the white wine over it. Snip the thyme sprigs over the fennel, drizzle with the oil and roast for 45 minutes.

2 Halve the tomatoes, add to the roasting tin and continue to roast for 30 minutes or until tender, basting with the juices halfway through.

Serves 6	EASY		NUTRITIONAL INFORMATION	
	Preparation Time 25 minutes	**Cooking Time** 1¼ hours	**Per Serving** 127 calories, 9g fat (of which 1g saturates), 7g carbohydrate, 0.1g salt	Vegetarian Gluten free • Dairy free

Hasselback Potatoes

8 potatoes, weighing about 75g (3oz) each

vegetable oil for brushing

salt and ground black pepper

1 Preheat the oven to 220°C (200°C fan oven) mark 7. Cut the potatoes across their width at 5mm (¼ in) intervals three-quarters of the way through.

2 Put in a single layer in an oiled baking tin. Brush with oil and season. Roast, uncovered, for 45 minutes.

EASY		NUTRITIONAL INFORMATION		Serves
Preparation Time 10 minutes	**Cooking Time** 45 minutes	**Per Serving** 162 calories, 6g fat (of which 1g saturates), 26g carbohydrate, 0.3g salt	Vegetarian Gluten free • Dairy free	4

Oven Chips

900g (2lb) Desirée potatoes
2–3 tbsp olive oil
salt and sea salt flakes

1 Preheat the oven to 240°C (220°C fan oven) mark 9. Peel the potatoes and cut into chips. Add to a pan of lightly salted boiling water, cover and bring to the boil, then boil for 2 minutes. Drain well, then pat dry with kitchen paper.

2 Tip the par-boiled potatoes into a large non-stick roasting tin, toss with the oil and season with sea salt. Roast for 40 minutes or until golden and cooked, turning from time to time. Drain on kitchen paper and serve.

Serves	EASY		NUTRITIONAL INFORMATION	
4	**Preparation Time** 10 minutes	**Cooking Time** 40 minutes	**Per Serving** 220 calories, 6g fat (of which 1g saturates), 39g carbohydrate, 0.3g salt	Vegetarian Gluten free • Dairy free

Freezing Tip

To freeze Complete the recipe to the end of step 2, then cool, seal in large freezer bags and freeze for up to one month.
To use Cook from frozen, allowing an additional 15–20 minutes total cooking time.

Crispy Roast Potatoes

1.8kg (4lb) potatoes, preferably King Edward, cut into two-bite pieces

2 tsp paprika

2–3 tbsp goose or white vegetable fat

salt

1 Put the potatoes into a pan of lightly salted cold water. Cover and bring to the boil. Boil for 7 minutes, then drain well in a colander.

2 Sprinkle the paprika over the potatoes in the colander, then cover and shake the potatoes roughly, so they become fluffy around the edges.

3 Preheat the oven to 220°C (200°C fan oven) mark 7. Heat the fat in a large roasting tin on the hob. When it sizzles, add the potatoes. Tilt the pan to coat, taking care as the fat will splutter. Roast in the oven for 1 hour.

4 Reduce the oven temperature to 200°C (180°C fan oven) mark 6 and roast for a further 40 minutes. Shake the potatoes only once or twice during cooking, otherwise the edges won't crisp and brown. Season with a little salt before serving.

Serves 8	EASY		NUTRITIONAL INFORMATION	
	Preparation Time 20 minutes	**Cooking Time** 1 hour 50 minutes	**Per Serving** 211 calories, 6g fat (of which 3g saturates), 37g carbohydrate, 0.1g salt	Dairy free Gluten free

Get Ahead

To prepare ahead Complete the recipe to the end of step 4, up to one day ahead. Cover and chill.
To use Reheat under the grill for 5 minutes.

Roasted Stuffed Peppers

40g (1½ oz) butter
4 Romano peppers, halved, with stalks on and seeded
3 tbsp olive oil
350g (12oz) chestnut mushrooms, roughly chopped
4 tbsp finely chopped fresh chives
100g (3½ oz) feta cheese (see Cook's Tip, page 26)
50g (2oz) fresh white breadcrumbs
25g (1oz) freshly grated Parmesan (see as above)
salt and ground black pepper

1 Preheat the oven to 180°C (160°C fan oven) mark 4. Use a little of the butter to grease a shallow ovenproof dish and put the peppers in it side by side, ready to be filled.

2 Heat the remaining butter and 1 tbsp oil in a pan. Add the mushrooms and fry until they're golden and there's no excess liquid left in the pan. Stir in the chives, then spoon the mixture into the pepper halves.

3 Crumble the feta over the mushrooms. Mix the breadcrumbs and Parmesan in a bowl, then sprinkle over the peppers.

4 Season with salt and pepper and drizzle with the remaining oil. Roast in the oven for 45 minutes or until golden and tender. Serve warm.

EASY		NUTRITIONAL INFORMATION		Serves
Preparation Time 20 minutes	**Cooking Time** 45 minutes	**Per Serving** 189 calories, 14g fat (of which 6g saturates), 11g carbohydrate, 0.9g salt	Vegetarian	**8**

Charred Courgettes

4 courgettes, halved lengthways

olive oil to brush

coarse sea salt to sprinkle

1 Preheat the barbecue or griddle. Score a criss-cross pattern on the fleshy side of the courgettes. Brush lightly with oil and sprinkle with sea salt.

2 Cook the courgettes on the barbecue or griddle for 10 minutes or until just tender, turning occasionally.

Try Something Different

Mix the olive oil with a good pinch of dried chilli flakes and a small handful of chopped fresh rosemary leaves.
Use a mixture of yellow and green courgettes if you like.

EASY		NUTRITIONAL INFORMATION		Serves
Preparation Time 5 minutes	**Cooking Time** 10 minutes	**Per Serving** 36 calories, 2g fat (of which trace saturates), 2g carbohydrate, 0g salt	Vegetarian Gluten free • Dairy free	**4**

Try Something Different

Use crushed garlic instead of chilli.

Roasted Butternut Squash

2 butternut squash

2 tbsp olive oil

25g (1oz) butter

2 tbsp freshly chopped thyme leaves

1 red chilli, seeded and finely chopped (see Cook's Tips, page 10)

salt and ground black pepper

1 Preheat the oven to 220°C (200°C fan oven) mark 7. Cut the squash in half lengthways and scoop out the seeds. Cut in half again, then put into a roasting tin. Drizzle with the oil, season with salt and pepper and roast for 40 minutes.

2 Meanwhile, put the butter into a bowl with the thyme and chilli. Mix together well. Add a little to each slice of cooked butternut squash and serve.

Serves 4	EASY		NUTRITIONAL INFORMATION	
	Preparation Time 15 minutes	**Cooking Time** 40 minutes	**Per Serving** 165 calories, 12g fat (of which 5g saturates), 11g carbohydrate, 0.1g salt	Vegetarian Gluten free

Try Something Different

Use basil-infused oil and increase the amount of oil to 2 tbsp.
Use pinenuts instead of almonds, drizzle with balsamic vinegar
and scatter with basil leaves to serve.

Green Beans and Flaked Almonds

200g (7oz) green beans

1 tsp olive oil

25g (1oz) flaked almonds

$^{1}/_{2}$ lemon

1 Bring a large pan of water to the boil. Add the green beans and cook for 4–5 minutes. Drain.

2 Meanwhile, heat the oil in a large frying pan. Add the almonds and cook for 1–2 minutes until golden. Turn off the heat, add the drained beans to the frying pan and toss. Squeeze a little lemon juice over just before serving.

EASY		NUTRITIONAL INFORMATION		Serves
Preparation Time 5 minutes	**Cooking Time** 5–7 minutes	**Per Serving** 57 calories, 5g fat (of which trace saturates), 2g carbohydrate, 0g salt	Vegetarian Gluten free • Dairy free	**4**

30 Minute Recipe

Caramelised Carrots

700g (1½lb) baby carrots, scraped

50g (2oz) butter

50g (2oz) light muscovado sugar

300ml (½ pint) chicken or vegetable stock

2 tbsp balsamic vinegar

salt and ground black pepper

2 tbsp freshly chopped parsley to serve

1 Thinly slice the carrots lengthways, then put into a pan with the butter, sugar and stock. Season with salt and pepper, then cover and bring to the boil. Reduce the heat and simmer for 5 minutes.

2 Remove the lid, add the balsamic vinegar and cook for a further 5–10 minutes until the carrots are tender and the liquid has reduced to form a glaze. Scatter with the chopped parsley to serve.

Serves 8	EASY		NUTRITIONAL INFORMATION	
	Preparation Time 15 minutes	**Cooking Time** 10–15 minutes	**Per Serving** 100 calories, 5g fat (of which 3g saturates), 13g carbohydrate, 0.8g salt	Gluten free

Slow-roasted Tomatoes

12 large ripe tomatoes
2 garlic cloves, roughly chopped
2 thyme sprigs, bruised
a pinch of sugar
4 tbsp extra virgin olive oil
squeeze of lemon juice
salt and ground black pepper
basil leaves to garnish

1 Preheat the oven to 150°C (130°C fan oven) mark 2. Halve the tomatoes and scoop out most of the seeds. Put the tomato halves into a baking dish in which they fit closely together and scatter the garlic, thyme, sugar, salt and pepper over.

2 Drizzle the oil over the tomatoes and add a good squeeze of lemon juice. Roast for $2\frac{1}{2}$–3 hours until the tomatoes are shrivelled (but not as dried as sun-dried tomatoes). Allow to cool.

3 Scatter basil leaves over the tomatoes and serve, as an accompaniment to cold meats and cheese.

EASY		NUTRITIONAL INFORMATION		Serves
Preparation Time 10 minutes	**Cooking Time** 2½–3 hours	**Per Serving** 170 calories, 14g fat (of which 2g saturates), 9g carbohydrate, 0.3g salt	Vegetarian Gluten free • Dairy free	**4**

savoury pies
and pastries

Goat's Cheese Parcels

125g (4oz) fresh spinach, coarse stalks removed

2 tbsp sunflower oil

1 onion, peeled and finely chopped

1 large garlic clove, peeled and chopped

250g (9oz) soft goat's cheese

275g (10oz) filo pastry, thawed if frozen

50g (2oz) butter, melted

sesame seeds to sprinkle

salt and ground black pepper

1 Plunge the spinach into a pan of boiling water, bring back to the boil for 1 minute, then drain and refresh under very cold water. Squeeze out all the excess liquid and chop finely.

2 Heat the oil in a pan, add the onion and garlic and cook until translucent, then leave to cool. Combine the spinach, onion mixture and goat's cheese in a bowl and season generously.

3 Cut the pastry into twenty-four 12.5cm (5in) squares. Brush one square with melted butter, cover with a second square and brush with more butter. Put to one side and cover with a damp teatowel. Repeat with the remaining squares, to make twelve sets.

4 Put a dessertspoonful of the filling on each square and join up the corners to form a parcel. Brush with a little more butter, sprinkle with sesame seeds and chill for 20 minutes. Meanwhile, preheat the oven to 220°C (200°C fan oven) mark 7. Bake the parcels for about 5 minutes until the pastry is crisp and browned.

Serves 6	EASY		NUTRITIONAL INFORMATION	
	Preparation Time 45 minutes, plus chilling	**Cooking Time** 10 minutes, plus cooling	**Per Serving (2 parcels)** 345 calories, 22g fat (of which 12g saturates), 26g carbohydrate, 0.8g salt	Vegetarian

Cook's Tips

Baking blind: Cooking the pastry before filling gives a crisp result. Prick the pastry base with a fork. Cover with foil or greaseproof paper 7.5cm (3in) larger than the tin. Spread baking beans on top and then place in the oven for the first stage of baking. Remove the foil or paper and beans and bake for the second stage, until the pastry is light golden.

To check the pie is cooked, insert a skewer into the centre for 30 seconds – it should feel hot when you pull it out. Cool the pie in the tin for 1 hour to serve warm, or 3 hours to serve at room temperature.

275g (10oz) plain flour, plus extra to dust

200g (7oz) chilled butter, cubed

pinch of salt

1 large egg, beaten, plus 1 large egg, beaten, to glaze

For the filling

2 large eggs and 2 large yolks, beaten

200ml (7fl oz) crème fraîche

3 tbsp freshly chopped dill

450g (1lb) fresh salmon fillet, cut into wide strips, 10cm (4in) long

200g (7oz) button mushrooms, sliced and fried in 25g (1oz) butter for 1–2 minutes, then cooled

150g (5oz) thick asparagus tips, blanched, drained and refreshed in iced water

salt and ground black pepper

Salmon and Asparagus Pie

1 Whiz the flour, butter and salt in a food processor until the mixture resembles breadcrumbs. Add 1 egg and 2 tbsp cold water and pulse until the mixture just comes together. Knead lightly on a floured surface. Cut off one-third, wrap both pieces and chill for 30 minutes.

2 Preheat the oven to 200°C (180°C fan oven) mark 6. Roll out the larger piece of pastry to a 28cm (11in) round and line a 20.5cm (8in) loose-based deep tin. Bake the pastry case blind for 25 minutes at the first stage and then 5–10 minutes for the second stage, using a little of the remaining egg to seal the pastry case.

3 Remove from the oven and leave to cool. Put a baking tray in the oven to heat up.

4 To make the filling, mix the eggs and yolks, crème fraîche and dill, and season. Put half the fish in the pie case, arrange the vegetables on top and season. Top with the remaining fish and pour the crème fraîche mixture over to within 1cm (½in) of the top. Brush the rim with beaten egg. Cut the remaining pastry into a 25.5cm (10in) round, place on top and seal the edges. Brush with egg and make a steam hole. Bake the pie on the hot tray for 40 minutes or until golden and the filling is cooked.

A LITTLE EFFORT		NUTRITIONAL INFORMATION	Serves
Preparation Time 40 minutes, plus chilling	**Cooking Time** 1 hour 10 minutes, plus cooling	**Per Serving** 782 calories, 59g fat (of which 32g saturates), 37g carbohydrate, 0.8g salt	**6**

Spinach and Feta Pie

1 tbsp vegetable oil

1 onion, peeled and finely chopped

1 garlic clove, peeled and crushed

1 tbsp cumin seeds

400g (14oz) baby leaf spinach

1.1kg (2½lb) waxy potatoes, such as Desirée, boiled in their skins until tender, cooled, peeled and sliced

2 x 200g packs vegetarian feta cheese, crumbled

2 medium eggs, beaten

50g (2oz) butter, melted, plus extra to grease

200g pack filo pastry, thawed if frozen

salt and ground black pepper

1 Heat the oil in a large pan and cook the onion for 10 minutes or until soft. Add the garlic and cumin and cook for 1–2 minutes. Add the spinach, cover and cook until the spinach has just wilted – 1–2 minutes. Tip into a bowl and leave to cool. Add the potatoes, cheese and eggs. Season and mix.

2 Preheat the oven to 200°C (180°C fan oven) mark 6. Lightly grease a 28cm (11in) tart tin with butter. Unroll the pastry and cut the sheets lengthways into three. Work with one-third of the strips at a time and cover the remainder with clingfilm. Lay a strip on the tin, starting from the middle so that half covers the tin and half hangs over the edge. Brush with melted butter, then lay another strip next to it, slightly overlapping, and brush again. Repeat, working quickly around the tin in a cartwheel shape.

3 Add the filling and level the surface. Fold in the overhanging pastry to cover the mixture, filling any gaps with leftover pastry. Drizzle with the remaining melted butter, then cook for 45 minutes or until golden.

Cook's Tip

If you don't eat all the pie, it's just as delicious cold the next day or, if you prefer, warm it in the oven at 200°C (180°C fan oven) mark 6 for 15–20 minutes. Cover with foil if it starts to over-brown.

Serves 10	EASY		NUTRITIONAL INFORMATION	
	Preparation Time 40 minutes	**Cooking Time** 45 minutes, plus cooling	**Per Serving** 311 calories, 15g fat (of which 9g saturates), 33g carbohydrate; 1.7g salt	Vegetarian

Try Something Different

Replace the artichoke hearts with 225g (8oz) brown-cap mushrooms, cooked in a little water with some sea salt and pepper and lemon juice.

Chicken and Artichoke Pie

3 boneless, skinless chicken breasts, about 350g (12oz)

150ml (¼ pint) dry white wine

225g (8oz) reduced-fat cream cheese with garlic and herbs

400g can artichoke hearts, drained and quartered

4 sheets filo pastry, thawed if frozen

olive oil to brush

1 tsp sesame seeds

salt and ground black pepper

1 Preheat the oven to 200°C (180°C fan oven) mark 6. Put the chicken and wine into a pan and bring to the boil, then cover, reduce the heat and simmer for 10 minutes. Remove the chicken with a slotted spoon and put to one side. Add the cheese to the wine and mix until smooth. Bring to the boil, then reduce the heat and simmer until thickened.

2 Cut the chicken into bite-size pieces, then add to the sauce with the artichokes. Season and mix well.

3 Put the mixture into an ovenproof dish. Brush the pastry lightly with oil, scrunch slightly and put on top of the chicken. Sprinkle with sesame seeds, then cook in the oven for 30–35 minutes until crisp. Serve hot.

Serves 4	EASY		NUTRITIONAL INFORMATION
	Preparation Time 20 minutes	**Cooking Time** 45 minutes	**Per Serving** 241 calories, 9g fat (of which 5g saturates), 7g carbohydrate, 0.2g salt

Get Ahead

To prepare ahead Assemble the pie, then cover and chill for up to two days.
To use Brush with beaten egg and complete the recipe.

Chicken and Bacon Pie

1 tbsp olive oil
4 chicken breasts, cut into 2.5cm (1in) cubes
1 medium onion, peeled and sliced
1 carrot, peeled and roughly chopped
50g (2oz) smoked streaky bacon, chopped
1 tbsp flour
200ml (7fl oz) chicken stock
100ml (3½fl oz) double cream
25g (1oz) frozen peas
1½ tsp wholegrain mustard
1 tbsp freshly chopped tarragon
175g (6oz) puff pastry, thawed if frozen
plain flour to dust
1 medium egg, beaten
salt and ground black pepper

1. Heat half the oil in a large pan, then brown the chicken in batches. Remove from the pan and put to one side. Add the remaining oil and fry the onion and carrot for 10 minutes. Add the bacon and cook for 3 minutes.

2. Stir in the flour and cook for 1 minute. Gradually add the stock, stirring well. Add the cream and return the chicken and any juices to the pan. Simmer for 5 minutes or until the chicken is cooked.

3. Add the peas, mustard and tarragon, then check the seasoning. Leave to cool a little.

4. Preheat the oven to 200°C (180°C fan oven) mark 6. Put a pie funnel, if you have one, in the centre of a 1 litre (1¾pint) pie dish or ovenproof casserole and tip in the filling. Roll out the pastry on a lightly floured surface to make a lid (make a slit for the pie funnel). Brush the pastry edges with the egg, then lay the pastry over the dish and trim with a sharp knife. Seal and brush with beaten egg and cook for 25–30 minutes until golden.

A LITTLE EFFORT		NUTRITIONAL INFORMATION	Serves
Preparation Time 30 minutes	**Cooking Time** about 55 minutes	**Per Serving** 554 calories, 34g fat (of which 6g saturates), 24g carbohydrate, 1.3g salt	**4**

Wild Mushroom Pithiviers

450g (1lb) wild mushrooms
300ml ($\frac{1}{2}$ pint) milk
200ml (7fl oz) double cream
2 garlic cloves, peeled and crushed
450g (1lb) floury potatoes, peeled and thinly sliced
freshly grated nutmeg
50g (2oz) butter
2 tsp freshly chopped thyme, plus fresh sprigs to garnish
2 x 500g packs puff pastry, thawed if frozen
plain flour to dust
1 large egg, beaten
salt and ground black pepper

Get Ahead

To prepare ahead Complete the recipe to the end of step 4, then cover and chill in the fridge overnight until ready to cook.
To use Complete the recipe.

1 Rinse the mushrooms in cold running water to remove any grit, then pat dry with kitchen paper. Roughly slice.

2 Pour the milk and cream into a large heavy-based pan and add the garlic. Bring to the boil, then add the potatoes. Bring back to the boil, then reduce the heat and simmer gently, stirring occasionally, for 15–20 minutes until the potatoes are tender. Season with salt, pepper and nutmeg. Leave to cool.

3 Melt the butter in a large frying pan. When it's sizzling, add the mushrooms and cook over a high heat, stirring all the time, for 5–10 minutes until the mushrooms are cooked and the juices have evaporated completely. Season. Stir in the chopped thyme, then set aside to cool.

4 Roll out the pastry thinly on a lightly floured surface. Cut into eight rounds, approximately 12.5cm (5in) in diameter, for the tops, and eight rounds, approximately 11.5cm (4$\frac{1}{2}$in) in diameter, for the bases. Put the smaller pastry rounds on baking sheets and brush the edges with beaten egg. Put a large spoonful of the cooled potato mixture in the centre of each round, leaving a 1cm ($\frac{1}{2}$in) border around the edge. Top with a spoonful of the mushroom mixture, then cover with the pastry tops. Press the edges together well to seal. Chill for 30 minutes–1 hour.

5 Meanwhile, preheat the oven to 220°C (200°C fan oven) mark 7 and put two baking trays in to heat up. Use the back of a knife to scallop the edges of the pastry and brush the top with the remaining beaten egg. If you like, use a knife to decorate the tops of the pithiviers.

6 Put the pithiviers, on their baking sheets, on the preheated baking trays. Cook for 15–20 minutes until deep golden brown, swapping the trays around in the oven halfway through cooking. Serve immediately, garnished with thyme sprigs.

EASY		NUTRITIONAL INFORMATION		Serves
Preparation Time 1 hour, plus chilling	**Cooking Time** about 1 hour, plus cooling	**Per Serving** 710 calories, 51g fat (of which 12g saturates), 58g carbohydrate, 1.2g salt	Vegetarian	**8**

Freezing Tip

To freeze Cover the uncooked galette in clingfilm and freeze on the baking sheet. When firm, remove from the baking tray. Wrap in baking parchment, and then in clingfilm.

To use Thaw for 3 hours at cool room temperature on baking parchment. Preheat the oven to 220°C (200°C fan oven) mark 7 and put a baking tray in the oven to heat. Brush the galette with beaten egg and sprinkle with cheese. Put the galette on the hot tray (this will keep the pastry base crisp) and bake for 40 minutes.

Leek and Ham Galette

25g (1oz) butter, plus extra to grease
350g (12oz) medium leeks, trimmed and cut into 2cm (½in) thick slices
25g (1oz) plain flour, plus extra to dust
50ml (2fl oz) milk
1 tbsp freshly chopped marjoram
50g (2oz) Gruyère cheese, cubed, plus 2 tbsp, grated
150g (5oz) cooked sliced ham, thickly shredded
225g (8oz) puff pastry, thawed if frozen
½ medium egg, beaten with a pinch of salt
salt and ground black pepper

1 Preheat the oven to 220°C (200°C fan oven) mark 7. Grease a baking sheet. Cook the leeks in lightly salted boiling water for 2–3 minutes until just beginning to soften. Drain, keeping the cooking liquid to one side. Plunge the leeks into cold water, drain and dry well on kitchen paper.

2 Melt the butter in a pan, remove from the heat and mix in the flour to form a smooth paste. Add 225ml (8fl oz) leek water and the milk and stir until smooth. Bring to the boil, then reduce the heat and simmer for 1–2 minutes. Remove from the heat, cover and leave to cool for 20 minutes or until cold. Add the marjoram, leeks, cubed cheese and ham and season.

3 Roll out the pastry on a lightly floured surface to a 30.5 x 33cm (12 x 13in) rectangle. Cut into two rectangles, one 15 x 30.5cm (6 x 12in) and the other 18 x 30.5cm (7 x 12in). Put the smaller piece on to the baking sheet. Spoon on the ham mixture, leaving a 2cm (¾in) border all the way around. Brush the border with beaten egg. Cover the filling with the larger pastry rectangle and press the edges together. Cut slashes in the top of the pastry to prevent the filling seeping out. Crimp the edges to seal, then cover and freeze for 20 minutes or until firm. Remove from the freezer, brush again with the beaten egg and sprinkle with the grated cheese. Bake for 20–30 minutes until brown and crisp. Serve hot.

Serves 4	EASY		NUTRITIONAL INFORMATION
	Preparation Time 30 minutes, plus chilling	**Cooking Time** 40 minutes, plus cooling	**Per Serving** 395 calories, 25g fat (of which 6g saturates), 29g carbohydrate; 2g salt

Freezing Tip

To freeze Complete the recipe but do not glaze or bake. Wrap the uncooked pie and freeze.

To use Thaw at cool room temperature overnight. Glaze the pastry and add 5–10 minutes to the cooking time, covering the pie with foil if the top starts to turn too brown.

Steak and Kidney Pie

700g (1½lb) stewing steak, cubed and seasoned

2 tbsp plain flour, plus extra to dust

3 tbsp vegetable oil

25g (1oz) butter

1 small onion, peeled and finely chopped

175g (6oz) ox kidney, cut into small pieces

150g (5oz) flat mushrooms, cut into large chunks

small pinch of cayenne pepper

1 tsp anchovy essence

350g (12oz) puff pastry, thawed if frozen

1 large egg, beaten with pinch of salt, to glaze

salt and ground black pepper

1 Preheat the oven to 170°C (150°C fan oven) mark 3. Toss half the steak with half the flour. Heat the oil in a flameproof, non-stick casserole and add the butter. Fry the steak in batches until brown, remove and put to one side. Repeat with the remaining steak.

2 Add the onion and cook gently until soft. Return the steak to the casserole with 200ml (7fl oz) water, the kidney, mushrooms, cayenne and anchovy essence. Bring to the boil, then reduce the heat, cover and simmer for 5 minutes.

3 Transfer to the oven and cook for 1 hour or until tender. The sauce should be syrupy. If not, transfer the casserole to the hob, remove the lid, bring to the boil and bubble for 5 minutes to reduce the liquid. Leave the steak mixture to cool.

4 Preheat the oven to 200°C (180°C fan oven) mark 6. Put the steak and kidney mixture into a 900ml (1½ pint) pie dish. Pile it high to support the pastry.

5 Roll out the pastry on a lightly floured surface to 5mm (¼ inch) thick. Cut off four to six strips, 1cm (½in) wide. Dampen the edge of the dish with cold water, then press the pastry strips on to the edge. Dampen the pastry rim and lay the sheet of pastry on top. Press the surfaces together, trim the edge and press down with the back of a knife to seal. Brush the pastry with the glaze and score with the back of a knife. Put the pie dish on a baking sheet and cook for 30 minutes or until the pastry is golden brown and the filling is hot to the centre.

EASY		NUTRITIONAL INFORMATION	Serves
Preparation Time 40 minutes	**Cooking Time** about 1½ hours, plus cooling	**Per Serving** 565 calories, 36g fat (of which 8g saturates), 26g carbohydrate, 0.9g salt	**6**

Freezing Tip

To freeze Complete the recipe and cool completely in the tin. Wrap in clingfilm and freeze for up to three months.
To use Thaw in the fridge overnight, then serve at room temperature, or heat for 25 minutes in an oven preheated to 150°C (130°C fan oven) mark 2.

Cook's Tip

Onions take a good 45 minutes to caramelise over a low heat, but chopping them finely and adding a touch of sugar and balsamic vinegar speeds up the process dramatically. You can make this recipe even faster by using a ready-cooked tart case.

Caramelised Onion and Goat's Cheese Tart

200g (7oz) ready-made shortcrust pastry

plain flour to dust

1 tbsp olive oil

2 red onions and 1 medium white onion, peeled and finely chopped

1 tbsp balsamic vinegar

1 tbsp light muscovado sugar

1 tbsp fresh oregano leaves, finely chopped

50g (2oz) goat's cheese, roughly chopped

2 medium eggs, beaten

200ml (7fl oz) double cream

salt and ground black pepper

1 Preheat the oven to 200°C (180°C fan oven) mark 6. Roll out the pastry on a lightly floured surface to the thickness of a £1 coin. Use to line a 20.5cm (8in) diameter, 2.5cm (1in) deep, fluted quiche tin and prick the base with a fork. Chill for 30 minutes. Bake blind (see page 237) for 10–12 minutes until pastry is set, then remove the beans and paper and bake for a further 10 minutes until the base feels sandy to the touch. Take out of the oven and set aside. Reduce the oven temperature to 150°C (130°C fan oven) mark 2.

2 Meanwhile, heat the oil in a pan. Add the onions and fry gently for 10 minutes. Turn up the heat, add the vinegar and sugar and cook for 10 minutes, stirring until the onions are golden. Add a little water if the pan dries out. Stir in most of the oregano.

3 Spoon the onion mixture into the pastry case and dot the cheese on top. Lightly beat the eggs, cream and seasoning in a small bowl. Pour over the onions, then use a fork to lift some onions to the surface. Sprinkle the remaining oregano over the surface, then cook for 30 minutes until just set. Serve warm or at room temperature.

Serves	EASY		NUTRITIONAL INFORMATION	
4	**Preparation Time** 20 minutes	**Cooking Time** about 50 minutes	**Per Serving** 627 calories, 34g fat (of which 17g saturates), 210g carbohydrate, 1g salt	Vegetarian

Get Ahead

To prepare ahead Complete the recipe to the end of step 4. Cover the prawns, vegetables and pastry separately and chill overnight.
To use Complete the recipe.

Freezing Tip

To freeze Complete the recipe to the end of step 4. Pack the pastry, prawns and vegetables separately and freeze for up to one month.
To use Thaw at cool room temperature then complete the recipe.

Prawn Tartlets

30 raw large prawns, shells on, about 400g (14oz) total weight

4 tbsp olive oil

2 shallots, peeled and finely chopped

2 garlic cloves, peeled and roughly chopped

1 bay leaf

150ml (¼ pint) brandy

150ml (¼ pint) white wine

400g can chopped tomatoes

2 tbsp freshly chopped tarragon

175g (6oz) celeriac, peeled and chopped

125g (4oz) carrots, peeled and chopped

175g (6oz) leeks (white part only), roughly chopped

2 tbsp vegetable oil

150ml (¼ pint) double cream

grated zest of ½ lemon

225g (8oz) puff pastry, thawed if frozen

plain flour to dust

salt and ground black pepper

fresh tarragon sprigs to garnish

celeriac and carrots, shredded, blanched and dressed with lemon juice and olive oil to serve

1 Cook the prawns in a pan of lightly salted boiling water for 1 minute until the shells are pink. Plunge into a bowl of cold water to cool. Remove the heads and shells and put to one side. Devein the prawns, then cover and chill.

2 Heat the olive oil in a large pan, add the shallots and cook gently for 5 minutes or until soft. Add the garlic, bay leaf and prawn heads and shells. Cook over a high heat for 1 minute, then add the brandy. (If you're cooking over gas, take care, as the brandy may ignite.) Allow the liquid to reduce by half, then add the wine. Bring to the boil and bubble until reduced by half, then add the tomatoes and season. Add 1 tbsp tarragon. Cook over a medium-low heat for 20 minutes. Put a colander over a large bowl, pour the contents of the pan into the colander and push through as much liquid as possible. Put the liquid to one side and discard the heads and shells.

3 Put the celeriac, carrots and leeks in a food processor and pulse until finely chopped. Heat the vegetable oil in a frying pan, add the vegetables and cook quickly for 2 minutes (don't allow them to colour). Add the prawn and tomato liquid and the cream, bring to the boil and bubble for 10–15 minutes until thick. Season and stir in the remaining tarragon and the lemon zest. Leave to cool.

4 Preheat the oven to 200°C (180°C fan oven) mark 6. Roll out the pastry on a lightly floured surface and use to line six 4cm (1½in) diameter (at base) brioche tins. Bake blind (see page 237), then remove from the oven and leave to cool.

5 Divide the vegetable mixture among the pastry cases and top each with five prawns. Put back in the oven for 10–15 minutes until hot to the centre. Season with pepper, garnish with tarragon and serve with a salad of finely shredded celeriac and carrots.

EASY		NUTRITIONAL INFORMATION	Serves
Preparation Time 50 minutes	**Cooking Time** 1¼–1½ hours, plus cooling	**Per Serving** 489 calories, 34g fat (of which 10g saturates), 21g carbohydrate, 1.4g salt	**6**

Cook's Tip

Tapenade is a strongly flavoured paste made from black olives, capers, anchovies, garlic and olive oil; originally from Provence in southern France.

30 Minute Recipe

Camembert and Tomato Tarts

½ x 375g pack ready-rolled puff pastry
2 tbsp tapenade (see Cook's Tip)
200g (7oz) cherry tomatoes, halved
75g (3oz) Camembert, sliced (see Cook's Tips, page 26)

1 Preheat the oven to 220°C (200°C fan oven) mark 7. Cut the puff pastry into four pieces. Put on a baking sheet and cook for 8–10 minutes until risen.

2 Press down the centre of each tart slightly with the back of a fish slice, then spread this area with the tapenade. Top with the tomatoes and sliced Camembert. Put back into the oven for a further 7–8 minutes until golden brown.

Serves	EASY		NUTRITIONAL INFORMATION	
4	**Preparation Time** 10 minutes	**Cooking Time** 15–20 minutes	**Per Serving** 253 calories, 17g fat (of which 4g saturates), 19g carbohydrate, 1.1g salt	Vegetarian

Cook's Tips

Shortcrust Pastry: Sift the flour and salt into a bowl, add the fat and mix lightly. Using your fingertips, rub the fat into the flour until the mixture resembles fine breadcrumbs. Sprinkle 3–4 tbsp cold water evenly over the surface and stir with a round-bladed knife until the mixture begins to stick together in large lumps. If the dough seems dry, add a little extra water. With one hand, collect the dough together to form a ball. Knead lightly on a lightly floured surface for a few seconds to form a smooth, firm dough; do not over-work. Form the pastry into a ball, wrap tightly in clingfilm and leave to rest in the fridge for at least 30 minutes before rolling out. (This allows the pastry to 'relax' and prevents shrinkage when it is baked.)

Fill the pastry case as full as possible. You may find you have a little mixture left, as flan tins vary in size.

Quiche Lorraine

1 Preheat the oven to 200°C (180°C fan oven) mark 6. Roll out the pastry thinly on a lightly floured surface and use to line a 23cm (9in), 3cm (1¼in) deep, loose-based tart tin. Bake the pastry case blind (see page 237). Meanwhile, lightly whisk the eggs for the filling. Use a little to brush the inside of the pastry case and return it to the oven for 5 minutes to seal any cracks. Reduce the oven temperature to 190°C (170°C fan oven) mark 5.

2 Cut the bacon into 5mm (¼in) strips. Put the bacon in a pan of cold water and bring to the boil. Drain, then refresh under cold water and dry on kitchen paper.

3 Melt the butter in a frying pan, add the shallots or onions and cook for 1 minute. Add the bacon and cook, stirring, until brown.

4 Mix the eggs with the crème fraîche and cheese and season. Put the bacon mixture in the pastry case and spoon the crème fraîche mixture on top (see Cook's Tip). Cook for 30–35 minutes until golden and just set. Cool for 10 minutes before serving. Garnish with bacon and fried spring onions.

Shortcrust Pastry (see Cook's Tip), made with 200g (7oz) plain flour, pinch of salt, 100g (3½oz) chilled butter and 1 large egg

plain flour to dust

For the filling

5 large eggs

225g (8oz) unsmoked streaky bacon, rind removed

40g (1½oz) butter

125g (4oz) shallots, onions or spring onions, peeled and finely chopped

400g (14oz) crème fraîche

100g (3½oz) Gruyère cheese, grated

salt and ground black pepper

crispy bacon and fried spring onions to garnish

EASY		NUTRITIONAL INFORMATION	Serves
Preparation Time 35 minutes, plus chilling	**Cooking Time** 1 hour	**Per Serving** 595 calories, 50g fat (of which 29g saturates), 22g carbohydrate, 1.5g salt	**8**

sweet pies
and pastries

Classic Apple Pie

900g (2lb) cooking apples, peeled, cored and sliced

50g (2oz) caster sugar, plus extra to sprinkle

Sweet Shortcrust Pastry (see Cook's Tips), made with 225g (8oz) plain flour, a pinch of salt, 100g (3½oz) chilled butter and 1 large egg

flour to dust

cream to serve

1 Preheat the oven to 190°C (170°C fan oven) mark 7.

2 Layer the apples and sugar in a 1.1 litre (2 pint) pie dish. Sprinkle with 1 tbsp water.

3 Roll out the pastry on a lightly floured surface to a round 2.5cm (1in) larger than the pie dish. Cut off a strip the width of the rim of the dish, dampen the rim of the dish and press on the strip. Dampen the pastry strip and cover with the pastry circle, pressing the edges together well. Decorate the edge of the pastry and make a slit in the centre to allow steam to escape.

4 Bake for 35–40 minutes until the pastry is lightly browned. Sprinkle with caster sugar before serving with cream.

Cook's Tips

Sweet Shortcrust Pastry: Sift the flour and salt into a mound on a clean surface. Make a large well in the centre and add the butter, egg yolks and sugar. Using the fingertips of one hand, work the sugar, butter and egg yolks together until well blended. Gradually work in all the flour to bind the mixture together. Knead the dough gently on a lightly floured surface until smooth, then wrap in clingfilm and leave to rest in the fridge for at least 30 minutes before rolling out.
Apple pie is also great served cold, with vanilla ice cream.

Serves	EASY		NUTRITIONAL INFORMATION	
6	Preparation Time 20 minutes	Cooking Time 35–40 minutes	Per Serving 268 calories, 11g fat (of which 4g saturates), 43g carbohydrate, 0.4g salt	Vegetarian

Sugar-crusted Fruit Pie

75g (3oz) hazelnuts
350g (12oz) cherries, stoned
75g (3oz) caster sugar, plus 2 tbsp
175g (6oz) plain flour, plus extra to dust
125g (4oz) butter
275g (10oz) cooking apples, peeled, cored and quartered

1 Spread the hazelnuts over a baking sheet. Toast under a hot grill until golden brown, turning them frequently. Put the hazelnuts in a clean teatowel and rub off the skins. Leave to cool. Put the cherries into a bowl with 25g (1oz) caster sugar. Cover and set aside.

2 For the hazelnut pastry, put 50g (2oz) hazelnuts into a food processor with the flour and pulse to a powder. Remove and set aside. In the food processor, whiz the butter with 50g (2oz) sugar. Add the flour mixture and pulse until it forms a dough. Turn out on to a lightly floured surface and knead lightly, then wrap and chill for 30 minutes. If the pastry cracks, just work it together.

3 Preheat the oven to 180°C (160°C fan oven) mark 4. Cut the apples into small chunks and put into a 900ml (1½ pint) oval pie dish. Spoon the cherries on top. Roll out the pastry on a lightly floured surface to about 5mm (¼in) thick. Cut into 1cm (½in) strips. Dampen the edge of the pie dish with a little water and press a few of the strips on to the rim to cover it. Dampen the pastry rim. Put the remaining strips over the cherries to create a lattice pattern.

4 Brush the pastry with water and sprinkle with the extra sugar. Bake for 30–35 minutes until the pastry is golden. Leave to cool for 15 minutes.

5 Chop the remaining toasted hazelnuts and sprinkle over the tart. Serve warm.

Serves 4	EASY		NUTRITIONAL INFORMATION	
	Preparation Time 30 minutes, plus chilling	**Cooking Time** about 40 minutes, plus cooling	**Per Serving** 673 calories, 38g fat (of which 17g saturates), 79g carbohydrate, 0.5g salt	Vegetarian

Cook's Tips

Improve the flavour of a jar of bought mincemeat by adding 2 tbsp brandy, the grated zest of 1 lemon and 25g (1oz) pecan nuts, chopped. Instead of the nuts, try a piece of preserved stem ginger, chopped.

For vegetarians, make sure you use mincemeat made with vegetable suet rather than beef suet.

Mince Pies

225g (8oz) plain flour, plus extra to dust

125g (4oz) unsalted butter, chilled and diced

100g (3½oz) cream cheese

1 egg yolk

finely grated zest of 1 orange

400g jar mincemeat (see Cook's Tips)

1 egg, beaten

icing sugar to dust

1   Put the flour into a food processor. Add the butter, cream cheese, egg yolk and orange zest and whiz until the mixture just comes together. Tip the mixture into a large bowl and bring the dough together with your hands. Shape into a ball, wrap in clingfilm and put in the freezer for 5 minutes.

2   Preheat the oven to 220°C (200°C fan) mark 7. Cut off about one-third of the pastry dough and set aside. Roll out the remainder on a lightly floured surface to 5mm (¼in) thick. Stamp out circles with a 6.5cm (2½in) cutter to make 24 rounds, re-rolling the dough as necessary. Use the pastry circles to line two 12-hole patty tins. Roll out the reserved pastry and use a star cutter to stamp out the stars.

3   Put 1 tsp mincemeat into each pastry case, then top with pastry stars. Brush the tops with beaten egg, then bake for 12–15 minutes until golden. Remove from the tins and leave to cool on a wire rack. Serve warm or cold, dusted with icing sugar. Store in an airtight container for up to four days.

EASY		NUTRITIONAL INFORMATION		Makes
Preparation Time 15 minutes, plus chilling	**Cooking Time** 12–15 minutes, plus cooling	**Per Serving** 150 calories, 8g fat (of which 4g saturates), 17g carbohydrate, 0.2g salt	Vegetarian	**24**

Try Something Different

Éclairs: Put the choux pastry into a piping bag fitted with a medium plain nozzle and pipe 9cm (3¹/₂in) long fingers on to the baking sheet. Trim with a wet knife. Bake at 200°C (180°C fan oven) mark 6 for about 35 minutes until crisp and golden. Using a sharp, pointed knife, make a slit down the side of each bun to release the steam, then transfer to a wire rack and leave for 20–30 minutes to cool completely. Just before serving, whip 300ml (¹/₂ pint) double cream until stiff and use it to fill the éclairs. Break 125g (4oz) plain chocolate into a bowl set over a pan of simmering water, making sure the base of the bowl doesn't touch the water. Stir until melted. Pour into a wide shallow bowl and dip the top of each filled éclair into it, drawing each one across the surface of the chocolate. Leave to set. Makes 12.

Cook's Tip

Choux Pastry: Sift 65g (2¹/₂oz) plain flour and a pinch of salt on to a large sheet of greaseproof paper. Pour 150ml (¹/₄ pint) cold water into a medium pan, add 50g (2oz) unsalted butter and melt over a low heat. Increase the heat and bring to a rolling boil. Take off the heat, immediately tip in all the flour and beat vigorously, using a wooden spoon. Continue beating until the mixture is smooth and leaves the sides of the pan to form a ball; do not over-beat. Leave to cool slightly, for 1–2 minutes, while you lightly beat 2 eggs. Then, gradually add the eggs to the pan, beating well between each addition, adding just enough to give a smooth dropping consistency. The choux pastry should be smooth and shiny. Use as required.

2 egg quantity Choux Pastry (see Cook's Tip)

For the filling

300ml (¹/₂ pint) double cream

1 tsp vanilla extract

1 tsp golden caster sugar

For the topping

200g (7oz) plain chocolate, in pieces

75g (3oz) butter, at room temperature

Chocolate Choux Buns

1. Preheat the oven to 220°C (200°C fan oven) mark 7. Sprinkle a non-stick baking sheet with a little water. Using two dampened tablespoons, spoon the choux paste into eight large mounds on the baking sheet, spacing them well apart to allow room for expansion.

2. Bake for about 30 minutes until risen and golden brown. Make a small hole in the side of each bun, then put back in the switched-off oven for 10–15 minutes to dry out. Transfer to a wire rack and leave to cool.

3. For the filling, whip the cream with the vanilla extract and sugar until soft peaks form. Split the choux buns and fill them with the cream.

4. For the topping, melt the chocolate with the butter in a heatproof bowl set over a pan of gently simmering water. Leave to cool until beginning to thicken. Top the choux buns with the warm melted chocolate to serve.

Makes 8	EASY		NUTRITIONAL INFORMATION	
	Preparation Time 25 minutes	**Cooking Time** 40–45 minutes, plus cooling	**Per Bun** 475 calories, 40g fat (of which 25g saturates), 25g carbohydrate, 0.3g salt	Vegetarian

Freezing Tip

To freeze Complete the recipe to the end of step 2, then cover, wrap and freeze.
To use Bake from frozen at 220°C (200°C fan oven) mark 7 for 40 minutes or until the pastry is golden. Complete the recipe.

Plum Tarte Tatin

75g (3oz) unsalted butter
125g (4oz) caster sugar
700g (1½ lb) plums, halved and stoned
350g pack all-butter dessert pastry
flour to dust
crème fraîche or cream to serve

1   Melt the butter and sugar in a heavy-based frying pan. Cook, stirring, for 2–3 minutes until the sugar begins to turn light brown. Immediately add the plums and cook for 5 minutes or until the juices begin to run and the plums start to soften. Increase the heat and bubble until the juices are very syrupy. Lift the plums out of the pan into a 23cm (9in) shallow ovenproof dish or cake tin, with some of them cut side up, and pour the juice over them. Leave to cool.

2   Roll out the pastry on a lightly floured surface into a circle slightly larger than the dish and about 5mm (¼ in) thick. Lay the pastry over the plums, tuck the edges down into the dish and make a few slits in the pastry with a knife to allow steam to escape. Chill for 20 minutes.

3   Preheat the oven to 220°C (200°C fan oven) mark 7. Bake for 20 minutes or until the pastry is golden. Cool for 5 minutes before carefully inverting on to a plate. Serve with crème fraîche or cream.

EASY		NUTRITIONAL INFORMATION		Serves
Preparation Time 30 minutes, plus chilling	**Cooking Time** 30 minutes, plus cooling	**Per Serving** 488 calories, 28g fat (of which 17g saturates), 59g carbohydrate, 0.5g salt	Vegetarian	**6**

Cook's Tip

The pastry will be easier to unroll if you remove it from the fridge 10–15 minutes beforehand.

30 Minute Recipe

Express Apple Tart

375g ready-rolled puff pastry

500g (1lb 2oz) dessert apples, such as Cox's Orange Pippins, cored and thinly sliced, then tossed in the juice of 1 lemon

golden icing sugar to dust

1 Preheat the oven to 200°C (180°C fan oven) mark 6. Unroll the pastry on to a 28 x 38cm (11 x 15in) baking sheet and lightly roll a rolling pin over it to smooth down the pastry. Score lightly around the edge, leaving a 3cm (1¼in) border.

2 Put the apple slices on top of the pastry, within the border. Turn the edge of the pastry inwards to reach the edge of the apples, pressing it down and using your fingers to crimp the edge.

3 Dust heavily with icing sugar. Bake for 20 minutes or until the pastry is cooked and the sugar has caramelised. Serve warm, dusted with more icing sugar.

Serves 8	EASY		NUTRITIONAL INFORMATION	
	Preparation Time 10 minutes	**Cooking Time** 20 minutes	**Per Serving** 197 calories, 12g fat (of which 0g saturates), 24g carbohydrate, 0.4g salt	Vegetarian

Freezing Tip

To freeze Complete the recipe, wrap and freeze for up to one month.
To use Thaw overnight. Put on a baking sheet, cover loosely with foil and reheat at 200°C (180°C fan oven) mark 6 for 20 minutes.

225g (8oz) macadamia nuts, halved

350g (12oz) ready-made shortcrust pastry, thawed if frozen

flour to dust

75g (3oz) unsalted butter, softened

75g (3oz) dark muscovado sugar

3 medium eggs, beaten

1 tsp cornflour

50ml (2fl oz) maple syrup, plus extra to drizzle

225ml (8fl oz) golden syrup

grated zest of 1 lemon and 2 tbsp lemon juice

1 tsp vanilla extract

Macadamia and Maple Tart

1 Put the macadamia nuts on a baking sheet and toast under a hot grill until golden brown. Leave to cool.

2 Roll out the pastry on a lightly floured surface and use to line a 23cm (9in), 4cm (1½ in) deep, loose-based tart tin, leaving the pastry hanging over the edges to allow for shrinkage. Prick all over with a fork, then freeze for 30 minutes.

3 Preheat the oven to 200°C (180°C fan oven) mark 6. Bake the tart case blind (see Cook's Tips, page 237). Using a sharp knife, trim the overhanging pastry to a neat edge.

4 Beat the butter with the sugar until pale and creamy, then gradually add the beaten eggs and the cornflour. Stir in all the remaining ingredients. The mixture will look curdled, but don't panic. Stir in the toasted nuts and pour into the cooked pastry case.

5 Bake for 35–40 minutes until the filling is just set. Leave to cool for 10 minutes before serving.

EASY		NUTRITIONAL INFORMATION		Serves
Preparation Time 15 minutes, plus freezing	**Cooking Time** about 40 minutes, plus cooling	**Per Serving** 608 calories, 38g fat (of which 11g saturates), 60g carbohydrate, 0.9g salt	Vegetarian	**8**

Chocolate and Cherry Amaretti Tart

400g (14oz) pitted bottled or canned morello cherries, drained

3 tbsp brandy, sloe gin or almond-flavoured liqueur

150g (5oz) unsalted butter, softened

50g (2oz) icing sugar, plus extra to dust

1 small egg, beaten

225g (8oz) plain flour, plus extra to dust

For the filling

100g (3½oz) plain chocolate, broken into pieces

125g (4oz) unsalted butter, softened

125g (4oz) caster sugar

3 large eggs, beaten

125g (4oz) ground almonds

25g (1oz) self-raising flour, sifted

50g (2oz) amaretti biscuits, finely crushed

75g (3oz) slivered or flaked almonds

1. Put the cherries into a bowl with the brandy, gin or liqueur and leave for 30 minutes or overnight. Put the butter, icing sugar and egg into a food processor and whiz until almost smooth. Add the flour and whiz until the mixture begins to form a dough. (Alternatively, rub the fat into the flour, by hand or using a pastry cutter, to resemble fine crumbs, then stir in the icing sugar and egg.) Knead the pastry lightly, then wrap and chill for 30 minutes. Roll out the pastry on a lightly floured surface and use to line a 23cm (9in) loose-based fluted tart tin. Chill for 20 minutes.

2. Preheat the oven to 200°C (180°C fan oven) mark 6. Bake the pastry case blind (see Cook's Tips, page 237). Remove from the oven. Reduce the oven temperature to 150°C (130°C fan oven) mark 2.

3. To make the filling, melt the chocolate in a heatproof bowl set over a pan of gently simmering water, making sure the base of the bowl doesn't touch the water. Stir once or twice until smooth. Cool.

4. Beat the butter with the sugar until pale and fluffy. Gradually beat in the eggs, alternating with the ground almonds and flour. Fold in the melted chocolate and biscuits. Spoon one-third of the mixture into the pastry case. Spoon the cherries and juice over it. Spread the remaining filling over the cherries. Sprinkle on the slivered almonds and bake for about 1 hour. The tart will have a thin top crust but will be soft underneath. Leave in the tin for 10–15 minutes to firm up, then unmould, dust with icing sugar and serve warm.

Freezing Tip

To freeze Complete the recipe but do not dust with icing sugar. Cool completely, wrap, seal, label and freeze for up to one month.
To use Thaw at a cool room temperature overnight. Warm through at 200°C (180°C fan oven) mark 6 for 10 minutes and dust with icing sugar before serving.

EASY		NUTRITIONAL INFORMATION		Serves
Preparation Time 30 minutes, plus marinating and chilling	**Cooking Time** 1½ hours, plus cooling	**Per Serving** 760 calories, 50g fat (of which 22g saturates), 67g carbohydrate, 0.8g salt	Vegetarian	**8**

Cook's Tip

Remember that ovens vary, so check the tart after 15 minutes of cooking. Turn it round if cooking unevenly, otherwise the eggs might curdle.

Freezing Tip

To freeze Complete the recipe, then cool the tart, wrap carefully in foil and freeze for up to three months.
To use Thaw for 3 hours at room temperature.

butter to grease

plain flour to dust

Sweet Shortcrust Pastry (see Cook's Tip, page 252), made with 150g (5oz) plain flour, 75g (3oz) unsalted butter, 50g (2oz) icing sugar and 2 large egg yolks

peach slices and fresh or frozen raspberries, thawed, to decorate

icing sugar to dust

For the filling

1 large egg, plus 4 large yolks

150g (5oz) caster sugar

grated zest of 4 lemons

150ml (¼ pint) freshly squeezed lemon juice (about 4 medium lemons)

150ml (¼ pint) double cream

Lemon Tart

1 Grease and flour a 23cm (9in), 2.5cm (1in) deep, loose-based flan tin. Roll out the pastry on a lightly floured surface into a circle – if the pastry sticks to the surface, gently ease a palette knife under it to loosen. Line the tin with the pastry and trim the excess. Prick the base all over with a fork. Chill for 30 minutes.

2 Preheat the oven to 190°C (170°C fan oven) mark 5. Put the tin on a baking sheet and bake the pastry case blind (see Cook's Tips, page 237). Remove from the oven, leaving the flan tin on the baking sheet. Reduce the oven temperature to 170°C (150°C fan oven) mark 3.

3 Meanwhile, to make the filling, put the whole egg, egg yolks and caster sugar into a bowl and beat together with a wooden spoon or balloon whisk until smooth. Carefully stir in the lemon zest, lemon juice and cream. Leave to stand for 5 minutes.

4 Ladle three-quarters of the filling into the pastry case, position the baking sheet on the oven shelf and ladle in the remainder. Bake for 25–30 minutes until the filling bounces back when touched lightly in the centre. Cool for 15 minutes to serve warm, or cool completely and chill. Decorate with peaches and raspberries and dust with icing sugar to serve.

Serves 8	EASY		NUTRITIONAL INFORMATION	
	Preparation Time 30 minutes, plus chilling	**Cooking Time** about 50 minutes	**Per Serving** 385 calories, 23g fat (of which 13g saturates), 42g carbohydrate, 0.2g salt	Vegetarian

Cook's Tip

To decorate, cut the fruits into thick slices and arrange on two non-stick baking sheets. Put the remaining caster sugar into a small, heavy-based pan and cook over a low heat until the sugar begins to dissolve, then turn up the heat and cook to a pale caramel. Cool a little and drizzle over the fruit. Allow to set. (The caramel will stay brittle for 1–2 hours.)

Cinnamon Custard Tart

250g (9oz) plain flour, plus extra to dust

100g (3½oz) unsalted butter

100g (3½oz) icing sugar

4 large eggs

450ml (¾ pint) milk

285ml (9½fl oz) double cream

1 vanilla pod, split

1 cinnamon stick, crumbled

275g (10oz) caster sugar

1 mango, 1 small pineapple, 2 clementines and 125g (4oz) kumquats to serve

1. Put the flour, butter and icing sugar into a food processor and pulse until the mixture forms fine crumbs. (Alternatively, rub the fat into the flour by hand or using a pastry cutter, then stir in the icing sugar.) Beat 1 egg and add to the flour mixture with 1 tbsp water. Process (or stir) until the crumbs make a dough. Wrap in clingfilm and chill for 30 minutes.

2. Use the pastry to line a 23cm (9in) loose-based tart tin. Prick the base all over with a fork. Chill for 30 minutes.

3. Preheat the oven to 200°C (180°C fan oven) mark 6. Bake the pastry case blind (see Cook's Tip, p237). Lightly whisk the remaining eggs. Use 1 tbsp egg to brush over the pastry. Return to the oven for 2 minutes. Remove from the oven. Reduce the oven temperature to 150°C (130°C fan oven) mark 2.

4. Put the milk, cream, vanilla pod and cinnamon into a pan and slowly bring to the boil. Leave to infuse for 20 minutes. Mix the whisked eggs with 150g (5oz) caster sugar. Stir the milk into the egg mixture, strain into a jug and pour into the tart. Cook for 40–50 minutes until the filling has just set. Turn the oven off and leave the tart in the oven for 15 minutes. Remove and cool in the tin for 20–30 minutes. Transfer to a wire rack to cool completely.

5. Make the caramelised fruit (see Finishing Touches). Cut the tart into portions and spoon the fruit over the top to serve.

EASY		NUTRITIONAL INFORMATION		Serves
Preparation Time 50 minutes, plus chilling and infusing	**Cooking Time** 1½ hours, plus standing and cooling	**Per Serving** 664 calories, 34g fat (of which 20g saturates), 87g carbohydrate, 0.4g salt	Vegetarian	**8**

White Chocolate and Raspberry Tart

150g (5oz) plain flour, plus extra to dust
a pinch of salt
65g (2½oz) cold, unsalted butter, diced
100g (3½oz) ground hazelnuts
25g (1oz) sugar
1 large egg, beaten
250g tub mascarpone cheese
200g (7oz) white chocolate
142ml carton double cream
400g (14oz) fresh raspberries
golden icing sugar to dust

1 Sift the flour and salt into a food processor. Add the butter and whiz until the mixture resembles fine breadcrumbs. (Alternatively, rub the butter into the flour in a large bowl by hand or using a pastry cutter to resemble fine crumbs.) Add the hazelnuts, sugar and just enough egg and pulse, or stir, to bring the mixture together. Shape the pastry into a disc, wrap in clingfilm and chill for 30 minutes.

2 Roll out the pastry on a lightly floured surface, then press into the base and sides of a 20.5cm (8in) fluted pastry tin. Prick all over. Cover with a large round of baking parchment and top with baking beans. Chill until firm. Preheat the oven to 190°C (170°C fan oven) mark 5.

3 Bake for 12–15 minutes until the pastry has set. Remove the beans and parchment and continue baking for 5–10 minutes until the pastry is dry and slightly sandy to the touch. Cool in the tin on a wire rack.

4 Melt the mascarpone and chocolate together in a heatproof bowl set over a pan of gently simmering water, making sure the base of the bowl doesn't touch the water. Don't stir, otherwise the mixture will thicken into a sticky mess.

5 Remove the bowl from the pan and leave to cool completely. Meanwhile, lightly whip the cream. Fold the chocolate into the cream. Spoon the filling into the pastry case and chill. To serve, top with fresh raspberries and dust with icing sugar.

Serves 12	EASY		NUTRITIONAL INFORMATION	
	Preparation Time 35 minutes, plus chilling	**Cooking Time** 30 minutes, plus cooling	**Per Serving** 391 calories, 32g fat (of which 16g saturates), 24g carbohydrate, 0.3g salt	Vegetarian

cakes and bakes

Cook's Tip

Store in an airtight container. It will keep for up to three months. If you like, after the cake has matured for two weeks, prick it all over with a metal skewer and sprinkle with 1 tbsp brandy. Leave to soak in, then rewrap and store as before.

Rich Fruit Cake

175g (6oz) unsalted butter, cubed, plus extra to grease

1kg (2¼lb) mixed dried fruit

100g (3½oz) ready-to-eat dried prunes, roughly chopped

50g (2oz) ready-to-eat dried figs, roughly chopped

100g (3½oz) dried cranberries

2 balls preserved stem ginger in syrup, grated and syrup reserved

grated zest and juice of 1 orange

175ml (6fl oz) brandy

2 splashes Angostura bitters

175g (6oz) dark muscovado sugar

200g (7oz) self-raising flour

½ tsp ground cinnamon

½ tsp freshly grated nutmeg

½ tsp ground cloves

4 medium eggs, beaten

1 Preheat the oven to 150°C (130°C fan oven) mark 2. Grease a 20.5cm (8in) round, deep cake tin and line base and sides with greaseproof paper.

2 Put all the dried fruit into a very large pan and add the ginger, 1 tbsp reserved ginger syrup, the orange zest and juice, brandy and Angostura bitters. Bring to the boil, then simmer for 5 minutes. Add the butter and sugar and heat gently to melt. Stir occasionally until the sugar dissolves. Take the pan off the heat and leave to cool for a couple of minutes.

3 Add the flour, spices and beaten eggs and mix well. Pour the mixture into the prepared tin and level the surface. Wrap the outside of the tin in brown paper and secure with string to protect the cake during cooking. Bake for 2–2½ hours – cover with greaseproof paper after about 1½ hours – until the cake is firm to the touch and a skewer inserted into the centre comes out clean.

4 Cool in the tin for 2–3 hours, then remove from the tin, leaving the greaseproof paper on, transfer to a wire rack and leave to cool completely. Wrap the cake in a layer of clingfilm, then in foil.

Serves 16	EASY		NUTRITIONAL INFORMATION	
	Preparation Time 30 minutes	**Cooking Time** 2½ hours, plus cooling	**Per Serving** 277 calories, 11g fat (of which 6g saturates), 38g carbohydrate, 0.2g salt	Vegetarian

Cook's Tip

Store in an airtight container. It will keep for up to three days. If stored in the fridge it will keep for up to one week.

The Perfect Victoria Sponge

175g (6oz) unsalted butter at room temperature, plus extra to grease

175g (6oz) golden caster sugar

3 medium eggs

175g (6oz) self-raising flour, sifted

3–4 tbsp jam

a little icing sugar to dust

1 Grease two 18cm (7in) sandwich tins and base-line with greaseproof paper. Preheat the oven to 190°C (170°C fan oven) mark 5.

2 Put the butter and caster sugar into a large bowl and, using a hand-held electric whisk, beat together until pale and fluffy. Add the eggs, one at a time, beating well after each addition and adding a spoonful of flour to the mixture if it looks as if it's about to curdle. Using a large metal spoon, fold in the remaining flour.

3 Divide the mixture evenly between the prepared tins and level the surface with a palette knife. Bake in the centre of the oven for 20–25 minutes until the cakes are well risen and spring back when lightly pressed in the centre. Loosen the edges with a palette knife and leave in the tins for 5 minutes.

4 Turn out, remove the lining paper and leave to cool on a wire rack. Sandwich the two cakes together with jam and dust icing sugar over the top. Slice and serve.

EASY		NUTRITIONAL INFORMATION		Serves
Preparation Time 20 minutes	**Cooking Time** about 25 minutes, plus cooling	**Per Serving** 445 calories, 21g fat (of which 11g saturates), 30g carbohydrate, 0.8g salt	Vegetarian	**10**

Cook's Tip

Store in an airtight container. Eat within two days. Alternatively, the cake will keep for up to one week in an airtight container if it is stored before the frosting is applied.

Carrot Cake

250ml (9fl oz) sunflower oil, plus extra to grease

225g (8oz) light muscovado sugar

3 large eggs

225g (8oz) self-raising flour

large pinch of salt

1/2 tsp each ground mixed spice, ground nutmeg and ground cinnamon

250g (9oz) carrots, peeled and coarsely grated

For the frosting

50g (2oz) butter, preferably unsalted, at room temperature

225g pack cream cheese

25g (1oz) golden icing sugar

1/2 tsp vanilla extract

8 pecan halves, roughly chopped

1 Preheat the oven to 180°C (160°C fan oven) mark 4. Grease two 18cm (7in) sandwich tins and base-line with greaseproof paper.

2 Using a hand-held electric whisk, whisk the oil and muscovado sugar together to combine, then whisk in the eggs, one at a time.

3 Sift the flour, salt and spices together over the mixture, then gently fold in, using a large metal spoon. Tip the carrots into the bowl and fold in.

4 Divide the cake mixture between the prepared tins and bake for 30–40 minutes until golden and a skewer inserted into the centre comes out clean. Remove from the oven and leave in the tins for 10 minutes, then turn out on to a wire rack and leave to cool completely.

5 To make the frosting, beat the butter and cream cheese together in a bowl until light and fluffy. Sift in the icing sugar, add the vanilla extract and beat well until smooth. Spread one-third of the frosting over one cake and sandwich together with the other cake. Spread the remaining frosting on top and sprinkle with the pecans.

Serves 12	EASY		NUTRITIONAL INFORMATION	
	Preparation Time 15 minutes	**Cooking Time** 40 minutes, plus cooling	**Per Serving** 383 calories, 32g fat (of which 10g saturates), 24g carbohydrate, 0.3g salt	Vegetarian

Cook's Tip

Wrap in clingfilm and store in an airtight container. It will keep for up to three days.

Sticky Lemon Polenta Cake

50g (2oz) unsalted butter, softened, plus extra to grease

3 lemons

250g (9oz) golden caster sugar

250g (9oz) instant polenta

1 tsp wheat-free baking powder

2 large eggs

50ml (2fl oz) semi-skimmed milk

2 tbsp natural yogurt

2 tbsp poppy seeds

1 Preheat the oven to 180°C (160°C fan oven) mark 4. Lightly grease a 900g (2lb) loaf tin and base-line with greaseproof paper.

2 Grate the zest of 1 lemon and put into a food processor with the butter, 200g (7oz) sugar, the polenta, baking powder, eggs, milk, yogurt and poppy seeds, then whiz until smooth. Spoon the mixture into the prepared tin and level the surface. Bake for 55 minutes–1 hour until a skewer inserted into the centre comes out clean. Leave to cool in the tin for 10 minutes.

3 Next, make a syrup. Squeeze the juice from the zested lemon plus 1 more lemon. Thinly slice the third lemon. Put the lemon juice into a pan with the remaining sugar and 150ml (¼ pint) water. Add the lemon slices, bring to the boil and bubble for about 10 minutes until syrupy. Take the pan off the heat and leave to cool for 5 minutes. Remove the lemon slices from the syrup and set aside.

4 Slide a knife around the edge of the cake and turn out on to a serving plate. Pierce the cake in several places with a skewer, spoon the syrup over it and decorate with the lemon slices.

EASY		NUTRITIONAL INFORMATION		Serves
Preparation Time 10 minutes	**Cooking Time** 1 hour, plus cooling	**Per Serving** 220 calories, 7g fat (of which 3g saturates), 37g carbohydrate, 0.1g salt	Vegetarian Gluten free	**12**

Orange Syrup Cake

175g (6oz) unsalted butter, plus extra to grease

225g (8oz) caster sugar

2 medium eggs, beaten

200g (7oz) rice flour

2 tsp baking powder

75g (3oz) ground almonds

grated zest and juice of 1 large orange

250ml carton orange juice

2 tbsp lemon juice

2 large oranges, peeled and thickly sliced

blueberries to serve

1 Preheat the oven to 190°C (170°C fan oven) mark 5. Grease a shallow 20.5cm (8in) round tin and base-line with baking parchment.

2 Cream the butter and 75g (3oz) sugar together. Gradually beat in the eggs. Fold in the rice flour, baking powder and ground almonds. Stir in the zest and juice of the orange and 8 tbsp orange juice. The mixture should be of a soft, dropping consistency. Spoon the mixture into the prepared tin and level the surface.

3 Bake for 40 minutes or until firm. Cool in the tin for 10 minutes, then turn out on to a wire rack and leave to cool completely.

4 Just before serving, combine the remaining sugar and orange juice plus the lemon juice in a small pan. Add the orange slices, bring to the boil and cook for 1–2 minutes. Take the pan off the heat and leave to cool for 5 minutes. Remove the orange slices from the syrup and set aside. Put the cake on a serving plate and, with a cocktail stick, prick the cake in a number of places. Drizzle with the syrup and leave to soak in for 30 minutes.

5 Serve with the orange slices and blueberries.

Freezing Tip

To freeze Complete the recipe to the end of step 3, wrap and freeze.
To use Thaw at cool room temperature for 2–3 hours. Complete the recipe.

Serves 10	EASY		NUTRITIONAL INFORMATION	
	Preparation Time 20 minutes, plus soaking	**Cooking Time** 30–40 minutes, plus cooling	**Per Serving** 291 calories, 20g fat (of which 10g saturates), 27g carbohydrate, 0.4g salt	Vegetarian

Cook's Tip

Store in an airtight container. It will keep for up to two days.

Try Something Different

If you can't find butterscotch chocolate, use a bar of plain dark chocolate instead.

Banana and Butterscotch Loaf

butter to grease
175g (6oz) plain flour, sifted
2 tsp baking powder
½ tsp bicarbonate of soda
½ tsp salt
175g (6oz) light muscovado sugar
2 large eggs
3 medium-size ripe bananas, peeled and mashed
150g carton natural yogurt
150g bar butterscotch chocolate, roughly chopped
100g (3½oz) pecan nuts, chopped
1–2 tbsp demerara sugar

1 Preheat the oven to 170°C (150°C fan oven) mark 3. Grease a 1.4kg (3lb) loaf tin and line with greaseproof paper.

2 Put the flour, baking powder, bicarbonate of soda and salt into a large bowl and mix together.

3 In a separate bowl, beat the muscovado sugar and eggs together with a hand-held electric whisk until pale and fluffy. Carefully stir in the bananas, yogurt, chocolate and 50g (2oz) pecan nuts, followed by the flour mixture.

4 Spoon the mixture into the prepared tin and level the surface. Sprinkle with the remaining chopped pecan nuts and the demerara sugar. Bake for 1 hour or until a skewer inserted into the centre comes out clean. Leave to cool in the tin on a wire rack, then turn out and slice.

Serves 15	EASY		NUTRITIONAL INFORMATION	
	Preparation Time 20 minutes	**Cooking Time** 1 hour, plus cooling	**Per Serving** 221 calories, 9g fat (of which 2g saturates), 34g carbohydrate, 0.2g salt	Vegetarian

Cook's Tip

Poached Rhubarb: Chop 250g (9oz) rhubarb into 6.5cm (2½in) pieces. Put into a pan with 50g (2oz) caster sugar, 25g (1oz) stem ginger, cut into slivers, and 75ml (3fl oz) water. Cover and simmer gently for 5 minutes.

Get Ahead

To prepare ahead Complete the recipe without icing sugar up to one day in advance. Store in an airtight container.
To use Dust with icing sugar to serve.

150g (5oz) unsalted butter, softened, plus extra to grease

400g (14oz) rhubarb, trimmed and cut into 2.5cm (1in) pieces

175g (6oz) golden caster sugar

2 large eggs, beaten

100g (3½oz) ground almonds

3 tbsp milk

125g (4oz) self-raising flour

1 tsp cinnamon

½ tsp ground ginger

50g (2oz) flaked almonds

icing sugar to dust

Poached Rhubarb to serve (see Cook's Tip)

For the crumble topping

40g (1½oz) cold unsalted butter, diced

50g (2oz) plain flour

40g (1½oz) demerara sugar

Rhubarb Crumble Cake

1 Preheat the oven to 180°C (160°C fan oven) mark 4. Grease a 20.5cm (8in) springform tin and line with greaseproof paper.

2 Put the rhubarb into a pan with 25g (1oz) caster sugar and 100ml (3½fl oz) water and simmer for 5 minutes. Strain and set aside.

3 To make the topping, rub the chilled diced butter into the flour until the mixture resembles breadcrumbs. Stir in the demerara sugar and set aside.

4 Beat the softened butter and remaining caster sugar together until pale and fluffy. Gradually add the eggs, beating well after each addition. Using a large metal spoon, fold in the ground almonds, milk, flour and spices, then fold in the flaked almonds. Turn into the prepared tin, level the surface and top with rhubarb, then sprinkle with the crumble topping.

5 Bake for 1–1¼ hours until a skewer inserted into the centre comes out clean. Leave to cool in the tin for 5 minutes, then remove from the tin. Dust with icing sugar and serve warm with custard and poached rhubarb, or cool on a wire rack and serve cold.

EASY		NUTRITIONAL INFORMATION		Serves
Preparation Time 25 minutes	**Cooking Time** 1 hour–1 hour 20 minutes	**Per Serving** 394 calories, 25g fat (of which 11g saturates), 37g carbohydrate, 0.5g salt	Vegetarian	**10**

Cappuccino and Walnut Cake

65g (2½oz) unsalted butter, melted and cooled, plus extra to grease

100g (3½oz) plain flour

1 tsp baking powder

4 medium eggs

125g (4oz) caster sugar

1 tbsp chicory and coffee essence

75g (3oz) walnuts, toasted, cooled and finely chopped

For the decoration

50g (2oz) walnuts

1 tbsp granulated sugar

¼ tsp ground cinnamon

For the icing

200g (7oz) good-quality white chocolate

4 tsp chicory and coffee essence

2 x 250g tubs mascarpone cheese

fresh unsprayed violets to decorate (optional)

Cook's Tip

Store in an airtight container in the fridge. It will keep for up to two days.

1 Preheat the oven to 190°C (170°C fan oven) mark 5. Grease two 20.5 x 4cm deep (8 x 1½in deep) round cake tins and base-line each with a circle of greased greaseproof paper. Sift the flour and baking powder together twice.

2 Using an electric mixer, whisk the eggs and caster sugar in a large heatproof bowl set over a pan of barely simmering water for 3–4 minutes until light, thick and fluffy. Remove the bowl from the heat and continue whisking until the mixture has cooled and the whisk leaves a ribbon trail for 8 seconds when lifted out of the bowl.

3 Fold in the butter, coffee essence and chopped walnuts. Sift half the flour over the mixture, then fold in carefully but quickly with a metal spoon. Sift and fold in the rest, taking care not to knock out too much air. Pour into the prepared tins and tap them lightly on the worksurface. Bake for 20–25 minutes until the tops feel springy. Cool in the tins for 10 minutes, then turn out on to a wire rack and leave to cool completely.

4 To make the decoration, whiz the walnuts in a food processor or blender with the granulated sugar and cinnamon until finely chopped. Take care not to overprocess the nuts or they'll become oily. Set aside.

5 To make the icing, break up the chocolate and put into a heatproof bowl set over a pan of gently simmering water, making sure the base of the bowl doesn't touch the water. Allow to melt slowly without stirring. In another bowl, add the coffee essence to the mascarpone and beat until smooth, then slowly beat in the melted chocolate.

6 Spread one-third of the icing on top of one cake, then sandwich with the other half. Smooth the remaining icing over the top and sides. Lift the cake on to a large piece of greaseproof paper and scatter the chopped nuts all around it. Then lift the greaseproof up to press nuts on to the sides. Transfer to a plate and decorate with the violets, if you like.

EASY		NUTRITIONAL INFORMATION		Serves
Preparation Time 30 minutes	**Cooking Time** about 45 minutes, plus cooling	**Per Serving** 449 calories, 30g fat (of which 13g saturates), 36g carbohydrate, 0.3g salt	Vegetarian	**10**

Cook's Tip

Store in an airtight container. It will keep for up to three days.

Freezing Tip

To freeze Complete the recipe to the end of step 5, wrap, seal, label and freeze; it will keep for up to one month.
To use Thaw the torte at a cool room temperature for 2 hours. Dust with sifted icing sugar to serve.

125g (4oz) unsalted butter, diced, plus extra to grease

225g (8oz) plain chocolate (at least 70% cocoa solids), broken into pieces

3 large eggs, separated

125g (4oz) light muscovado sugar

50ml (2fl oz) brandy

75g (3oz) self-raising flour, sifted

50g (2oz) ground almonds

icing sugar to dust

crème fraîche to serve

Chocolate Brandy Torte

1 Preheat the oven to 180°C (160°C fan oven) mark 4. Grease a 20.5cm (8in) springform cake tin and base-line with baking parchment.

2 Melt the diced butter and chocolate in a heatproof bowl set over a pan of gently simmering water, making sure the base of the bowl doesn't touch the water, stirring occasionally. Take the bowl off the pan and leave to cool a little.

3 Put the egg yolks and muscovado sugar into a bowl and whisk together until pale and creamy, then whisk in the brandy and melted chocolate at a slow speed. Using a large metal spoon, fold in the flour and ground almonds. Put the mixture to one side.

4 Put the egg whites into a clean, grease-free bowl and whisk until soft peaks form. Beat a large spoonful of the egg white into the chocolate mixture to lighten it, then carefully fold in the remainder with a large metal spoon.

5 Pour the mixture into the prepared tin and bake for 45 minutes or until a skewer inserted into the centre comes out clean. Leave to cool in the tin for 10 minutes, then turn out on to a wire rack to cool completely. Remove the lining paper from the base of the cake when it's cold.

6 To serve, dust the top of the cake with sifted icing sugar and serve with crème fraîche.

Serves 6	EASY		NUTRITIONAL INFORMATION	
	Preparation Time 10 minutes	**Cooking Time** 45 minutes, plus cooling	**Per Serving** 531 calories, 35g fat (of which 19g saturates), 47g carbohydrate, 0.5g salt	Vegetarian

Raspberry Cheesecake

100g (3½oz) unsalted butter, melted, plus extra to grease

25g (1oz) blanched almonds, lightly toasted, then finely chopped

225g (8oz) almond butter biscuits, finely crushed

a few drops of almond extract

450g (1lb) raspberries

300g (11oz) Greek-style yogurt

150g (5oz) low-fat cream cheese

1 tbsp powdered gelatine

2 medium egg whites

50g (2oz) icing sugar

1 Grease a 20.5cm (8in) round springform cake tin. Mix the almonds with the crushed biscuits and melted butter and add the almond extract. Tip the crumb mixture into the prepared tin and press evenly on to the bottom, using the back of a metal spoon to level the surface. Chill for 1 hour or until firm.

2 To make the filling, purée 225g (8oz) raspberries in a blender, then press through a sieve. Put three-quarters of the purée to one side and return the rest to the blender. Add the yogurt and cheese, then whiz to blend. Transfer to a bowl. Sprinkle the gelatine over 2 tbsp cold water in a heatproof bowl and leave to soak for 2–3 minutes. Put the bowl over a pan of simmering water until the gelatine has dissolved. Leave to cool.

3 Whisk the egg whites with the sugar until thick and shiny. Fold into the cheese mixture. Add the cooled gelatine. Arrange half the remaining berries over the biscuit base, then pour the cheese mixture over the berries. Add the reserved purée and swirl with a knife to marble. Top with the remaining berries and chill for 3–4 hours.

EASY		NUTRITIONAL INFORMATION		Serves
Preparation Time 25 minutes, plus chilling	**Cooking Time** 5 minutes, plus cooling and chilling	**Per Serving** 270 calories, 19g fat (of which 10g saturates), 20g carbohydrate, 0.5g salt	Vegetarian	**10**

Black Forest Gateau

125g (4oz) unsalted butter, melted

200g (7oz) plain flour

50g (2oz) cornflour

50g (2oz) cocoa powder, plus extra to dust

2 tsp espresso instant coffee powder

1 tsp baking powder

4 large eggs, separated

300g (11oz) golden caster sugar

2 x 300g jars morello cherries in syrup

2 tbsp Kirsch

200ml (7fl oz) double cream

2 tbsp icing sugar, sifted

fresh cherries and chocolate curls to decorate

1 Preheat the oven to 180°C (160°C fan oven) mark 4. Brush a little of the melted butter over the base and sides of a 20.5cm (8in) round x 9cm (3½in) deep cake tin. Line the base and sides with baking parchment.

2 Sift the flour, cornflour, cocoa powder, coffee powder and baking powder together three times – this helps to add air and makes sure the ingredients are well mixed.

3 Put the egg yolks, caster sugar and 100ml (3½fl oz) cold water into a freestanding mixer and whisk for 8 minutes until the mixture leaves a trail for 3 seconds when the whisk is lifted.

4 Add the rest of the melted butter, pouring it around the edge of the bowl so that the mixture doesn't lose any air, then quickly fold it in, followed by the sifted flour mixture in two batches.

5 In another bowl, whisk the egg whites until stiff peaks form, then fold a spoonful into the cake mixture to loosen. Carefully fold in the rest of the egg whites, making sure there are no white blobs left. Pour into the prepared tin and bake in the oven for 45–50 minutes until a skewer inserted into the centre comes out clean. Leave in the tin for 10 minutes, then turn out on to a wire rack to cool completely.

6 When the cake is cold, trim the top to make a flat surface. Turn the cake over so that the top becomes the base. Using a long serrated bread knife, carefully cut into three horizontally. Drain the cherries, reserving 250ml (9fl oz) of the syrup. Put the syrup into a pan and simmer to reduce by half. Stir in the Kirsch. Brush the hot syrup on to each layer of the cake – including the top – using up all the liquid.

7 Lightly whip the cream with the icing sugar. Spread one-third over the bottom layer of cake and cover with half the cherries. Top with the next cake layer and repeat with another third of the cream and the remaining cherries. Top with the final cake layer and spread the remaining cream over. Decorate with fresh cherries, chocolate curls and a dusting of cocoa powder.

Cook's Tip

Make the gateau up to two hours ahead to allow the flavours to mingle and the syrup to moisten the cake.

Serves	EASY		NUTRITIONAL INFORMATION	
12	**Preparation Time** 30 minutes	**Cooking Time** about 50 minutes, plus cooling	**Per Serving** 440 calories, 22g fat (of which 12g saturates), 59g carbohydrate, 0.8g salt	Vegetarian

Cook's Tip

Cover and store in the fridge. It will keep for up to two weeks.

Refrigerator Cake

175g (6oz) unsalted butter, cut into 8 pieces, plus extra to grease

200g (7oz) natural glacé cherries, halved

2 tbsp Kirsch

150g (5oz) dark chocolate with fruit, broken into pieces

200g (7oz) plain chocolate, broken into pieces

100g (3½oz) golden syrup

200g (7oz) digestive biscuits, roughly crushed

1 Grease a 20.5cm (8in) round tin and base-line with greaseproof paper. Put the cherries into a bowl, add the Kirsch and leave to soak.

2 Put all the chocolate, the butter and syrup into a large heatproof bowl and melt in a 900W microwave oven on medium for 2 minutes. Stir and cook for a further 2 minutes or until the chocolate has melted. (Alternatively, put into a heatproof bowl set over a pan of simmering water, making sure the base of the bowl doesn't touch the water, and leave until melted.)

3 Add half the soaked cherries and all the biscuits to the chocolate, then stir together. Spoon into the prepared tin and level the surface.

4 Arrange the remaining cherries around the edge of the cake and chill for at least 15 minutes.

5 Cut into slices to serve.

Serves 12	EASY		NUTRITIONAL INFORMATION	
	Preparation Time 10 minutes, plus chilling	**Cooking Time** 4 minutes	**Per Serving** 411 calories, 24g fat (of which 14g saturates), 48g carbohydrate, 0.6g salt	Vegetarian

Banana and Chocolate Ice Cream Pie

500ml tub chocolate ice cream

75g (3oz) butter, plus extra to grease

200g (7oz) plain chocolate digestive biscuits, crushed

2 large bananas, sliced

juice of ½ lemon

1 king-size Mars Bar, cut into thin slivers and chilled

1 Take the ice cream out of the freezer to let it soften. Grease a 20.5cm (8in) loose-based fluted flan tin and base-line with greaseproof paper. Put the butter into a small pan and melt over a medium heat.

2 Put the biscuits into a bowl, add the melted butter and mix until well combined. Tip the crumb mixture into the prepared tin and press evenly on to the base, using the back of a spoon to level the surface.

3 Toss the bananas in the lemon juice and scatter over the base. Upturn the ice cream tub on to the bananas and use a palette knife to spread the ice cream evenly, covering the fruit. Scatter the Mars Bar slices over the ice cream and freeze for at least 1 hour. Slice to serve.

EASY		NUTRITIONAL INFORMATION	Serves
Preparation Time 15 minutes, plus freezing		**Per Serving** 406 calories, 26g fat (of which 15g saturates), 42g carbohydrate, 0.6g salt	Vegetarian	**8**

Cook's Tip

Confectioner's Custard: Scrape the vanilla seeds from 1 vanilla pod into a pan. Add the pod and 450ml (¾ pint) milk, bring to the boil, then set aside for 30 minutes. Remove the vanilla pod. Whisk 4 large egg yolks and 75g (3oz) caster sugar until pale. Mix in 50g (2oz) plain flour. Strain in a quarter of the infused milk, mix, then stir in the remainder. Return to the pan and bring to the boil over a low heat, stirring. Pour into a bowl, cover with clingfilm, cool and chill for 3–4 hours.

Raspberry Millefeuilles

550g (1¼lb) puff pastry, thawed if frozen

plain flour to dust

25g (1oz) caster sugar, plus 3 tbsp

50g (2oz) hazelnuts, toasted and chopped

225g (8oz) raspberries

1 tbsp lemon juice

1 x quantity Confectioner's Custard (see Cook's Tip)

300ml (½ pint) double cream

50g (2oz) icing sugar, sifted

1 Cut the pastry into three and roll out each piece on a lightly floured surface into an 18 x 35.5cm (7 x 14in) rectangle. Put each on a baking sheet, prick and chill for 30 minutes.

2 Preheat the oven to 220°C (200°C fan oven) mark 7. Bake the pastry for 10 minutes, then turn the pieces over and cook for another 3 minutes. Sprinkle each sheet with 1 tbsp caster sugar and one-third of the nuts. Return to the oven for 8 minutes or until the sugar dissolves. Cool slightly, then transfer to wire racks to cool.

3 Sprinkle the raspberries with 25g (1oz) caster sugar and the lemon juice. Beat the custard until smooth and whip the cream until thick, then fold the cream into the custard with the raspberries and juices. Cover and chill.

4 Put the icing sugar into a bowl, then stir in 2 tbsp water. Trim each pastry sheet to 15 x 30.5cm (6 x 12in), then drizzle with the icing. Leave for 15 minutes.

5 Spoon half the custard over a sheet of pastry. Put another sheet on top and spoon on the remaining custard. Top with the final sheet and press down lightly. Leave for 30 minutes before slicing.

Slices 8	EASY		NUTRITIONAL INFORMATION	
	Preparation Time 40 minutes, plus chilling	**Cooking Time** 40 minutes, plus cooling and standing	**Per Serving** 828 calories, 57g fat (of which 23g saturates), 65g carbohydrate, 1.4g salt	Vegetarian

Eccles Cakes

212g pack puff pastry, thawed if frozen
plain flour to dust
25g (1oz) butter, softened
25g (1oz) dark brown soft sugar
25g (1oz) fine chopped mixed peel
50g (2oz) currants
caster sugar to sprinkle

1 Roll out the puff pastry on a lightly floured surface and cut into 9cm (3½in) rounds.

2 For the filling, mix the butter, sugar, mixed peel and currants in a bowl.

3 Place 1 tsp of the fruit and butter mixture in the centre of each pastry round. Draw up the edges of each pastry round to enclose the filling, brush the edges with water and pinch together firmly, then reshape. Turn each round over and roll lightly until the currants just show through. Prick the top of each with a fork. Leave to rest for about 10 minutes in a cool place. Preheat the oven to 230°C (210°C fan oven) mark 8.

4 Put the pastry rounds on a damp baking sheet and bake for about 15 minutes until golden. Transfer to a wire rack and leave to cool for 30 minutes. Sprinkle with caster sugar while still warm.

EASY		NUTRITIONAL INFORMATION		Makes
Preparation Time 10 minutes, plus resting	**Cooking Time** 15 minutes, plus cooling	**Per Cake** 158 calories, 9g fat (of which 2g saturates), 19g carbohydrate, 0.3g salt	Vegetarian	**8**

Freezing Tip

To freeze Complete the recipe and allow the cookies to cool. Wrap, seal, label and freeze.
To use Thaw the cookies individually, as needed, at room temperature for 1–2 hours.

Cook's Tip

Store in an airtight container. They will keep for up to one week.

30 Minute Recipe

Chocolate Chip Oat Cookies

125g (4oz) unsalted butter, softened, plus extra to grease

125g (4oz) golden caster sugar

1 medium egg

1 tsp vanilla extract

125g (4oz) porridge oats

150g (5oz) plain flour

$\frac{1}{2}$ tsp baking powder

200g (7oz) plain chocolate (at least 70% cocoa solids), cut into 1cm ($\frac{1}{2}$in) chunks

1 Preheat the oven to 180°C (160°C fan oven) mark 4. Lightly grease two baking sheets.

2 Cream the butter and sugar together in a bowl until pale and creamy. Add the egg, vanilla extract and oats. Sift the flour and baking powder together over the mixture and mix until evenly combined. Stir in the chocolate chunks.

3 Put dessertspoonfuls of the mixture on to the prepared baking sheets, spacing them well apart to allow room for spreading. Flatten each one slightly with the back of a fork.

4 Bake for 12–15 minutes until risen and turning golden, but still quite soft. Leave on the baking sheet for 5 minutes, then transfer to a wire rack and leave to cool completely.

Makes 18	EASY		NUTRITIONAL INFORMATION	
	Preparation Time 15 minutes	**Cooking Time** 12–15 minutes, plus cooling	**Per Cookie** 197 calories, 10g fat (of which 6g saturates), 26g carbohydrate, 0.2g salt	Vegetarian

Freezing Tip

To freeze Complete the recipe to the end of step 4, then open-freeze a tray of unbaked cookies. When frozen, pack into bags or containers.
To use Cook from frozen for 18–20 minutes.

Cook's Tip

Store in an airtight container. They will keep for up to one week.

30 Minute Recipe

Sultana and Pecan Cookies

225g (8oz) unsalted butter, at room temperature, plus extra to grease

175g (6oz) light muscovado sugar

2 medium eggs, lightly beaten

225g (8oz) pecan nut halves

300g (11oz) self-raising flour, sifted

¼ tsp baking powder

125g (4oz) sultanas

2 tbsp maple syrup

1 Preheat the oven to 190°C (170°C fan oven) mark 5. Lightly grease four baking sheets.

2 Cream the butter and sugar together until the mixture is pale and fluffy. Gradually beat in the eggs until thoroughly combined.

3 Put 20 pecan nut halves to one side, then roughly chop the rest and fold into the mixture with the flour, baking powder, sultanas and syrup.

4 Roll the mixture into 20 balls and place them, spaced well apart, on the prepared baking sheets. Using a dampened palette knife, flatten the cookies and top each with a piece of pecan nut.

5 Bake for 12–15 minutes until pale golden. Leave on the baking sheets for 5 minutes, then transfer to a wire rack and leave to cool completely.

EASY		NUTRITIONAL INFORMATION		Makes **20**
Preparation Time 15 minutes	**Cooking Time** 12–15 minutes, plus cooling	**Per Cookie** 276 calories, 18g fat (of which 7g saturates), 27g carbohydrate, 0.2g salt	Vegetarian	

Cook's Tip

Store in an airtight container. They will keep for up to one week.

30 Minute Recipe

Almond Macaroons

2 medium egg whites

125g (4oz) caster sugar

125g (4oz) ground almonds

¼ tsp almond extract

22 blanched almonds

1 Preheat the oven to 180°C (fan oven 160°C) mark 4. Line baking trays with baking parchment.

2 Whisk the egg whites in a clean, grease-free bowl until stiff peaks form. Gradually whisk in the sugar, a little at a time, until thick and glossy. Gently stir in the ground almonds and almond extract.

3 Spoon teaspoonfuls of the mixture on to the prepared baking trays, spacing them slightly apart. Press an almond into the centre of each one and bake in the oven for 12–15 minutes until just golden and firm to the touch.

4 Leave on the baking sheets for 10 minutes, then transfer to wire racks and leave to cool completely. On cooling, these biscuits have a soft, chewy centre; they harden up after a few days.

Makes 22	EASY		NUTRITIONAL INFORMATION	
	Preparation Time 10 minutes	**Cooking Time** 12–15 minutes, plus cooling	**Per Macaroon** 86 calories, 6g fat (of which 1g saturates), 7g carbohydrate, 0g salt	Vegetarian

Cook's Tip

Store in an airtight container. They will keep for up to two weeks.

Florentines

65g (2½oz) unsalted butter, plus extra to grease

50g (2oz) golden caster sugar

2 tbsp double cream

25g (1oz) sunflower seeds

20g (¾oz) chopped mixed candied peel

20g (¾oz) sultanas

25g (1oz) natural glacé cherries, roughly chopped

40g (1½oz) flaked almonds, lightly crushed

15g (½oz) plain flour

125g (4oz) plain chocolate (at least 70% cocoa solids), broken into pieces

1 Preheat the oven to 180°C (160°C fan oven) mark 4. Lightly grease two large baking sheets.

2 Melt the butter in a small heavy-based pan. Add the sugar and heat gently until dissolved, then bring to the boil. Take off the heat and stir in the cream, seeds, peel, sultanas, cherries, almonds and flour. Mix until evenly combined. Put heaped teaspoonfuls on to the prepared baking sheets, spaced well apart to allow for spreading.

3 Bake one sheet at a time, for 6–8 minutes, until the biscuits have spread considerably and the edges are golden brown. Using a large plain metal biscuit cutter, push the edges into the centre to create neat rounds. Bake for a further 2 minutes or until deep golden. Leave on the baking sheet for 2 minutes, then transfer to a wire rack and leave to cool completely.

4 Melt the chocolate in a heatproof bowl set over a pan of gently simmering water, making sure the base of the bowl doesn't touch the water, stirring occasionally. Spread on the underside of each Florentine and mark wavy lines with a fork. Put, chocolate-side up, on a sheet of baking parchment and leave to set.

EASY		NUTRITIONAL INFORMATION		Makes
Preparation Time 15 minutes	**Cooking Time** 16–20 minutes, plus cooling and setting	**Per Biscuit** 115 calories, 8g fat (of which 4g saturates), 11g carbohydrate, 0.1g salt	Vegetarian	**18**

Freezing Tip

To freeze Complete the recipe to the end of step 3. Open-freeze, then wrap and freeze.
To use Thaw for about 1 hour, then complete the recipe.

Orange and Poppy Seed Cupcakes

175g (6oz) unsalted butter, softened
175g (6oz) caster sugar
3 medium eggs
175g (6oz) self-raising flour, sifted
grated zest and juice of 1 large orange
2 tbsp poppy seeds
1 tsp baking powder

For the icing and decoration
125g (4oz) unsalted butter, softened
250g (9oz) icing sugar, sifted
1 tbsp orange flower water
12 orange jelly slices and orange edible glitter (optional)

1 Preheat the oven to 190°C (170°C fan oven), mark 5. Line a 12-hole muffin tin with paper muffin cases.

2 Using a hand-held electric whisk, whisk the butter and caster sugar in a bowl until pale and creamy, or beat with a wooden spoon. Gradually whisk in the eggs until just combined. Using a metal spoon, fold in the flour, orange zest and juice, poppy seeds and baking powder until combined. Divide the mixture equally between the paper cases.

3 Bake for 20 minutes or until golden and risen. Cool in the tin for 5 minutes, then transfer to a wire rack and leave to cool completely.

4 For the decoration, put the butter into a bowl and whisk until fluffy. Gradually add the icing sugar and orange flower water and whisk until light and fluffy.

5 Insert a star nozzle into a piping bag, then fill the bag with the buttercream and pipe a swirl on to the top of each cake. Decorate each with an orange slice, and edible glitter, if you like.

Makes 12	EASY		NUTRITIONAL INFORMATION	
	Preparation Time 30 minutes	**Cooking Time** 20 minutes, plus cooling	**Per Cupcake** 408 calories, 24g fat (of which 14g saturates), 49g carbohydrate, 0.5g salt	Vegetarian

Freezing Tip

To freeze Complete the recipe to the end of step 4. Open-freeze, then wrap and freeze.
To use Thaw for about 1 hour, then complete the recipe.

50g (2oz) seedless raspberry jam

50g (2oz) fresh raspberries

125g (4oz) unsalted butter, softened

100g (3½ oz) caster sugar

2 medium eggs

1 tbsp milk

150g (5oz) self-raising flour, sifted

For the icing and decoration

150g (5oz) fresh raspberries

300ml (½ pint) whipping cream

50g (2oz) icing sugar, sifted

Raspberry Ripple Cupcakes

1 Preheat the oven to 190°C (170°C fan oven), mark 5. Line a 12-hole muffin tin with 9 paper muffin cases.

2 Mix the raspberry jam with the 50g (2oz) raspberries, lightly crushing the raspberries. Set aside.

3 Using a hand-held electric whisk, whisk the butter and caster sugar in a bowl, or beat with a wooden spoon, until pale and creamy. Gradually whisk in the eggs and milk until just combined. Using a metal spoon, fold in the flour until just combined, then carefully fold in the raspberry jam mixture until just marbled, being careful not to overmix. Divide the mixture equally between the paper cases.

4 Bake for 20 minutes or until golden and risen. Cool in the tin for 5 minutes, then transfer to a wire rack and leave to cool completely.

5 For the decoration, reserve 9 raspberries. Mash the remaining raspberries in a bowl with a fork. Pass through a sieve into a bowl to remove the seeds. Using a hand-held electric whisk, whisk the cream and icing sugar together until stiff peaks form. Mix the raspberry purée into the cream until combined.

6 Insert a star nozzle into a piping bag, then fill the bag with the cream and pipe a swirl on to the top of each cake. Decorate each with a raspberry.

EASY		NUTRITIONAL INFORMATION		Makes
Preparation Time 30 minutes	**Cooking Time** 20 minutes, plus cooling	**Per Cupcake** 385 calories, 26g fat (of which 16g saturates), 36g carbohydrate, 0.5g salt	Vegetarian	**9**

Fairy Cakes

125g (4oz) self-raising flour, sifted
1 tsp baking powder
125g (4oz) caster sugar
125g (4oz) unsalted butter, very soft
2 medium eggs
1 tbsp milk

For the icing and decoration
225g (8oz) icing sugar, sifted
assorted food colourings (optional)
sweets, sprinkles or coloured sugar

1 Preheat the oven to 200°C (180°C fan oven) mark 6. Put paper cases into 18 of the holes in 2 bun tins.

2 Put the flour, baking powder, sugar, butter, eggs and milk into a mixing bowl and beat with a hand-held electric whisk for 2 minutes or until the mixture is pale and very soft. Half-fill each paper case with the mixture.

3 Bake for 10–15 minutes until golden brown. Transfer to a wire rack and leave to cool completely.

4 Put the icing sugar into a bowl and gradually blend in 2–3 tbsp warm water until the icing is fairly stiff, but spreadable. Add a couple of drops of food colouring, if you like.

5 When the cakes are cold, spread the tops with the icing and decorate.

Freezing Tip

To freeze Complete the recipe to the end of step 3. Open-freeze, then wrap and freeze.
To use Thaw for about 1 hour, then complete the recipe.

Try Something Different

Chocolate Fairy Cakes: Replace 2 tbsp of the flour with the same amount of cocoa powder. Stir 50g (2oz) chocolate chips, sultanas or chopped dried apricots into the mixture at the end of step 1. Complete the recipe.

Makes	EASY		NUTRITIONAL INFORMATION	
18	**Preparation Time** 20 minutes	**Cooking Time** 10–15 minutes, plus cooling and setting	**Per Cake** 160 calories, 6g fat (of which 4g saturates), 6g carbohydrate, 0.2g salt	Vegetarian

Freezing Tip

To freeze Complete the recipe to the end of step 3. Open-freeze, then wrap and freeze.
To use Thaw for about 1 hour, then complete the recipe.

125g (4oz) unsalted butter, softened

125g (4oz) light muscovado sugar

2 medium eggs, beaten

15g (½ oz) cocoa powder

100g (3½ oz) self-raising flour

100g (3½ oz) plain chocolate (at least 70% cocoa solids), roughly chopped

Chocolate Cupcakes

For the topping

150ml (¼ pint) double cream

100g (3½ oz) plain chocolate (at least 70% cocoa solids), broken up

1 Preheat the oven to 190°C (170°C fan oven) mark 5. Line a 12-hole and a 6-hole bun tin or muffin tin with paper muffin cases.

2 Beat the butter and sugar together until light and fluffy. Gradually beat in the eggs. Sift the cocoa powder with the flour and fold into the creamed mixture with the chopped chocolate. Divide the mixture among the paper cases and lightly flatten the surface with the back of a spoon.

3 Bake for 20 minutes, then transfer to a wire rack and leave to cool completely.

4 For the topping, put the cream and chocolate into a heavy-based pan over a low heat and heat until melted, then allow to cool and thicken slightly. Spoon on to the cooled cakes, then stand the cakes upright on the wire rack and leave for 30 minutes to set.

Makes 18	EASY		NUTRITIONAL INFORMATION	
	Preparation Time 15 minutes	Cooking Time 25 minutes, plus cooling and setting	Per Cupcake 203 calories, 14g fat (of which 8g saturates), 19g carbohydrate, 0.2g salt	Vegetarian

Freezing Tip

To freeze Complete the recipe to the end of step 3.
Open-freeze, then wrap and freeze.
To use Thaw for about 1 hour, then complete the recipe.

Nutty Cupcakes

150g (5oz) unsalted butter, softened
175g (6oz) self-raising flour, sifted
50g (2oz) caster sugar
100g (3½ oz) golden syrup
3 medium eggs
1 tsp baking powder
1 tsp ground mixed spice
50g (2oz) mixed chopped nuts

For the topping
3 tbsp double cream
1 tbsp milk
50g (2oz) milk chocolate, finely chopped
25g (1oz) plain chocolate, finely chopped
75g (3oz) roasted chopped hazelnuts

1 Preheat the oven to 190°C (170°C fan oven), mark 5. Line a 12-hole muffin tin with paper muffin cases.

2 Using a hand-held electric whisk, whisk the butter, flour, sugar, syrup, eggs, baking powder, mixed spice and nuts in a large bowl until pale and creamy. Divide the mixture equally between the paper cases.

3 Bake for 20 minutes or until golden and risen. Leave to cool in the tin for 5 minutes, then transfer to a wire rack to cool completely.

4 For the topping, heat the cream and milk in a small saucepan until nearly boiling. Put both chocolates into a bowl and pour the hot cream over them. Leave to stand for 5 minutes, then gently stir until smooth.

5 Put the hazelnuts into a shallow bowl. Dip the top of each cake into the chocolate cream, allow the excess to drip off, then dip into the hazelnuts until coated all over. Stand the cakes upright on the wire rack and leave for about 1 hour to set.

EASY		NUTRITIONAL INFORMATION		Makes
Preparation Time 40 minutes	**Cooking Time** 25 minutes, plus cooling and setting	**Per Cupcake** 338 calories, 23g fat (of which 10g saturates), 31g carbohydrate, 0.4g salt	Vegetarian	**12**

Spiced Carrot Muffins

125g (4oz) unsalted butter, softened

125g (4oz) light muscovado sugar

3 pieces preserved stem ginger, drained and chopped

150g (5oz) self-raising flour, sifted

1½ tsp baking powder

1 tbsp ground mixed spice

25g (1oz) ground almonds

3 medium eggs

finely grated zest of ½ orange

150g (5oz) carrots, peeled and grated

50g (2oz) pecan nuts, chopped

50g (2oz) sultanas

3 tbsp white rum or orange liqueur (optional)

For the icing and decoration

200g (7oz) cream cheese

75g (3oz) icing sugar

1 tsp lemon juice

12 unsprayed rose petals (optional)

1 Preheat the oven to 180°C (160°C fan oven) mark 4. Line a 12-hole bun tin or muffin tin with paper muffin cases.

2 Beat the butter, muscovado sugar and stem ginger together until pale and creamy. Add the flour, baking powder, spice, ground almonds, eggs and orange zest and beat well until combined. Stir in the carrots, pecan nuts and sultanas. Divide the mixture equally among the paper cases.

3 Bake for 20–25 minutes until risen and just firm. A skewer inserted into the centre should come out clean. Transfer to a wire rack and leave to cool completely.

4 For the topping, beat the cream cheese in a bowl until softened. Beat in the icing sugar and lemon juice to give a smooth icing that just holds its shape.

5 Drizzle each cake with a little liqueur, if using. Using a small palette knife, spread a little icing over each cake. Decorate with a rose petal, if you like.

Freezing Tip

To freeze Complete the recipe to the end of step 3. Once the muffins are cold, pack, seal and freeze.

To use Thaw at cool room temperature and complete the recipe.

EASY		NUTRITIONAL INFORMATION		Makes
Preparation Time 30 minutes	**Cooking Time** 20–25 minutes, plus cooling	**Per Muffin** 333 calories, 22g fat (of which 11g saturates), 31g carbohydrate, 0.5g salt	Vegetarian	**12**

Freezing Tip

To freeze Complete the recipe to the end of step 4. Once the muffins are cold, pack, seal and freeze.
To use Thaw at cool room temperature. Complete the recipe.

Wholemeal Banana Muffins

50g (2oz) raisins
finely grated zest and juice of 1 orange
125g (4oz) wholemeal flour
25g (1oz) wheatgerm
3 tbsp caster sugar
2 tsp baking powder
pinch of salt
1 large egg, beaten
50ml (2fl oz) milk
50ml (2fl oz) sunflower oil
2 medium-sized ripe bananas, about 225g (8oz) when peeled, roughly mashed

For the topping
5 tbsp orange marmalade
50g (2oz) banana chips, roughly chopped
50g (2oz) walnuts, roughly chopped

1 Preheat the oven to 200°C (180°C fan oven) mark 6. Line a 6-hole bun tin or muffin tin with paper muffin cases. Put the raisins into a bowl, pour the orange juice over them and leave to soak for 1 hour.

2 Put the orange zest into a bowl with the flour, wheatgerm, sugar, baking powder and salt and mix together. Make a well in the centre.

3 In a separate bowl, mix the egg, milk and oil, then pour into the flour mixture and stir until just blended. Drain the raisins, reserving 1 tbsp juice, and stir into the mixture with the bananas. Don't overmix. Fill each muffin case two-thirds full.

4 Bake for 20–25 minutes until a skewer inserted into the centre comes out clean. Transfer to a wire rack and leave to cool slightly.

5 For the topping, gently heat the marmalade with the reserved orange juice until melted. Simmer for 1 minute, then add the banana chips and walnuts. Spoon on top of the muffins. Serve while still warm.

Makes 6	EASY		NUTRITIONAL INFORMATION	
	Preparation Time 15 minutes	**Cooking Time** 25–30 minutes	**Per Muffin** 341 calories, 13g fat (of which 2g saturates), 51g carbohydrate, 0.6g salt	Vegetarian

Freezing Tip

To freeze Complete the recipe. Once the muffins are cold, pack, seal and freeze.
To use Thaw at cool room temperature.

Try Something Different

Double Chocolate Chip Muffins: Omit the blueberries and lemon zest. Replace 40g (1½ oz) of the flour with cocoa powder, then add 150g (5oz) chopped dark chocolate to the dry ingredients in step 3.

Blueberry Muffins

2 medium eggs
250ml (9fl oz) semi-skimmed milk
250g (9oz) golden granulated sugar
2 tsp vanilla extract
350g (12oz) plain flour
4 tsp baking powder
250g (9oz) blueberries, frozen
finely grated zest of 2 lemons

1 Preheat the oven to 200°C (180°C fan oven) mark 6. Line a 12-hole bun tin or muffin tin with 10 paper muffin cases.

2 Put the eggs, milk, sugar and vanilla extract into a bowl and mix well.

3 In another bowl, sift the flour and baking powder together, then add the blueberries and lemon zest. Toss together and make a well in the centre.

4 Pour the egg mixture into the flour and blueberries and mix in gently – overbeating will make the muffins tough. Divide the mixture equally between the paper cases.

5 Bake for 20–25 minutes until risen and just firm. Transfer to a wire rack and leave to cool completely. These are best eaten on the day they are made.

EASY		NUTRITIONAL INFORMATION		Makes
Preparation Time 10 minutes	**Cooking Time** 20–25 minutes, plus cooling	**Per Muffin** 218 calories, 2g fat (of which trace saturates), 49g carbohydrate, 0.5g salt	Vegetarian	**10**

Get Ahead

To prepare ahead Complete the recipe to the end of step 5, then store in an airtight container. It will keep for up to one week.
To use Complete the recipe.

Try Something Different

Try making these brownies without butter – believe it or not, this recipe will still work. But you'll need to eat them within an hour of taking them out of the oven – fat is what makes cakes moist and allows them to be stored.

Double-chocolate Brownies

250g (9oz) butter, plus extra to grease

250g (9oz) plain chocolate (at least 50% cocoa solids), broken into pieces

100g (3½oz) white chocolate, broken into pieces

4 medium eggs

175g (6oz) light muscovado sugar

1 tsp vanilla extract

75g (3oz) plain flour, sifted

¼ tsp baking powder

1 tbsp cocoa powder, sifted, plus extra to dust

100g (3½oz) pecan nuts, chopped

pinch of salt

a little icing sugar to dust

1 Preheat the oven to 200°C (180°C fan oven) mark 6. Grease a 20.5cm (8in) square shallow tin and base-line with baking parchment. Melt the butter and plain chocolate in a heatproof bowl set over a pan of gently simmering water, making sure the base of the bowl doesn't touch the water. Remove the bowl from the pan and put to one side.

2 In a separate bowl, melt the white chocolate over a pan of gently simmering water, making sure the base of the bowl doesn't touch the water. Remove the bowl from the pan and put to one side.

3 Put the eggs into a separate large bowl. Add the muscovado sugar and vanilla extract and whisk until the mixture is pale and thick. Add the flour, baking powder, cocoa powder, nuts and salt to the bowl, then pour in the dark chocolate mixture. Using a large metal spoon, gently fold the ingredients together to make a smooth batter – if you fold too roughly, the chocolate will seize up and become unusable.

4 Pour the brownie mixture into the prepared tin. Spoon dollops of the white chocolate over the top, then swirl a skewer through it several times to create a marbled effect. Bake for 20–25 minutes. The brownie should be fudgy inside and the top should be cracked and crispy. Leave to cool in the tin.

5 Transfer the brownies to a board and cut into 16 individual brownies. To serve, dust with a little icing sugar and cocoa powder.

Cuts into 16	EASY		NUTRITIONAL INFORMATION	
	Preparation Time 15 minutes	**Cooking Time** 20–25 minutes, plus cooling	**Per Serving** 352 calories, 25g fat (of which 13g saturates), 29g carbohydrate, 0.3g salt	Vegetarian

Cook's Tip

Store in an airtight container. They will keep for up to one week.

Freezing Tip

To freeze Complete the recipe up to the end of step 2. Remove from the tin, wrap and freeze.
To use Thaw at cool room temperature for about 5 hours. Complete the recipe.

Cherry Chocolate Fudge Brownies

150g (5oz) unsalted butter, plus extra to grease
200g (7oz) plain chocolate (at least 70% cocoa solids)
175g (6oz) caster sugar
2 tsp vanilla extract
5 medium eggs
175g (6oz) plain flour
$^3/_4$ tsp baking powder
250g (9oz) glacé cherries, halved

For the icing
150g (5oz) plain chocolate (at least 70% cocoa solids)
2 tbsp Kirsch
4 tbsp double cream

1 Preheat the oven to 180°C (160°C fan oven) mark 4. Grease an 18cm (7in) square shallow cake tin and base-line with greaseproof paper. Put the butter and chocolate into a heatproof bowl set over a pan of gently simmering water, making sure the base of the bowl doesn't touch the water. Leave the chocolate to melt without stirring. Remove the bowl from the pan and stir until smooth. Leave to cool.

2 Whisk the sugar, vanilla extract and eggs until pale and thick. Stir the chocolate into the egg mixture. Sift the flour and baking powder together and lightly fold into the mixture with the cherries. Pour the mixture into the prepared tin and bake for 40 minutes or until just set. Cool slightly in the tin before icing.

3 To make the icing, put the chocolate and Kirsch into a heatproof bowl set over a pan of gently simmering water, making sure the base of the bowl doesn't touch the water. Once melted, add the cream and 4 tbsp water and stir well. Pour over the brownie and leave to set. Cut into 12 individual brownies.

EASY		NUTRITIONAL INFORMATION		Cuts into
Preparation Time 20 minutes	**Cooking Time** 50 minutes, plus cooling and 1 hour setting	**Per Serving** 462 calories, 24g fat (of which 14g saturates), 59g carbohydrate, 0.3g salt	Vegetarian	**12**

Cook's Tips

Store in an airtight container. They will keep for up to one week.
Don't over-cook the flapjacks or they will be hard and dry. When they are cooked, they should still be sticky and slightly soft when you press them in the middle.

Sticky Ginger Flapjacks

350g (12oz) unsalted butter, plus extra to grease
275g (10oz) caster sugar
225g (8oz) golden syrup
450g (1lb) rolled oats
1 tbsp ground ginger

1 Preheat the oven to 180°C (160°C fan oven) mark 4. Grease a 28 x 18cm (11 x 7in) shallow cake tin and base-line with baking parchment.

2 Put the butter, sugar and syrup into a large pan and heat gently until melted. Mix in the rolled oats and ground ginger until they are thoroughly combined. Pour the mixture into the tin and level the surface.

3 Bake for 30–35 minutes until golden brown around the edges. Leave to cool in the tin for 15 minutes.

4 While still warm, score into 24 pieces with a sharp knife. Leave in the tin to cool completely, then turn out and cut out the pieces.

Cuts into 24	EASY		NUTRITIONAL INFORMATION	
	Preparation Time 10 minutes	**Cooking Time** 40 minutes, plus cooling	**Per Serving** 259 calories, 14g fat (of which 8g saturates), 33g carbohydrate, 0.3g salt	Vegetarian

Cook's Tip

Store in an airtight container. They will keep for up to two days.

Chocolate Pecan Bars

200g (7oz) unsalted butter, softened, plus extra to grease

125g (4oz) plain flour, sifted

25g (1oz) icing sugar

1 large egg yolk and 2 large eggs

125g (4oz) self-raising flour

1 tsp baking powder

125g (4oz) caster sugar

3–4 drops vanilla extract

150g (5oz) milk chocolate chips

75g (3oz) pecan nuts, chopped

6 tbsp chocolate and hazelnut spread

1 Preheat the oven to 200°C (180°C fan oven) mark 6. Grease a 25.5 x 15cm (10 x 6in) shallow baking tin and base-line with baking parchment.

2 Put the plain flour and icing sugar into a food processor with 75g (3oz) roughly chopped butter and whiz until crumb-like in texture. (Alternatively, rub the butter into the dry ingredients in a large bowl by hand or using a pastry cutter.) Add the egg yolk and whiz for 10–15 seconds, or add to the bowl with the dry ingredients and stir until the mixture begins to come together. Turn into the tin and press into a thin layer. Bake for 15 minutes or until golden.

3 Meanwhile, put the self-raising flour, baking powder, caster sugar, vanilla extract and the remaining eggs into the food processor with the remaining softened butter and blend for 15 seconds or until smooth (or put the ingredients into a bowl and mix well with a wooden spoon). Remove the blade and fold in the chocolate chips and pecan nuts. Set aside.

4 Spread the chocolate and hazelnut spread over the cooked base and top with the cake mixture. Reduce the oven temperature to 180°C (160°C fan oven) mark 4 and bake for 45–50 minutes until golden – cover the top of the cake with foil if it appears to be browning too quickly. Cool in the tin for about 10 minutes, then turn out on to a wire rack and leave to cool completely. Cut into 25 pieces.

EASY		NUTRITIONAL INFORMATION		Cuts into
Preparation Time 15 minutes	**Cooking Time** 1¼ hours, plus cooling	**Per Serving** 189 calories, 13g fat (of which 6g saturates), 18g carbohydrate, 0.2g salt	Vegetarian	**25**

Blackberry Traybake

275g (10oz) unsalted butter, softened, plus extra to grease

275g (10oz) golden caster sugar

400g (14oz) self-raising flour

1½ tsp baking powder

5 medium eggs, beaten

finely grated zest of 1 large orange

1 tbsp vanilla extract

4–5 tbsp milk

250g (9oz) blackberries

40g (1½oz) flaked almonds

For the icing

150g (5oz) icing sugar

1 tsp vanilla extract

about 2 tbsp orange juice

1 Preheat the oven to 190°C (170°C fan oven) mark 5. Grease a shallow 30.5 x 20.5cm (12 x 8in) baking tin and line with greaseproof paper.

2 Put the butter and caster sugar into a large bowl. Sift in the flour and baking powder, then add the eggs, orange zest and juice, vanilla extract and milk and beat together until light and fluffy.

3 Using a metal spoon, fold in half the blackberries. Spoon into the prepared tin and dot with the remaining blackberries, then the almonds.

4 Bake for 40–45 minutes until springy to the touch. Cool in the tin for 5 minutes, then turn out on to a wire rack and leave to cool completely.

5 When the cake is cool, make the icing. Sift the icing sugar into a bowl, then add the vanilla extract and orange juice, mixing as you go, until smooth and runny. Drizzle over the cake and leave for 30 minutes to set. Cut into 24 squares to serve.

Cook's Tip

Wrap in clingfilm and store in an airtight container. It will keep for up to four days.

Freezing tip

To freeze Complete the recipe to the end of step 4. Leave to cool completely, keeping the cake in its greaseproof paper, then wrap in clingfilm. Freeze for up to one month.
To use Thaw overnight at cool room temperature. Complete the recipe.

Cuts into 24	EASY		NUTRITIONAL INFORMATION	
	Preparation Time 20 minutes	**Cooking Time** about 45 minutes, plus cooling and setting	**Per Serving** 239 calories, 12g fat (of which 7g saturates), 32g carbohydrate, 0.4g salt	Vegetarian

puddings

Apple Crumble

125g (4oz) plain flour

50g (2oz) unsalted butter, cubed

50g (2oz) golden caster sugar

450g (1lb) apples, peeled, cored and sliced

custard or double cream to serve

1 Preheat the oven to 180°C (160°C fan oven) mark 4. Put the flour into a bowl, add the butter and rub in with your fingertips until the mixture resembles fine breadcrumbs. Stir in half the sugar. Put to one side.

2 Arrange half the apples in a 1.1 litre (2 pint) pie dish and sprinkle with the rest of the sugar. Add the remaining apple slices to the dish. Spoon the crumble mixture over the fruit.

3 Bake in the oven for about 45 minutes until the fruit is soft. Serve hot with custard or a drizzle of double cream.

Serves 4	EASY		NUTRITIONAL INFORMATION	
	Preparation Time 15 minutes	**Cooking Time** 45 minutes	**Per Serving** 425 calories, 18g fat (of which 7g saturates), 74g carbohydrate, 0.3g salt	Vegetarian

Rhubarb and Pear Crumble

450g (1lb) rhubarb, cut into 2.5cm (1in) pieces

2 ripe pears, peeled, cored and roughly chopped

75g (3oz) demerara sugar

1 tsp ground cinnamon

50g (2oz) unsalted butter, chilled

75g (3oz) self-raising flour

2 shortbread fingers

50g (2oz) hazelnuts

Greek yogurt to serve

1 Preheat the oven to 180°C (160°C fan oven) mark 4. Put the fruit into a small shallow baking dish and sprinkle with 25g (1oz) sugar and the cinnamon. Mix together well.

2 Next, make the crumble mixture. Put the butter in a food processor, add the flour and the remaining sugar and whiz until it looks like rough breadcrumbs. (Alternatively, rub the fat into the flour by hand or using a pastry cutter, then stir in the sugar.)

3 Break the shortbread fingers into pieces and add to the processor with the hazelnuts, or crush the shortbread with a rolling pin and chop the hazelnuts. Whiz again for 4–5 seconds until the crumble is blended but still looks rough. Sprinkle the crumble over the fruit, spreading it up to the edges and pressing down with the back of a wooden spoon.

4 Bake for 40–45 minutes until the topping is golden brown and crisp. Serve with yogurt.

Serves 6	EASY		NUTRITIONAL INFORMATION	
	Preparation Time 25 minutes	Cooking Time 40–45 minutes	Per Serving 255 calories, 14g fat (of which 6g saturates), 32g carbohydrate, 0.2g salt	Vegetarian

butter to grease

125g (4oz) short-grain pudding rice

1.1 litres (2 pints) milk

50g (2oz) golden caster sugar

1 tsp vanilla extract

grated zest of 1 orange (optional)

freshly grated nutmeg to taste

Rice Pudding

1 Preheat the oven to 170°C (150°C fan oven) mark 3. Lightly grease a 1.7 litre (3 pint) ovenproof dish.

2 Put the rice, milk, sugar, vanilla extract and orange zest, if using, into the dish and stir everything together. Grate the nutmeg over the top of the mixture.

3 Bake the pudding in the middle of the oven for 1½ hours or until the top is golden brown.

EASY		NUTRITIONAL INFORMATION		Serves
Preparation Time 5 minutes	**Cooking Time** 1½ hours	**Per Serving** 239 calories, 8g fat (of which 5g saturates), 34g carbohydrate, 0.2g salt	Vegetarian	**6**

Cook's Tip

Use thick-skinned oranges, such as navel oranges, as they are easier to peel.

Oranges with Caramel Sauce

6 oranges

25g (1oz) butter

2 tbsp golden caster sugar

2 tbsp Grand Marnier

2 tbsp marmalade

grated zest and juice of 1 large orange

crème fraîche to serve

1 Preheat the oven to 200°C (180°C fan oven) mark 6. Cut away the peel and pith from the oranges, then put them into a roasting tin just large enough to hold them.

2 Melt the butter in a pan and add the sugar, Grand Marnier, marmalade, orange zest and juice. Heat gently until the sugar dissolves. Pour the mixture over the oranges in the tin, then bake in the oven for 30–40 minutes until the oranges are caramelised. Serve warm, with crème fraîche.

Serves 6	EASY			NUTRITIONAL INFORMATION	
	Preparation Time 15 minutes	**Cooking Time** 30–40 minutes		**Per Serving** 139 calories, 4g fat (of which 2g saturates), 24g carbohydrate, 0.1g salt	Vegetarian Gluten free

Freezing Tip

To freeze Cool the puddings completely. Wrap in clingfilm. Pour the sauce into a freezerproof container and leave to cool. Freeze both for up to one month.

To use Thaw the puddings and sauce overnight in the fridge. Warm the sauce. Meanwhile, put the puddings on a microwaveable plate. Spoon 1 tbsp sauce over each. Warm in the microwave on full power for 2 minutes. Serve with the remaining sauce.

Cherry and Tangerine Sticky Puddings

about 25g (1oz) white vegetable fat, melted
200g (7oz) dried cherries
2 tbsp orange-flavoured liqueur
³/₄ tsp bicarbonate of soda
75g (3oz) unsalted butter, softened
150g (5oz) golden caster sugar
2 medium eggs, beaten
175g (6oz) self-raising flour

For the sauce

175g (6oz) light muscovado sugar
125g (4oz) unsalted butter
6 tbsp double cream
25g (1oz) pecan nuts, chopped
juice of 1 tangerine

1 Preheat the oven to 180°C (160°C fan oven) mark 4. Using the melted fat, lightly oil eight 175ml (6fl oz) metal pudding basins or ramekins, then put a circle of non-stick baking parchment into the bottom of each.

2 Put 175g (6oz) dried cherries into a bowl and pour 150ml (¹/₄ pint) boiling water over them. Stir in the liqueur and bicarbonate of soda, then leave to soak for 1 hour.

3 Whisk the butter and sugar in a large bowl until pale and fluffy, then beat in the eggs a little at a time. Fold in the cherry mixture.

4 Add the flour and fold in with a large metal spoon. Divide the mixture equally among the basins, then place on a baking sheet and bake for about 25 minutes or until well risen and firm.

5 Meanwhile, make the sauce. Put the sugar, butter, cream, pecans and remaining cherries in a pan. Heat gently until the sugar has dissolved, then stir in the tangerine juice.

6 Leave the puddings to cool for 5 minutes, then turn out. Serve topped with the sauce.

EASY		NUTRITIONAL INFORMATION		Serves
Preparation Time 20 minutes, plus soaking	**Cooking Time** 25 minutes	**Per Serving** 664 calories, 39g fat (of which 22g saturates), 79g carbohydrate, 0.7g salt	Vegetarian	**8**

Cook's Tip

To reheat, remove the foil and clingfilm wrapping. Re-cover the top of the basin with baking parchment and foil. Cook the pudding as in step 4 for 2 hours. Discard the foil and parchment. Slide a knife around the edge of the pudding, then turn out on to a plate and leave to stand for 15 minutes before serving.

Fig, Orange and Cranberry Christmas Pudding

125g (4oz) each sultanas, currants and raisins

75g (3oz) dried cranberries

75g (3oz) dried figs, finely chopped

75ml (3fl oz) orange liqueur, such as Cointreau

zest and juice of 1 orange

butter to grease

1 pear

2 medium eggs

50g (2oz) each shredded vegetarian suet and self-raising flour

75g (3oz) fresh white breadcrumbs

1/2 tsp each mixed spice and ground cinnamon

pinch of freshly grated nutmeg

100g (3 1/2oz) soft dark brown sugar

25g (1oz) brazil nuts, roughly chopped (optional)

1 Put the dried fruit into a large non-metallic bowl and stir in the liqueur, orange zest and juice. Cover and leave to soak overnight at room temperature.

2 Lightly grease a 1 litre (1 3/4 pint) pudding basin and line the bottom with a circle of baking parchment. Lay a 35.5cm (14in) square of foil on top of a square of baking parchment the same size. Fold a 4cm (1 1/2in) pleat down the centre of both and set aside.

3 Core the pear, then grate into the soaked fruit mixture. Beat the eggs and add to the bowl, then add all the remaining ingredients and stir well. Spoon into the prepared basin, pressing down firmly, and level the top. Put the pleated foil square (foil side up) on top of the pudding and smooth down to cover. Using a long length of string, securely tie down the square just under the lip of the basin and knot it. Bring the excess string over the top of the bowl and tie it to the string under the lip on the other side to make a handle. Scrunch the edge of the parchment up underneath the foil.

4 Put an upturned heatproof saucer into a deep pan and balance the pudding on top. Pour in enough water to come halfway up the sides of the basin, cover the pan with a tight-fitting lid and bring to a simmer. Cook for 4 1/2–5 hours, checking the water level regularly and topping up as necessary with boiling water. Remove the pudding from the pan and cool. Once it is cold, wrap the entire basin tightly in clingfilm and a layer of foil. Store in a cool, dark place for up to two months.

Serves 8	EASY		NUTRITIONAL INFORMATION	
	Preparation Time 20 minutes, plus overnight soaking	**Cooking Time** 4–5 hours	**Per Serving** 435 calories, 12g fat (of which 5g saturates), 75g carbohydrate, 0.8g salt	Vegetarian

Cook's Tip

The puddings can also be baked in a conventional oven, although this takes a little longer. Preheat the oven to 200°C (180°C fan oven) mark 6. Spoon the mixture into greased heatproof cups and cover with foil, then put on to a baking sheet. Bake for 30 minutes or until soft and springy and a skewer inserted into the middle comes out clean.

75g (3oz) butter, softened, plus extra to grease

75g (3oz) mixed dried fruit

75g (3oz) pitted dates, roughly chopped

3/4 tsp bicarbonate of soda

150g (5oz) light muscovado sugar

2 medium eggs, beaten

1/2 tsp vanilla extract

175g (6oz) self-raising flour

For the toffee sauce

125g (4oz) butter

175g (6oz) light muscovado sugar

4 tbsp double cream

25g (1oz) pecan nuts, roughly chopped

30 Minute Recipe

Speedy Sticky Toffee Puddings

1 Grease and baseline six 250ml (9fl oz) cups. Put the dried fruit and bicarbonate of soda into a bowl and pour 175ml (6fl oz) boiling water over them. Put to one side.

2 Beat the sugar and butter in another bowl for 1–2 minutes until light and fluffy. Beat in the eggs and vanilla extract, then sift the flour over and fold it into the fruit mixture.

3 Spoon the mixture into the prepared cups. Cover very loosely with microwave film and cook three cups in the microwave oven on medium power or 600W for 6 minutes. Remove the microwave film from the puddings and leave to stand for 1 minute. Repeat with the remaining cups.

4 To make the sauce, put the butter, sugar and cream into a pan and heat gently, stirring well. Pour the sauce over the puddings and sprinkle with the chopped nuts.

EASY		NUTRITIONAL INFORMATION		Serves
Preparation Time 15 minutes	**Cooking Time** 12 minutes	**Per Serving** 720 calories, 38g fat (of which 22g saturates), 96g carbohydrate, 1g salt	Vegetarian	**6**

Tiramisu

200g carton mascarpone
1 vanilla pod, split lengthways
450ml ($^{3}/_{4}$ pint) warm strong black coffee
4 medium egg yolks
75g (3oz) golden caster sugar
284ml carton double cream
100ml (3$^{1}/_{2}$fl oz) grappa
200g pack savoiardi or sponge fingers
cocoa powder to dust

1 Put the mascarpone into a bowl with the seeds from the vanilla pod.

2 Pour the coffee into a shallow dish, add the empty vanilla pod and set aside to infuse.

3 In a large bowl, whisk the egg yolks and sugar together until pale and thick, then whisk in the mascarpone until smooth.

4 Whip the cream in another bowl to soft peaks, then fold into the mascarpone mixture with the grappa.

5 Take half of the sponge fingers and dip each in turn into the coffee mixture, then arrange over the base of a 2.4 litre (4$^{1}/_{4}$ pint) shallow dish. Spread a layer of mascarpone mixture over the sponge fingers, then dip the remaining sponge fingers into the coffee and arrange on top. Finish with a top layer of mascarpone. Cover and chill for at least 2 hours.

6 Dust with cocoa and cut into portions with a sharp knife. Use a spatula to lift them neatly on to plates.

Cook's Tip

For optimum flavour, prepare a day ahead.

EASY	NUTRITIONAL INFORMATION		Serves
Preparation Time 20 minutes, plus chilling	**Per Serving** 333 calories, 22g fat (of which 11g saturates), 31g carbohydrate, 0.5g salt	Vegetarian	**10**

Try Something Different

Use raspberries or blueberries instead of the strawberries.

Strawberry Brûlée

250g (9oz) strawberries, hulled and sliced

2 tsp golden icing sugar

1 vanilla pod, split in half lengthways

400g (14oz) Greek yogurt

100g (3½oz) golden caster sugar

1 Divide the strawberries among four ramekins and sprinkle with icing sugar.

2 Scrape the seeds from the vanilla pod and stir into the yogurt, then spread the mixture evenly over the fruit.

3 Preheat the grill to high. Sprinkle the caster sugar evenly over the yogurt until it is well covered.

4 Put the ramekins on a baking sheet or into the grill pan and grill until the sugar turns dark brown and caramelises. Leave for 15 minutes or until the caramel is cool enough to eat, or chill for up to 2 hours before serving.

Serves 4	EASY		NUTRITIONAL INFORMATION	
	Preparation Time 15 minutes, plus chilling (optional)	**Cooking Time** 5 minutes, plus cooling	**Per Serving** 240 calories, 10g fat (of which 5g saturates), 35g carbohydrate, 0.2g salt	Vegetarian Gluten free

Cook's Tip

Remember to remove the carton of custard from the fridge 20 minutes before you start to make the trifle, to bring it to room temperature.

White Chocolate and Red Fruit Trifle

3 × 500g bags frozen mixed berries

125g (4oz) golden caster sugar, plus 1 tsp

250g (9oz) biscotti or cantuccini biscuits, plus crushed biscuits to decorate

5 tbsp dessert wine or fruit juice (such as cranberry and orange)

For the topping

450ml (³⁄₄ pint) double cream, lightly whipped

200g (7oz) white chocolate, broken into pieces and melted (see page 273)

500g carton fresh custard (at room temperature)

500ml (18fl oz) crème fraîche, beaten until smooth

1 Put the berries into a large pan with 125g (4oz) caster sugar and heat gently for about 5 minutes or until the sugar has dissolved and the berries have thawed. Sieve the mixture over a bowl to catch the juices. Pour the juices back into the pan, then tip the berries into the bowl. Bring the juices to the boil, then reduce the heat and simmer for 10 minutes or until reduced to about 150ml (¹⁄₄ pint). Pour over the berries and leave to cool.

2 Lay the biscuits over the bottom of a 3 litre (5¹⁄₄ pint) trifle dish and sprinkle with the dessert wine or fruit juice. Scatter the cooled berries over the top.

3 To make the topping, transfer half the cream to a bowl, cover and chill; leave the rest of the cream at room temperature. Pour the melted chocolate into a cold bowl and gradually fold in the custard. Fold in the room-temperature whipped cream. Pour the chocolate custard over the fruit to cover it evenly. Fold the chilled cream into the crème fraîche with the 1 tsp sugar, then spoon over the custard. Chill for 2 hours. Remove from the fridge 20 minutes before serving. Scatter crushed biscuits over the top.

EASY		NUTRITIONAL INFORMATION		Serves
Preparation Time 45 minutes, plus chilling	**Cooking Time** 15 minutes, plus cooling	**Per Serving** 943 calories, 68g fat (of which 41g saturates), 82g carbohydrate, 0.5g salt	Vegetarian	**8**

Chocolate Panettone Pudding

125g (4oz) raisins

100ml (3½ fl oz) brandy

75g (3oz) softened butter, plus extra to grease

700g (1½ lb) panettone

2 x 500g cartons fresh custard, or 750ml (1¼ pints) home-made

600ml (1 pint) semi-skimmed milk

200g (7oz) plain chocolate (at least 70% cocoa solids), roughly chopped

icing sugar to dust

1 Put the raisins into a bowl, pour the brandy over them, cover and leave to soak overnight.

2 Preheat the oven to 180°C (160°C fan oven) mark 4. Grease a 3.4 litre (6 pint) ovenproof dish. Slice the panettone into slices about 5mm (¼ in) thick. Spread with the butter and cut into quarters. Stir the custard and milk together and pour a thin layer over the base of the prepared dish. Arrange a layer of panettone on top and scatter some of the raisins and chocolate on top. Pour on another thin layer of custard. Continue to layer up the panettone, raisins, chocolate and custard, finishing with a layer of custard. Leave to rest for 1 hour.

3 Stand the dish in a roasting tin and pour hot water around the dish to come halfway up the sides. Bake in the oven for 1–1¼ hours until the custard is set and the top has turned a deep brown, covering lightly with foil after 40 minutes to prevent over-browning. Dust the surface lightly with icing sugar to serve.

Serves 8	A LITTLE EFFORT		NUTRITIONAL INFORMATION	
	Preparation Time 30 minutes, plus soaking and resting	**Cooking Time** 1–1¼ hours	**Per Serving** 685 calories, 25g fat (of which 10g saturates), 97g carbohydrate, 0.9g salt	Vegetarian

Quick Gooey Chocolate Puddings

100g (3½ oz) unsalted butter, plus extra to grease

100g (3½ oz) golden caster sugar, plus extra to dust

100g (3½ oz) plain chocolate (at least 70% cocoa solids), broken into pieces

2 large eggs

20g (¾ oz) plain flour

icing sugar to dust

1 Preheat the oven to 200°C (180°C fan oven) mark 6. Grease four 200ml (7fl oz) ramekins and dust with caster sugar. Melt the chocolate and butter in a heatproof bowl set over a pan of gently simmering water, making sure the base of the bowl doesn't touch the water. Take the bowl off the pan and leave to cool for 5 minutes.

2 Whisk the eggs, caster sugar and flour together in a bowl until smooth. Fold in the chocolate mixture and pour into the ramekins.

3 Stand the dishes on a baking tray and bake for 12–15 minutes until the puddings are puffed and set on the outside, but still runny inside.

4 Turn out, dust with icing sugar and serve immediately.

EASY		NUTRITIONAL INFORMATION		Serves
Preparation Time 15 minutes	**Cooking Time** 12–15 minutes	**Per Serving** 468 calories, 31g fat (of which 19g saturates), 46g carbohydrate, 0.6g salt	Vegetarian	**4**

breads and rolls

White Farmhouse Loaf

1 tsp easy-blend dried yeast

500g (1lb 2oz) strong white bread flour, plus extra to sprinkle

1 tbsp caster sugar

2 tbsp milk powder

1½ tsp salt

25g (1oz) butter

350ml (12fl oz) water

1 Put the ingredients into the bread maker bucket, following the order and method specified in the manual.

2 Fit the bucket into the bread maker and set to the basic programme with a crust of your choice. Press start.

3 Just before baking starts, brush the top of the dough with water and sprinkle with flour. If preferred, slash the top of the bread lengthways with a sharp knife, taking care not to scratch the bucket.

4 After baking, remove the bread from the machine and shake out on to a wire rack to cool.

Slices 12	EASY		NUTRITIONAL INFORMATION	
	Preparation Time 20 minutes, plus rising	**Cooking Time** 30–35 minutes, plus cooling	**Per Serving** 180 calories, 3g fat (1g saturates), 34g carbohydrate, 0.9g salt	Vegetarian

Freezing Tip

To freeze Follow the recipe and cooking times in step 3, but don't glaze and bake for the final 5 minutes. Leave to cool in the tin. Wrap and freeze for up to two months.
To use Thaw, uncovered, at room temperature for 6 hours. Glaze the bread, put it on a hot baking sheet and bake at 220°C (200°C fan oven) mark 7 for 8–10 minutes until hot throughout.

Walnut and Garlic Bread

oil to grease

500g (1lb 2oz) strong white bread flour with kibbled grains of rye and wheat, plus extra to dust

7g sachet fast-action dried yeast

2 tsp salt

1 tbsp malt extract

50g (2oz) butter, softened

3 garlic cloves, peeled and crushed

100g (3½oz) walnut pieces

1 tbsp milk mixed with 1 tbsp malt extract to glaze

1 Lightly oil a 20.5cm (8in) springform cake tin. Put the flour, yeast and salt into a freestanding mixer with a dough hook. Add 300ml (½ pint) lukewarm water and the malt extract, then mix to a pliable dough. Increase the speed and machine-knead for 5 minutes.

2 Turn out on to a lightly floured surface and roll the dough into a rectangle about 40.5 x 28cm (16 x 11in). Mix the butter with the garlic and spread over the dough, then scatter the walnuts over. Starting at one long edge, roll up the dough into a sausage. Cut into eight slices and put in the prepared tin. Cover with lightly oiled clingfilm and leave to rise in a warm place for 45 minutes or until doubled in size.

3 Preheat the oven to 220°C (200°C fan oven) mark 7 and put a baking sheet in to heat. Remove the clingfilm, cover the bread with foil and put on the hot baking sheet. Bake for 20 minutes. Reduce the oven temperature to 200°C (180°C fan oven) mark 6 and bake for 1 hour 10 minutes. Brush with the glaze and bake, uncovered, for a further 5 minutes or until golden brown. Leave in the tin to cool slightly. Serve warm.

Slices 8	EASY		NUTRITIONAL INFORMATION	
	Preparation Time 25 minutes, plus rising	**Cooking Time** about 1 hour 35 minutes	**Per Serving** 359 calories, 15g fat (of which 4g saturates), 52g carbohydrate, 1.3g salt	Vegetarian

Oatmeal Soda Bread

25g (1oz) butter, plus extra to grease
275g (10oz) plain wholemeal flour
175g (6oz) coarse oatmeal
2 tsp cream of tartar
1 tsp salt
about 300ml (½ pint) milk and water, mixed

1 Preheat the oven to 220°C (200°C fan oven) mark 7. Grease and base-line a 900g (2lb) loaf tin.

2 Mix together all the dry ingredients in a bowl. Rub in the butter, then add the milk and water to bind to a soft dough. Spoon into the prepared tin.

3 Bake in the oven for about 25 minutes until golden brown and well risen. Turn out on to a wire rack and leave to cool slightly. It is best eaten on the day it is made.

EASY		NUTRITIONAL INFORMATION		Slices
				10
Preparation Time 15 minutes	**Cooking Time** 25 minutes, plus cooling	**Per Slice** 183 calories, 4g fat (of which 2g saturates), 31g carbohydrate, 0.6g salt	Vegetarian	

Cook's Tip

Use dried polenta grains for this recipe.

oil to grease

125g (4oz) plain flour

175g (6oz) polenta (see Cook's Tip) or cornmeal

1 tbsp baking powder

1 tbsp caster sugar

1/2 tsp salt

300ml (1/2 pint) buttermilk, or equal quantities of natural yogurt and milk, mixed together

2 medium eggs

4 tbsp extra virgin olive oil

CornBread

1 Preheat the oven to 200°C (180°C fan oven) mark 6. Generously oil a 20.5cm (8in) square shallow tin.

2 Put the flour into a large bowl, then add the polenta or cornmeal, the baking powder, sugar and salt. Make a well in the centre and pour in the buttermilk or yogurt and milk mixture. Add the eggs and olive oil and stir together until evenly mixed.

3 Pour into the tin and bake for 25–30 minutes until firm to the touch. Insert a skewer into the centre – if it comes out clean, the cornbread is done.

4 Leave the cornbread to rest in the tin for 5 minutes, then turn out and cut into chunky triangles. Serve warm with butter.

Serves 8	EASY		NUTRITIONAL INFORMATION	
	Preparation Time 5 minutes	**Cooking Time** 25–30 minutes	**Per Serving** 229 calories, 8g fat (of which 1g saturates), 33g carbohydrate, 1.3g salt	Vegetarian

BREAD MACHINE *recipe*

Floury Baps

1 tsp easy-blend dried yeast
450g (1lb) strong white bread flour, plus extra to dust
1 tsp salt
1 tsp golden caster sugar
15g (½oz) butter
150ml (¼ pint) milk, plus extra to brush
oil to grease

1 Put all the ingredients except the oil into the bread maker bucket with 125ml (4fl oz) water, following the order and method specified in the manual.

2 Fit the bucket into the bread maker and set to the dough programme. Press start. Lightly oil a large baking sheet.

3 Once the dough is ready, turn it out on to a lightly floured surface and punch it down to deflate. Divide into 8 even-sized pieces. Shape each piece into a round and flatten with the palm of your hand until about 10cm (4in) in diameter.

4 Space slightly apart on the baking sheet and brush lightly with milk. Sprinkle generously with flour, cover loosely with a cloth and leave to rise for 30–40 minutes until doubled in size.

5 Preheat the oven to 200°C (180°C fan oven) mark 6. Using your thumb, make a deep impression in the centre of each bap. Dust with a little more flour and bake for 18–20 minutes until risen and pale golden around the edges. Eat warm or transfer to a wire rack to cool.

EASY		NUTRITIONAL INFORMATION		Makes
Preparation Time 10 minutes, plus kneading and rising	**Cooking Time** 18–20 minutes, plus cooling	**Per Serving** 220 calories, 3g fat (of which 1g saturates), 45g carbohydrate, 0.7g salt	Vegetarian	**8**

Glossary

Al dente Italian term commonly used to describe food, especially pasta and vegetables, which are cooked until tender but still firm to the bite.

Antipasto Italian selection of cold meats, fish, salads, etc., served as a starter.

Au gratin Describes a dish that has been coated with sauce, sprinkled with breadcrumbs or cheese and browned under the grill or in the oven. Low-sided gratin dishes are used.

Bain-marie Literally, a water bath, used to keep foods, such as delicate custards and sauces, at a constant low temperature during cooking. On the hob a double saucepan or bowl over a pan of simmering water is used; for oven cooking, the baking dish(es) is placed in a roasting tin containing enough hot water to come halfway up the sides.

Baking blind Pre-baking a pastry case before filling. The pastry case is lined with greaseproof paper and weighted down with dried beans or ceramic baking beans.

Baking powder A raising agent consisting of an acid, usually cream of tartar, and an alkali, such as bicarbonate of soda, which react to produce carbon dioxide. This expands during baking and makes cakes and breads rise.

Bard To cover the breast of game birds or poultry, or lean meat with fat to prevent the meat from drying out during roasting.

Baste To spoon the juices and melted fat over meat, poultry, game or vegetables during roasting to keep them moist. The term is also used to describe spooning over a marinade.

Beat To incorporate air into an ingredient or mixture by agitating it vigorously with a spoon, fork, whisk or electric mixer. The technique is also used to soften ingredients.

Béchamel Classic French white sauce, used as the basis for other sauces and savoury dishes.

Beurre manié Equal parts of flour and butter kneaded together to make a paste. Used to thicken soups, stews and casseroles. It is whisked into the hot liquid a little at a time at the end of cooking.

Bind To mix beaten egg or other liquid into a dry mixture to hold it together.

Blanch To immerse food briefly in fast-boiling water to loosen skins, such as peaches or tomatoes, or to remove bitterness, or to destroy enzymes and preserve the colour, flavour and texture of vegetables (especially prior to freezing).

Bone To remove the bones from meat, poultry, game or fish, so that it can be stuffed or simply rolled before cooking.

Bottle To preserve fruit, jams, pickles or other preserves in sterile glass jars.

Bouquet garni Small bunch of herbs – usually a mixture of parsley stems, thyme and a bay leaf – tied in muslin and used to flavour stocks, soups and stews.

Braise To cook meat, poultry, game or vegetables slowly in a small amount of liquid in a pan or casserole with a tight-fitting lid. The food is usually first browned in oil or fat.

Brochette Food cooked on a skewer.

Brûlée A French term, literally meaning 'burnt', used to refer to a dish with a crisp coating of caramelised sugar.

Butterfly To split a food, such as a large prawn or poussin, almost in half and open out flat, so that it will cook more quickly.

Calorie Strictly a kilocalorie, this is used in dietetics to measure the energy value of foods.

Canapé Small appetiser, served with drinks.

Candying Method of preserving fruit or peel by impregnating with sugar.

Caramelise To heat sugar or sugar syrup slowly until it is brown in colour; ie forms a caramel.

Carbonade Rich stew or braise of meat, which includes beer.

Casserole A dish with a tight-fitting lid used for slow-cooking meat, poultry and vegetables, now used to describe food cooked in this way.

Charcuterie French term for cooked pork products, including hams, sausages and terrines.

Chill To cool food in the refrigerator.

Chine To sever the rib bones from the backbone, close to the spine. This is done to meat joints, such as loin of pork or lamb, to make them easier to carve into chops after cooking.

Clarify To remove sediment or impurities from a liquid. Stock is clarified by heating with egg white, while butter is clarified by melting and skimming. Butter that has been clarified will withstand a higher frying temperature. To clarify butter, heat until melted and all bubbling stops. Take off the heat and let stand until the sediment has sunk to the bottom, then gently pour off the fat, straining it through muslin to remove sediment.

Compote Fresh or dried fruit stewed in sugar syrup. Served hot or cold.

Concassé Diced fresh ingredient, used as a garnish. The term is most often applied to skinned, deseeded tomatoes.

Consistency Term used to describe the texture of a mixture, eg firm, dropping or soft.

Coulis A smooth fruit or vegetable purée, thinned if necessary to a pouring consistency.

Court bouillon Aromatic cooking liquid containing wine, vinegar or lemon juice, used for poaching delicate fish, poultry or vegetables.

Cream To beat together fat and sugar until the mixture is pale and fluffy, and resembles whipped cream in texture and colour. The method is used in cakes and puddings that contain a high proportion of fat and require the incorporation of a lot of air.

Crêpe French term for a pancake.

Crimp To decorate the edge of a pie, tart or shortbread by pinching it at regular intervals to give a fluted effect.

Croquette Seasoned mixture of cooked potato and fish, meat, poultry or vegetables shaped into a small roll, coated with egg and breadcrumbs and shallow-fried.

Croûte Circle or other shaped piece of fried bread, typically used as a base for serving small game birds.

Croûtons Small pieces of fried or toasted bread, served with soups and salads.

Crudités Raw vegetables, usually cut into slices or sticks, typically served with a dipping sauce as an appetiser.

Crystallise To preserve fruit in sugar syrup.

Curdle To cause sauces or creamed mixtures to separate once the egg is added, usually by overheating or over-beating.

Cure To preserve fish, meat or poultry by smoking, drying or salting.

Daube Braising meat and vegetables with stock, often with wine and herbs added.

Deglaze To heat stock, wine or other liquid with the cooking juices left in the pan after roasting or sautéeing, scraping and stirring vigorously to dissolve the sediment on the bottom of the pan.

Dégorge To draw out moisture from a food, eg salting aubergines to remove bitter juices.

Dice To cut food into small cubes.

Draw To remove the entrails from poultry or game.

Dredge To sprinkle food generously with flour, sugar, icing sugar, etc.

Dress To pluck, draw and truss poultry or game. The term is also used to describe tossing a salad in vinaigrette or other dressing.

Dry To preserve food such as fruit, pasta and pulses by dehydration.

Dust To sprinkle lightly with flour, cornflour, icing sugar, etc.

Emulsion A mixture of two liquids, which do not dissolve into one another, such as oil and vinegar. Vigorous shaking or heating will emulsify them, as for a vinaigrette.

En croûte Term used to describe food that is wrapped in pastry before cooking.

En papillote Term used to describe food that is baked in a greaseproof paper or baking parchment parcel and served from the paper.

Escalope Thin slice of meat, such as pork, veal or turkey, from the top of the leg, usually pan-fried.

Extract Concentrated flavouring, which is used in small quantities, eg yeast extract, vanilla extract.

Fillet Term used to describe boned breasts of birds, boned sides of fish, and the undercut of a loin of beef, lamb, pork or veal.

Flake To separate food, such as cooked fish, into natural pieces.

Flambé Flavouring a dish with alcohol, usually brandy or rum, which is then ignited so that the actual alcohol content is burned off.

Folding in Method of combining a whisked or creamed mixture with other ingredients by cutting and folding so that it retains its lightness. A large metal spoon or plastic-bladed spatula is used.

Frosting To coat leaves and flowers with a fine layer of sugar to use as a decoration. Also an American term for icing cakes.

Fry To cook food in hot fat or oil. There are various methods: shallow-frying in a little fat in a shallow pan; deep-frying where the food is totally immersed in oil; dry-frying in which fatty foods are cooked in a non-stick pan without extra fat; see also Stir-frying.

Galette Cooked savoury or sweet mixture shaped into a round.

Garnish A decoration, usually edible, such as parsley or lemon, which is used to enhance the appearance of a savoury dish.

Glaze A glossy coating given to sweet and savoury dishes to improve their appearance and sometimes flavour. Ingredients for glazes include beaten egg, egg white, milk and syrup.

Grate To shred hard food, such as cheese and carrots, with a grater or food processor attachment.

Griddle A flat, heavy, metal plate used on the hob for cooking scones or for searing savoury ingredients.

Grind To reduce foods such as coffee beans, nuts and whole spices to small particles using a food mill, pestle and mortar, electric grinder or food processor.

Gut To clean out the entrails from fish.

Hang To suspend meat or game in a cool, dry place for a number of days to tenderise the flesh and develop flavour.

Hull To remove the stalk and calyx from soft fruits, such as strawberries.

Infuse To immerse flavourings, such as aromatic vegetables, herbs, spices and vanilla, in a liquid to impart flavour. Usually the infused liquid is brought to the boil, then left to stand for a while.

Julienne Fine 'matchstick' strips of vegetables or citrus zest, sometimes used as a garnish.

Knead To work dough by pummelling with the heel of the hand.

Knock back To knead a yeast dough for a second time after rising, to ensure an even texture.

Lard To insert small strips of fat or streaky bacon into the flesh of game birds and dry meat before cooking. A special larding needle is used.

Macerate To soften and flavour raw or dried foods by soaking in a liquid, eg soaking fruit in alcohol.

Mandolin A flat wooden or metal frame with adjustable cutting blades for slicing vegetables.

Marinate To soak raw meat, poultry or game – usually in a mixture of oil, wine, vinegar and flavourings – to soften and impart flavour. The mixture, which is known as a marinade, may also be used to baste the food during cooking.

Medallion Small round piece of meat, usually beef or veal.

Mince To cut food into very fine pieces, using a mincer, food processor or knife.

Mocha Term which has come to mean a blend of chocolate and coffee.

Parboil To boil a vegetable or other food for part of its cooking time before finishing it by another method.

Pare To finely peel the skin or zest from vegetables or fruit.

Pâté A savoury mixture of finely chopped or minced meat, fish and/or vegetables, usually served as a starter with bread or toast.

Patty tin Tray of cup-shaped moulds for cooking small cakes and deep tartlets. Also called a bun tin.

Pectin A naturally occurring substance found in most varieties of fruit and some vegetables, which is necessary for setting jams and jellies. Commercial pectin and sugar with pectin are also available for preserve-making.

Pickle To preserve meat or vegetables in brine or vinegar.

Pith The bitter white skin under the thin zest of citrus fruit.

Pluck To remove the feathers from poultry and game birds.

Poach To cook food gently in liquid at simmering point; the surface should be just trembling.

Pot roast To cook meat in a covered pan with some fat and a little liquid.

Prove To leave bread dough to rise (usually for a second time) after shaping.

Purée To pound, sieve or liquidise vegetables, fish or fruit to a smooth pulp. Purées often form the basis for soups and sauces.

Reduce To fast-boil stock or other liquid in an uncovered pan to evaporate water and concentrate the flavour.

Refresh To cool hot vegetables very quickly by plunging into ice-cold water or holding under cold running water in order to stop the cooking process and preserve the colour.

Render To melt fat slowly to a liquid, either by heating meat trimmings, or to release the fat from fatty meat, such as duck or goose, during roasting.

Rennet An animal-derived enzyme used to coagulate milk in cheese-making. A vegetarian alternative is available.

Roast To cook meat by dry heat in the oven.

Roulade Soufflé or sponge mixture rolled around a savoury or sweet filling.

Roux A mixture of equal quantities of butter (or other fat) and flour cooked together to form the basis of many sauces.

Rub-in Method of incorporating fat into flour by rubbing between the fingertips, used when a short texture is required. Used for pastry, cakes, scones and biscuits.

Salsa Piquant sauce made from chopped fresh vegetables and sometimes fruit.

Sauté To cook food in a small quantity of fat over a high heat, shaking the pan constantly – usually in a sauté pan (a frying pan with straight sides and a wide base).

Scald To pour boiling water over food to clean it, or loosen skin, eg tomatoes. Also used to describe heating milk to just below boiling point.

Score To cut parallel lines in the surface of food, such as fish (or the fat layer on meat), to improve its appearance or help it cook more quickly.

Sear To brown meat quickly in a little hot fat before grilling or roasting.

Seasoned flour Flour mixed with a little salt and pepper, used for dusting meat, fish etc., before frying.

Shred To grate cheese or slice vegetables into very fine pieces or strips.

Sieve To press food through a perforated sieve to obtain a smooth texture.

Sift To shake dry ingredients through a sieve to remove lumps.

Simmer To keep a liquid just below boiling point.

Skim To remove froth, scum or fat from the surface of stock, gravy, stews, jam etc. Use either a skimmer, a spoon or kitchen paper.

Smoke To cure meat, poultry and fish by exposure to wood smoke.

Souse To pickle food, especially fish, in vinegar flavoured with spices.

Steam To cook food in steam, usually in a steamer over rapidly boiling water.

Steep To immerse food in warm or cold liquid to soften it, and sometimes to draw out strong flavours.

Sterilise To destroy bacteria in foods by heating.

Stew To cook food, such as tougher cuts of meat, in flavoured liquid which is kept at simmering point.

Stir-fry To cook small even-sized pieces of food rapidly in a little fat, tossing constantly over a high heat, usually in a wok.

Suet Hard fat of animal origin used in pastry and steamed puddings. A vegetarian alternative is readily available.

Sugar syrup A concentrated solution of sugar in water used to poach fruit and make sorbets, granitas, fruit juices, etc.

Sweat To cook chopped or sliced vegetables in a little fat without liquid in a covered pan over a low heat to soften.

Tepid The term used to describe temperature at approximately blood heat, ie 37°C (98.7°F).

Truss To tie or skewer poultry or game into shape prior to roasting.

Unleavened Flat bread, such as pitta, made without a raising agent.

Vanilla sugar Sugar in which a vanilla pod has been stored to impart its flavour.

Whipping (whisking) Beating air rapidly into a mixture either with a manual or electric whisk. Whipping usually refers to cream.

Zest The thin coloured outer layer of citrus fruit, which can be removed in fine strips with a zester.

Index

Picture credits

Photographers: Marie-Louise Avery (pages 327 and 331); Neil Barclay (pages 13, 37, 84 and 92); Martin Brigdale (pages 127, 164, 167, 168, 171, 175, 180, 254, 257, 278, 286, 289 and 322); Nicki Dowey (pages 10, 11, 14, 18, 19, 21, 22, 23, 24, 25, 27, 28, 29, 33, 35, 36, 41, 42, 43, 45, 49, 50, 52, 59, 61, 63, 64, 68, 69, 72, 76, 77, 85, 88, 89, 93, 101, 105, 107, 111, 119, 120, 121, 122, 124, 125, 128, 130, 135, 142, 144, 147, 150, 160, 169, 170, 178, 185, 186, 187, 188, 189, 190, 192, 193, 195, 202, 206, 207, 212, 213, 215, 216, 218, 219, 226, 228, 237, 240, 244, 248, 253, 255, 260, 265, 268, 274, 275, 279, 284, 287, 288, 296, 298, 300, 301, 302, 303, 304, 305, 314, 315, 317, 320, 328 and 330); Will Heap (pages 51, 201, 222 and 231) Emma Lee (page 281); Craig Robertson (pages20, 34, 38, 40, 53, 60, 74, 86, 94, 96, 100, 102, 110, 116, 131, 134, 137, 140, 141, 145, 149, 152, 159, 174, 179, 200, 217, 230, 236, 239, 242, 245, 246, 247, 249, 258, 259, 262, 283 and 313) Clive Streeter (pages 83 and 117); Brett Stevens (page 241); Roger Stowell (page 204); Lucinda Symons (pages 15, 55, 65, 71, 73, 79, 91, 94, 103, 106, 108, 113, 133, 148, 153, 156, 161, 165, 172, 177, 199, 203, 209, 223, 225, 227, 232, 233, 256, 263, 270, 271, 273, 276, 282, 285, 292, 283, 285, 287, 307, 311, 312, 319, 321, 323 and 329); Martin Thompson (page 269); Philip Webb (pages 155 and 316)

Home Economists for Anova Books: Joanna Farrow, Emma Jane Frost, Teresa Goldfinch, Alice Hart, Lucy McKelvie, Kim Morphew, Aya Nishimura, Bridget Sargeson and Mari Mererid Williams

Stylists for Anova Books: Wei Tang, Helen Trent and Fanny Ward